DATE DUE

The Political Influence
of Ideas

The Political Influence of Ideas

POLICY COMMUNITIES AND THE SOCIAL SCIENCES

Edited by
Stephen Brooks and Alain-G. Gagnon

PRAEGER

Westport, Connecticut
London

Library of Congress Cataloging-in-Publication Data

The Political influence of ideas : policy communities and the social
  sciences / edited by Stephen Brooks and Alain-G. Gagnon.
      p.   cm.
  Includes bibliographical references and index.
  ISBN 0–275–94333–X
  1. Policy sciences. 2. Social sciences. 3. Pressure groups.
I. Brooks, Stephen. II. Gagnon, Alain.
H97.P665 1994
321.6'1—dc20   93–23680

British Library Cataloguing in Publication Data is available.

Library of Congress Catalog Card Number: 93–23680
ISBN: 0–275–94333–X

First published in 1994

Praeger Publishers, 88 Post Road West, Westport, CT 06881
An imprint of Greenwood Publishing Group, Inc.

Printed in the United States of America

The paper used in this book complies with the Permanent
Paper Standard issued by the National Information Standards
Organization (Z39.48-1984).

10 9 8 7 6 5 4 3 2 1

To Kenneth D. McRae,

Teacher and Scholar

Contents

The Political Influence
of Ideas

Introduction

Policy Communities and the Social Sciences

Stephen Brooks

Students of interest groups have long recognized the fragmented character of policy-making. The founders of liberal group theory, Bentley, Latham, and Truman, conceived of policy as the outcome of a dynamic process of group interaction in which the state's role was mainly passive. E.E. Schattschneider and Theodore Lowi refined this approach in the 1960s, emphasizing the undemocratic biases and illiberal aspects of the interest group system (in the United States), but retaining the notion that policy-making was best understood in terms of congeries of interests active around particular issues or policy fields. Clientelist theories of policy-making, the "iron triangle" model of relations between congressional committees, specialized administrative agencies and interest groups, and the "capture theory" of regulation also viewed policy-making as a fragmented process.

Although none of these early works on interest groups and policy-making used the terms "policy community" or "policy network," their approach clearly presaged the more systematic theory building that began by the late 1970s. The policy community literature that has emerged since then is different from this earlier work in several ways. First, it pays greater attention to the boundaries of policy communities—what interests, organizations, and individuals are part of the community. Second, it places greater emphasis on theorizing the relations between participants in a community, particularly those between state and societal actors. This emphasis is in part due to a third difference between the policy community literature and its liberal group theory antecedents, namely European influences on the policy community approach. Whereas the earlier work was mainly American and stood accused of being largely irrelevant to the experience of other advanced industrial democracies, more recent work on policy communities has been strongly influenced by European work on corporatism and has a trans-Atlantic flavor that was missing from earlier writings.

A fourth difference, one that interests us particularly, is the greater stress that the policy community literature places on ideas and those who generate and communicate them. The work of Hugh Heclo, Peter Hall (1989, 1990), and others has been important here. Nevertheless, the role of ideas and intellectuals within policy communities remains an underexamined corner of this approach. Theorizing about intellectuals, interests, and the state is more commonly done in the tradition of grand sociology—Intellectuals and the State—or focuses on particular sets of intellectuals (e.g., economists), institutions (e.g., think tanks), or issues (e.g., privatization). What someone like Peter Hall does, however, is weave together these individual strands of intellectuals' participation in policy-making in the context of a larger policy community, viewed through the lens of a theory—like the idea of learning within a community—that makes sense of their role.

The policy community approach has become the dominant paradigm in the study of interest groups. Its only rival is what in the United States is called political economy (in Canada and Britain, public choice), an approach that applies microeconomic theory to political behavior. The popularity of the policy community approach (we call it an approach rather than a model because it has not developed a single body of formal propositions about interest group behavior, state-society relations, etc.) is due to several factors. One is its empirical accuracy. It simply is undeniable that policy-making is a fragmented process in which the state, societal actors, and attentive publics whose behavior and attitudes matter, differ between issues and policy fields. A second part of the policy community approach's appeal is its avoidance of the pitfalls of grand generalization. This was one of the main weaknesses of classic group theory: its tendency to explain most everything in terms of the resources and behavior of organized interests, stressing particularly those of societal groups. But it was also a flaw in other macro-level theories like Marxism, both structuralist and instrumentalist, and systems theory, in which broad generalizations about the state and societal forces tended to obscure the nuanced reality of policy-making. The policy community approach has embedded within it the assumption that broad generalizations about, say, state-society relations are hazardous, so it avoids grand macro-level theorizing in preference for what is sometimes referred to as meso-level generalization.

A third reason for the popularity of the policy community approach is that it permits—even requires—a certain agnosticism on the issue of whether state or societal factors are the more important determinants of public policy. If in a comparatively statist political tradition like that of France one finds cases in which state agencies are the pliant instruments of power-ful interest groups, this suggests that caution and qualification are advisable when generalizing about state versus society. This is in some ways a more comfortable and certainly more easily defensible position than either of the extremes in the debate on state autonomy.

A fourth reason for the approach's appeal involves its open-ended qual-ity. By this we mean that it avoids the functionalism that is a problematic characteristic of elite theory and class-based approaches to interest groups and their influence. Relationships and roles tend to be viewed as contingent rather than necessary. A policy community may be more or less dynamic, but embedded in this approach is an unscripted element that E.E. Schattschneider described in explaining what he called the "contagiousness of conflict." The scope of conflict (i.e., the boundaries of the policy commu-nity) and the particular configuration of interests within it are fluid. Not per-fectly, of course. Some policy communities are quite exclusive and behav-ior/roles within them are highly routinized. But many others are not. As David Vogel demonstrates in *Fluctuating Fortunes* (1989), an analysis of the political influence of business in the United States, patterns of policy-making influence and participation are more open than is allowed by either liberal critics of the business elite like Charles Lindblom or by those who employ the language and analysis of dominant and subordinate classes.

The attraction of the policy community approach for those who are inter-ested in the political influence of intellectuals should be obvious. It enables one to conceptualize intellectuals' role(s) in the context of the organizations and interests active around a particular issue or policy field. It does not require generalization about their relationship to the state or society, only to those parts of them that are members of a policy community. Moreover, and perhaps most important, the policy community approach conforms to the way most intellectuals actually participate in politics and policy-making, through their work for a state agency or private organization, as experts and activists attempting to influence elite or public opinion, as critics or defend-ers of particular interests, and as key architects of the policy discourse that structures communication within a policy community. Engagé intellectuals may play many different roles, and the policy community approach is flexi-ble enough to recognize this variety.

The same cannot be said for much writing on the policy role of intellec-tuals. The approach of Noam Chomsky is typical. Chomsky portrays intel-lectuals as either defenders (wittingly or otherwise) of dominant class inter-ests, or their critics. This characterization follows naturally enough from his class analysis of politics, according to which society's key feature is its divi-sion into dominant and subordinate classes (when he turns his eyes to global politics he views it through the same eyes, as chiefly divided into dominant and subordinate states). Given the fundamental premise, it comes as no surprise that Chomsky's analysis of the role played by journalists, think tanks, government experts, and other groups of intellectuals is almost purely in terms of a simplistic class dichotomy: do their efforts tend to support or undermine the status quo?

Without denying the importance of the implicit question—whose side are the intellectuals on?—we would argue that things are not so simple. As the chapters in this volume demonstrate, the relationships between state, private interests, and social science intellectuals are more complex than can be captured through a dichotomous framework. The problem of conceptualizing the role of intellectuals in fact goes back to the modern emergence of politically engagé intellectuals at the time of the Dreyfus Affair in France. Emile Zola's ringing declaration, "J'accuse," and the events that followed seemed to indicate that real intellectuals stood outside of and opposed to conventional structures of power. In *La trahison des clercs* Julien Benda turned this dichotomy on its head, arguing that the true vocation of the intellectual required detachment from the grubby business of politics so as to protect his single-minded pursuit of the truth (an Enlightenment notion that is no longer very fashionable among members of a generation trained in the relativist quagmire of post-modernism). Sartre, Nizan, Chomsky, and other intellectuals of the left have also understood the intellectual's role in politics in essentially dichotomous terms. Denying the possibility of Benda's detached intellectual, they have tended to view intellectuals as being on one or the other side of the "class war." Left-wing intellectuals' development of increasingly complicated "class maps" and their insistence on "contradictory" class locations have not fundamentally altered this view.

When intellectuals or their works enter politics, they do so as combatants in the struggle to establish meaning. This is their primary function, to help fashion and communicate the information and arguments that are used to support and attack particular policies. In doing so, however, they perform several more specialized roles. These include the selection of issues, the construction of meaning, the promotion of cohesion and identity among members of a group, and the establishing of social legitimacy for a group's values and goals.

SELECTION

Issues emerge in a number of ways. John Kingdon argues that an issue may reach the public agenda as a result of problems, politics, policies, or some combination of these. By problems Kingdon means circumstances that are so compelling they inevitably give rise to calls for government action. By politics he refers to the efforts of individuals and groups to achieve public recognition for some problem. What Kingdon calls policies involve information, analyses, and arguments that are intended to bring attention to some condition and promote public action to address it. Intellectuals are particularly important in generating these policies. Indeed, their efforts can sometimes be the crucial factor responsible for propelling an issue onto the public agenda or raising the profile of one that already has the status of a public issue.

It is useful to distinguish between two levels at which intellectuals affect the selection of public issues. One involves conceptualization, the other what is commonly called gatekeeping. Conceptualization involves the construction of idea frameworks that purport to explain reality. This grand intellectual function is performed by relatively few. The work of Simone de Beauvoir, Germaine Greer, and Betty Friedan played this role in constructing female subordination as a political problem. Rachel Carson, Barry Commoner, Paul Ehrlich, and the authors of *The Limits to Growth* played the same sort of role in defining—redefining, really—the environmental issue. Allan Bloom's best-seller, *The Closing of the American Mind*, is an example of grand conceptualization that provided an intellectual focus for the political reaction to contemporary American liberalism and the policies associated with it.

It does not matter whether policymakers have actually read the works of de Beauvoir, a Carson, or a Bloom, or even whether they have heard of them at all. These grand conceptualizations enter the mainstream of policy discourse through the activities of those who operate at the second level of the issue selection process, the gatekeepers. These are the journalists, editors, producers, university teachers, bureaucrats, and researchers whose choices about what problems to report, write about, communicate through teaching, investigate, and make recommendations on are influenced by the grand conceptualizations they have learned through formal education and professional socialization. They are the gatekeepers of ideas; their decisions have a significant impact on what are defined as public issues and the prominence accorded to them.

MEANING

"The facts of modern life do not spontaneously take a shape in which they can be known," observed Walter Lippman in his book *Public Opinion*; "they must be given a shape by somebody" (1922: 345). This is the cardinal truth and major premise for any serious investigation of the process of mass communication. It is also a key function of intellectuals in policy communities. Indeed, their distinctive role is to provide information and arguments that construct the meaning of an issue. Take, for example, the issue of the predominantly black underclass in the United States. Sociologists like

William J. Wilson have defined the issue as one of economic marginaliza-
tion leading to increasing social and cultural exclusion. According to this
view, which is popular among American liberals, the underclass has been
produced by the decline of well-paying manufacturing industries in the cities
of the northeast and midwest, to which southern blacks were attracted particularly after World War II. Unemployed and lacking the education and skills
required for the information economy, inner-city black males have been
caught in a downward spiral of desperation of which poverty, crime, violence, and drugs are the main symptoms. The collapse of the black family in
America is, according to this view, a function of the increasing undesirabil-
ity of young black males as husbands.

Charles Murray and others attach a very different meaning to the underclass. Rather than seeing it as the victim of larger economic and social
forces, they interpret the underclass as primarily the product of liberal-
inspired welfare laws that have encouraged a subculture of dependence and
despair. This is an interpretation favored by American conservatives.

Think tanks, particularly in the United States, have come to play an
increasingly important role in shaping the public agenda and establishing the
meaning of issues that already have public significance. However, the struggle to impose meaning on issues takes place in many venues and involves
the participation of intellectuals in many guises. Teachers, in universities and
at lower levels, are important transmitters of meaning. They are part of what
George Ross calls the "massification of intellectual life" (1991: 61), the
explosive growth in the number of people whose work involves manipulating and disseminating ideas, but also in the market for these intellectual
products. So too are those who contribute to the products of the mass media.
Publicly recognized "experts"—men and women interviewed by the media,
called upon to testify before government commissions or to participate
directly in policy-making—lend the weight of their socially consecrated
authority to the meaning(s) associated with public issues. Task forces, commissions, and panels, whether publicly or privately sponsored, also perform
this function. Finally, one should not overlook the army of intellectual workers within the state—economists, social workers, psychologists, sociologists,
defense specialists, accountants, and others—whose interpretations of issues
are important and sometimes decisive in terms of what does or does not hap-
pen in public policy.

COHESION AND IDENTITY

An important but often overlooked role of intellectuals is their contribution to the collective identity and sense of moral correctness of those whose
interests and beliefs they defend. This is a role that may be played con-

sciously or inadvertently. Some intellectuals, like Charles Murray, George Gilder, or George Will, are very clearly identified with conservative policies, just as William J. Wilson, Daniel Patrick Moynihan, and Robert Reich are associated with liberal ones. Their arguments provide a sense of intellectual justification and self-affirmation for groups and individuals who are sympathetic to the issue definitions they create and the policy recommendations they make.

The cohesion/identity role of intellectuals in policy communities is most important in the case of groups that rely on ideological incentives for member solidarity. These are often referred to as public-interest organizations (e.g., consumer groups, environmental organizations, and civil rights groups) or ideological interest groups (e.g., the pro-life or pro-choice coalitions on the abortion issue, women's groups, the American Conservative Union and Americans for Democratic Action, or the ideological arms of organized business or labor). For these groups, ideas play a crucial role in helping to forge a sense of collective identity. Intellectuals articulate this identity, providing for group members a coherent justification of their beliefs and political demands.

LEGITIMACY

Policy communities generally are portrayed as having a center, occupied by individuals and organizations whose involvement and influence are greatest, expanding outward to a periphery consisting of segments of public opinion that are usually attentive to an issue and that may be mobilized in ways that affect the behavior of those nearer the center of the community. Intellectuals often play an important role at the edge of the policy community where the popular legitimacy of policies and their intellectual and moral premises are established or contested. The prominence of this role increases as the scope of conflict, and therefore public controversy, over the issue(s) within the community's domain expands.

Left-wing social critics argue that most of this intellectual activity supports the privileged status of dominant groups in society. Why this should be so is not obvious. Alvin Gouldner explains this bias by arguing that the needs of the welfare state for information and personnel have shaped the institutionalization of the social sciences. State funding of research has been a major factor orienting the social sciences toward the sort of problem solving that is congenial to the needs of the welfare state, treating social and economic disorders as problems for which there are solutions that do not require the negation of the values on which liberal capitalist society rests. According to Gouldner, the complicity between social scientists and the state goes further to include a legitimation function whereby social scientists lend their authority as scholars to problems that the state recognizes and is prepared to address. Noam Chomsky points to the influence that business has on public opinion, through an advertising-dependent media system and business-financed experts.

Conservative critics claim the opposite, arguing that intellectuals from the social sciences and humanities tend to be left-of-center, unsympathetic to business, and automatically critical of established authority. They argue that the left-wing intelligentsia behaves as a sort of moralizing priesthood, promoting an "adversary culture" through the media, academe, and the welfare state. While cloaking itself and its preferred policies in the garments of democracy and social justice, the intelligentsia behaves (according to conservative critics) in a profoundly undemocratic way. It tends to be condescending and dismissive of "uninformed" public opinion. Moreover, one of the main effects of the Culture of Critical Discourse that it promotes is to legitimize the left-wing intelligentsia's own status as a class whose rewards and influence rely on control over the means of intellectual production and dissemination.

If instead of examining the legitimacy function of intellectuals in macrosocietal terms one looks at the process of building, maintaining, and refuting legitimacy at the edge of policy communities, grand generalizations appear hazardous. The welfare policy community in the United States is a case in point. Not only is there an enormous range of diversity in the intellectual and moral arguments of leading intellectual figures, but there is nothing that could reasonably be labeled a dominant point of view. The individual responsibility morality of thinkers like Andrew Hacker, Charles Murray, or William Raspberry is in sharp contrast to the social responsibility morality of thinkers like William J. Wilson or John Kenneth Galbraith. Their analyses of the poverty problem and recommendations for policy reform are miles apart.

The chapters in this volume explore various dimensions of social scientists' participation in policy-making, with special emphasis on their roles within policy communities and their relationship to the state. Several chapters examine the role of research institutes and think tanks within policy communities in the United States, Canada, and Eastern Europe. Others address broader issues of how to conceptualize the role of social scientists in policy communities. Together, the contributions to this third volume in a series on intellectuals and politics (Gagnon, 1987; Brooks and Gagnon, 1990b) should enrich our appreciation of the complexities of this relationship.

Much of the research and theorizing on policy communities, particularly in Europe, has focused on corporatism. The most influential work views corporatism in structuralist terms, as the product of economic imperatives and class struggles operating within the framework of a particular national political system. The role of cultural factors has, according to Appel and Gagnon, received too little attention. Moreover, the tendency has been to treat culture as a factor separate from economics and political institutions. Appel and Gagnon argue that a return to the comparative politics approach of Tocqueville and Montesquieu allows for a better appreciation of how culture influences the network of private-public relations that is characteristic of corporatism.

Chapter 1 does not address the role of social scientists in corporatist policy communities. Instead, it offers an approach for understanding the relations that exist within such a community, but also at the macro-level in a corporatist society. Appel and Gagnon cite approvingly Peter Katzenstein's work on how public and private spheres, and the "public-private" distinction, are constituted differently in different societies. This, they argue, is very much in the spirit of Tocqueville and Montesquieu, whose analyses of *les corps intermédiaires* were sensitive to national differences in the characteristic *mœurs* of a society, but who also saw the institutions linking state to society as crucial to the health of democracy. Appel and Gagnon acknowledge that the appropriateness of corporatist arrangements, and the "right" mix of market mechanisms and state coordination ("right" from the standpoint of both efficiency and democracy), will depend on the particular characteristics of each society. But they conclude with Katzenstein that corporatism, if only at the meso-level of policy communities and not that of society as a whole, can "accommodate . . . the logic of the market by compensating for it, and . . . tolerate . . . the power of the state by circumscribing it" (Katzenstein, 1985: 38).

In Chapter 2 Martin Smith addresses a different theoretical issue. He notes that most advocates of a policy network approach to understanding policy-making view groups primarily as constraints on state autonomy. But in fact, Smith argues, the autonomy of state actors within a policy network may be considerable, so that there is no theoretical incompatibility between the concepts of policy networks and state autonomy. He demonstrates this by examining various policy networks in Britain and the United States.

"Policy networks," Smith concludes, "increase autonomy by creating mechanisms of infrastructural power and by sealing off sectors of policy from wider interests within government and society." In such circumstances the autonomy of state actors requires that they give groups a role in the policy process. Thus, state autonomy should not be viewed as something in opposition to powerful societal groups, but as a condition that may depend on the resources of these groups. Martin's analysis suggests that strong state/weak state distinctions often used in comparative analyses of state autonomy are at the very least misleading. State autonomy, he argues, depends more on the degrees of integration and closure characteristic of a

policy community, and on ideological consensus among its members, than
on the weakness of societal actors.

Whereas Chapters 1 and 2 deal with theoretical issues raised by the policy community approach, in Chapter 3 Susan Phillips shifts the focus to the
role of ideas within these communities. She argues that the ways in which a
social movement produces and uses knowledge have an important impact on
its collective identity, political strategies, alliances, and demands. The institutionalization of a social movement, a theme that goes back to Robert
Michels, changes the ways in which it produces and consumes knowledge
and the basis on which its demands for representation are made. Phillips
illustrates this through an examination of the environmental and women's
movements in Canada.

Ideas are likewise the focus of Neil Bradford's chapter. In Chapter 4 he
addresses the issue of how ideas enter the process of policy innovation. He
argues that neither a state-centered social learning explanation that emphasizes the role of bureaucratic experts nor a society-centered approach that
stresses the role of parties and their leaders is adequate. Instead, he proposes
the concept of a learning network, comprised of state and societal actors,
that constructs the policy discourse characteristic of a particular policy community. Bradford argues that what is needed is "a middle-level analysis paying close attention to institutional settings where state officials and societal
forces create 'authoritative' interpretations of so-called objective conditions."

Examining Canadian and Swedish responses to the economic crisis of
the Great Depression, Bradford shows how different configurations of institutional structures and social forces produced different policy discourses
within the economic policy communities of these two countries. Whereas
political parties and interest groups were key actors in generating new ideas
and ensuring the transition to the Keynesian welfare state in Sweden, policy
intellectuals—within the state or closely allied to it—were the main agents
of economic policy change in Canada. Differences in these national learning
networks produced different economic discourses and, ultimately, different
patterns of policy innovation.

In Part II of this volume the focus shifts to organizations whose raison
d'être is the generation and dissemination of ideas. In Chapter 5 Stephen
McDowell examines the contribution made by policy research institutes to
the liberalization of organizations whose activities involved the international
production and exchange of services, particularly within the context of the
General Agreement on Tariffs and Trade (GATT). He very carefully documents the policy network whose core members included state and international organization officials with responsibility for services negotiations, as
well as policy researchers and policy advocates. McDowell demonstrates
that policy research institutes played a key role in providing links, both

physically (through forums, seminars, informal meetings, and other relational activities between members of the international services policy community) and intellectually (through supplying the empirical data and arguments in support of international services liberalization and helping to
generate a consensus within the services policy community).

Evert Lindquist approaches the subject of intellectuals' contribution to a
policy community rather differently. Based on a study of four Canadian
think tanks on Asia-Pacific issues, in Chapter 6 Lindquist explores how government agencies and foundations may encourage the development of a policy community through the contracts and grants they provide to academic
think tanks, but in the process influence the behavior and research agendas
of social scientists within a policy community. Unlike McDowell, whose
focus is the impact that intellectuals have on the choices of state actors and
ultimately policy, Lindquist is more interested in the effects that state agencies and their policy preferences have on the choices of intellectuals within a
policy community.

Lindquist concludes that the cost to social scientists within contract-
oriented academic think tanks is not their intellectual freedom. "Academic
centers," he argues, "can be viewed as a form of organizational defense
whereby social scientists, for a minimal amount of time spent performing
administrative chores, are able to convince outside funders that they are conducting policy-relevant work, although most of that work is conducted by
others and helps directly their own research agendas." The project-driven,
state-funded research so often characteristic of policy communities does not
mean, Lindquist believes, that social scientists are mere hired guns, coopted
into an agenda set elsewhere.

Dependence on outside funding is also examined in Chapter 7 by Joan
Roelofs and Erkki Berndtson. They focus on the interaction between Eastern
European social scientists and the western research foundations that are
important sources of research funding and scholarly exchanges. Given the
scarcity of domestic resources for social scientific research in the formerly
communist countries of Eastern Europe, the siren call of western support is
irresistible. Roelofs and Berndtson argue, however, that the asymmetrical
relations of influence and dependency between western foundations (whose
research agendas are themselves shaped in some cases by their dependence
on government agencies and in others by their ideological commitment to
western-style liberal pluralist democracy) and Eastern European social scientists may produce a sort of intellectual imperialism in the developing
social sciences of Eastern Europe. This, they argue, has implications for the
policy communities of these countries insofar as the discourses, agendas,
and intellectual contacts of social scientists within Eastern Europe depend
heavily on the West.

Although the role of research foundations in Eastern Europe is fairly recent, they have been active participants in American policy-making for several decades. In Chapter 8, William Buxton examines the pivotal role played by one of the most prominent, the Rockefeller Foundation, in the institutionalization of mass communications research during World War II. He shows how the efforts of the foundation's communications specialists, especially those of John Marshall, were crucial in building a communications policy community that included state agencies and private researchers. Their common concern, Buxton argues, was "to generate research of practical relevance to building public consent to new lines of policy made necessary by the 'emergency period' [of World War II]." The intellectual coherence of this fledgling communications policy community, as well as infrastructural support through financial and organizational resources, were provided by the Rockefeller Foundation.

Buxton's chapter gives a fascinating account of the institutionalization of a policy community. He shows that the Rockefeller Foundation's mediating role, and particularly the intellectual guidance of John Marshall, were crucial in generating an expert "communications group" and ensuring that the lines of private research were closely tied to considerations of policy relevance. These efforts paved the way toward the development of the communications intelligence function that would be assumed during the Cold War era by organizations like Radio Free Europe and the Voice of America.

PART I

THEORETICAL ISSUES

1

Rethinking Corporatism and Comparative Social Science: An Old-New Approach

Fredrick Appel and Alain-G. Gagnon

This chapter focuses on a number of seemingly unrelated concepts that have attracted the attention of social scientists in recent years. We say "seemingly" because the links between "policy communities," "civil society," "new social movements," and "corporatism" are not always self-evident.[1] These apparently disparate research areas do, however, have something in common: a preoccupation with the social and political interaction, innovation, and policy formation situated between the micro-level of individuals and the macro-sphere of the state and economy. In modern liberal democracies, this is the site of group formation based on social, political, and economic locations or statuses that serves as the launching pad for trade unions; business groups; health, educational, and religious organizations; women's groups; and so on. The literature on corporatism, which we will examine in some detail, is noted for its analysis of the conditions under which groups like these meet with political parties and public bureaucracies in organized forums to discuss, formulate, and in some cases arrange for the implementation of policy.

Peter Katzenstein's term for this middle level, the "para-public," suggests how close attention to this space leads us to reconsider our often overdrawn distinctions between the concepts of public and private. Admittedly, if we view these two concepts in the narrow sense and associate the former exclusively with state bureaucracies and political office holders, the undeniably public dimension of the para-public can remain obscure, since it also involves the participation of a wide variety of non-state actors. Nonetheless, since it treats issues of public concern that touch all or most citizens, it may be considered part of the public sphere in the larger sense (Katzenstein, 1987).

Corporatist arrangements in the para-public sphere have no shortage of critics these days, especially in English-speaking countries, where the phenomenon has been routinely attacked across the ideological spectrum. On the right, criticism is advanced by economists who, believing in the efficacy of unfettered market forces, argue for the state's disengagement from as many economic activities as possible. State and market-driven society should remain separate, with each pursuing its proper course (e.g., Krauss, 1984; Olson, 1982). Ironically, the argument for a strong separation of state and society is echoed in much of the recent literature from the left, which identifies corporatist tendencies with attempts to (1) increase bureaucratic control of everyday life in the name of technological efficacy (e.g., Maheu, 1983; Melucci, 1985, 1988) and (2) "coopt" labor movements into the agendas of the business class and their pro-capitalist allies in government (Panitch, 1979, 1980). The discourses of the left and the right criticize corporatism for very different reasons: whereas the conservative critics of corporatism associate it with now-discredited Leninist models of the command economy, many on the left dismiss it either as a right-wing conspiracy or as a technocratic nightmare.[2]

In the face of this two-pronged attack, how have theorists who favor corporatism both as an analytical concept and a political project responded? Sensitive to the popular association of the term with fascist statism in Spain, Portugal, and Italy, theorists of corporatism tend to follow Philippe Schmitter in carefully distinguishing an authoritarian or statist corporatism, involving the subordination of all organized social groups to the will of the state, from the benign, "societal" or democratic corporatism of post-war Sweden, the Netherlands, the Federal Republic of Germany, and elsewhere (Schmitter, 1974). Corporatism in these countries, it is now widely agreed, can be seen at two analytically distinct levels. On a country-wide level, democratic corporatist practice, characterized by tripartite bargaining structures involving governments as well as the umbrella organizations or "peak associations" representing organized labor and business, can permeate the industrial economy. On the less ambitious sectoral (or meso) level, corporatist structures of negotiation tend to involve specific state agencies and organized interest groups tied either to particular sectors of production (e.g., steel workers, dairy farmers) or to the delivery of professional services (e.g., teachers, health care workers) (Cawson, 1985; Tuohy, 1990).

For theorists defending corporatism, the corporatist economic and social arrangements found in contemporary Europe have emerged as necessary structural adjustments to certain post-war problems. At one time, it is suggested, in a simpler, earlier phase of competitive capitalism, market processes and mechanisms had a "quasi-natural justification" and government intervention was limited to monetary policy and (later on) Keynesian techniques of macroeconomic demand management. With the onset of "stagflation" in various western economies in the 1970s, however, an unprecedented instability marked the world economy. This situation called for the development of new, innovative means of ensuring continued growth: namely, the recruitment and coordination of organized interest groups and other exogenous institutional bodies, with their policy expertise at the sectoral level, into policy planning with the state bureaucracy (Lehmbruch, 1979; Goldthorpe, 1984). Thus, according to this literature, the formation of corporatist relations between business groups, labor unions, and governmental agencies at the sectoral level came about because of certain "basic imperatives" or "functional exigencies" of both the post-war economy (i.e., the "need" of the capitalist system to reproduce its conditions of existence and to accumulate further resources) and the modern state (its "need" for professional expertise, specialized information, and prior aggregation of opinion in order to fulfill its role as the guardian of capitalist reproduction) (Schmitter, 1974; Lehmbruch, 1979).

These theoretical assumptions are as characteristic of the neo-Marxist "anti-corporatist" writings as they are of the "pro-corporatist" literature. Claus Offe, for example, suggests that the growing public policy–making role of organized interest groups can only be explained against the backdrop of the accumulation and legitimation crises of late capitalism. In the face of what are seen as two central failures of contemporary capitalist society—the inability of political parties to propose coherent economic programs and the declining effectiveness of traditional bureaucratic techniques in managing the crisis-ridden capitalist economy—corporatism is identified as part of the latest, desperate effort of the increasingly interventionist (and relatively autonomous) state to shore up the capitalist system by extra-parliamentary means (Offe, 1981, 1985; see also Panitch, 1980). From both ends of the ideological spectrum, then, the para-public level is interpreted through the rubric of structures or institutions that allegedly loom over and above societies, imposing their "imperatives."[3]

Theorists of corporatism disagree about the efficacy of the corporatist response to post-war economic crises. On the left, the tendency is to see it ultimately as an inadequate attempt at shoring up capitalist arrangements. Once these inadequacies are exposed, presumably the foundations are laid for a more just, socialist response to the structural problems of contemporary capitalism. For pro-corporatist theorists, post-war corporatism has been a success story: corporatist responses to the structural crises have, by and large, achieved their goal of sustained economic growth. Their analyses assume that sustained growth has been and remains the primary goal of modern societies, a precondition for the attainment of other collective and individual goals, and thus a rationale for corporatist practice. Growth—the increased output of goods and services, full employment, a high standard of living for the population—is the good to which these authors wish to contribute through the formulation of corporatist theory and successful corporatist economic policy.

Recent theoretical work on corporatist practice has focused on explaining corporatism's raison d'être by (1) generating structural accounts of how corporatist relations and institutions come into being and are perpetuated, and (2) adopting a strictly instrumentalist criterion for assessing corporatist practice (i.e., corporatism as laudable [or repugnant] because of its ability [or inability] to generate economic growth).[4]

Taking a closer look at the genesis story of corporatism as recounted in the structuralist narrative, we see that this literature posits an all-powerful, all-determining independent variable—the capitalist system, or a combination of economic and political structures—that is claimed to be at the origin of a one-way causal determination of the dependent variable—corporatism. Authors as diverse as Schmitter, Lehmbruch, Offe, and Panitch have helped us appreciate how global economic realities and class relations on a country-wide level have influenced the development and character of corporatist structures and, indeed, of the para-public realm as a whole. The question remains, however, whether a discussion couched strictly in terms of economic imperatives and/or class struggles can account for all the features of this realm in particular societies. As we will argue, cultural factors that are, by definition, specific to particular societies appear to play a significant role in the constitution of corporatist structures in particular and the para-public realm in general.[5] In this light, the aforementioned broad structuralist approaches, which rest (for the most part) upon acultural and ahistorical assumptions about the workings of macro-economic and political structures as such, appear to leave us with an unfinished canvas.

Our corrective to this one-sidedness involves reintroducing an important, yet often ignored, body of work into the debate, a tradition of political analysis that is in many ways foundational to the discipline of comparative politics.[6] This tradition has long been concerned with the complex, multifaceted network of intermediary bodies (*les corps intermédiaires*) that exist between the individual on the one hand and the bureaucratic state and market economy on the other. Dating back at least to the eighteenth century and most readily associated with the French thinkers Charles Louis de Montesquieu (1689–1755) and Alexis de Tocqueville (1805–1859), this tradition of comparative politics has also been concerned with the manner in which culture and institutions influence one another. Montesquieu and Tocqueville remained attuned to the way in which norms, habits, and traditions of different nations and peoples help to shape institutional constellations and social practices, which in turn contribute to changes in these norms, habits, and traditions. Their multifaceted accounts of social and political reality may help us steer clear of the excessively one-sided institutionalist orientation of much of the contemporary literature.[7]

With respect to the instrumentalist bias of most contemporary analyses of corporatism, we have no wish to dismiss instrumentalist arguments for corporatist practices altogether. Considering that the countries that have demonstrated the most consistent levels of growth in the post-war period have shown resolutely corporatist tendencies—for example, West Germany, Japan, the Scandinavian countries (Reich, 1983, 1991)—it is not difficult to sympathize with those attempting to assess and justify corporatist practice strictly in this light. It appears that the societies of the industrial world will require increasing amounts of coordination and cooperation between various governmental and non-governmental organizations and firms if they are to ensure growth. Those who insist that there is another path to competitive success on world markets, devoid of any government activism and coordination between government and society whatsoever, seem captive to a nostalgic illusion common in the Anglo-Saxon countries, one that evokes an earlier, braver era of Manchesterian laissez-faire capitalism (Taylor, 1991a: 119). Moreover, the case for taking corporatist options seriously appears even more compelling as the soaring debt loads of western governments and the growing realization of the limits of state power have caused the arguments for single-handed state direction of the economy to fall into disfavor. Recent reflections on "state capacities" have shown that the prospect for an even relatively modest level of state autonomy for the purposes of economic *dirigisme* is circumscribed by many factors, namely runaway deficits, economic globalization, and the plurality of social forces within contemporary societies (Evans, Rueschemeyer, and Skocpol, 1985; Katzenstein, 1987).

Though a strong case for corporatist practices can be made in terms of their encouraging economic growth, this does not exhaust the advantages of corporatism; and theoretical accounts that stress the instrumental dimension tend to lose sight of a potentially more evocative position: namely, that corporatist practice is laudable not simply because it is conducive to growth but also because it helps to foster an overall, societal orientation toward consensus-building in public policy. This normative dimension of democratic corporatism is rarely discussed in the social science literature, perhaps because arguments for corporatism that stress this might appear to stray too far from what are often assumed to be the value-free standards of contemporary social science.

Yet in spite of themselves, some social scientists continue to evoke this normative dimension, however inconsistently and unsystematically. Cawson, for example, in the course of an article stressing an instrumental concern with growth, notes with approval that those who show an interest in democratic forms of corporatism presume that power should not always be seen as a zero-sum affair, that it is possible, in cases of conflict between two or more social interests, for both or all groups to benefit from collectively negotiated policy (Cawson, 1985: 7–8). As we shall see, the work of both Montesquieu and Tocqueville suggests how the best social scientific investigation is inseparable from normative commitments (to political freedom, tolerance, consensus-building, etc.) that lend further power and credence to the analysis.

In the course of the following discussion of the Montesquieuian-Tocquevillian approach to the political space between the public and the private, we hope to outline a form of inquiry into corporatist practice (and other political phenomena) that, we believe, is of continued relevance not simply to the historian of philosophy and political thought but also to the contemporary social scientist.

Neither Montesquieu nor Tocqueville were interested in developing a *grande théorie* of society containing general laws that attempt to explain the inner workings of all societies in the same manner. As an entry in one of Montesquieu's notebooks illustrates, the eighteenth-century *homme de lettres* was particularly hostile to excessively abstract theorization: "the worst possible representation of man, containing a heap of generalizations [*un amas de propositions générales*] and almost always false, is that found in books" (quoted in Berlin, 1982: 138. Our translation.). These lines could have been written just as easily by Tocqueville, the man described by John Stuart Mill as the "Montesquieu of the nineteenth century," who also believed that insight in the field of comparative social science comes about not simply through abstract theorizing but through close attention to the constellation of practices, institutions, and beliefs that constitute the culture of particular countries.[8] Indeed, for both Montesquieu and Tocqueville, where societies or polities are concerned, no two are alike: different communities have different moral habits and institutions and hence different traditions of public-private interaction. Observation on a country-by-country basis of the interplay between cultural and acultural factors emerges as a methodological imperative.[9]

According to this approach, the laws, institutions, and practices typical of a given society are inextricably linked to that society's *mœurs*, a term invoked by Tocqueville to refer to the "habits of the heart . . . to the various notions and opinions current among men and to the mass of those ideas which constitute their character of mind [*les habitudes de l'esprit*]. I comprise under this term, therefore, the whole moral and intellectual condition of a people" (*Democracy in America*, I.2.9: 310). *Mœurs* are conceived neither as epiphenomena of particular institutional configurations nor as all-powerful forces exerting hegemony over institutions and practices. Rather, in the reciprocal or circular causal picture developed by Montesquieu and Tocqueville, a society's mores are seen as both greatly influential in shaping the framework of its institutions and practices, and, at the same time, as subject to constant evolution in and through this framework.

We can see this circular or reciprocal causality at work in Montesquieu's discussion of the changing means of settling legal disputes in France from the Middle Ages to the early modern period. He notes that as the *mœurs* became "gentler" and more refined, legal proceedings became progressively less violent, passing from the hands of warrior-aristocrats into those of literate jurists. The development of autonomous legal structures monopolized by jurists in turn further dissuaded society's warrior elements from participation in the legal arena, as legal battles came to be seen less as *combat par armes* than as *querelles de plume* (*Spirit of the Laws*, 28.18 & 27). In a similar fashion, Tocqueville described the participatory political structures of early nineteenth-century New England as simultaneously undergirded by the moral habits of a free people and responsible for the reproduction of that very spirit of freedom. On the one hand, "until the independence of the townships [*la liberté communale*] is amalgamated with the manners [*mœurs*] of a people, it is easily destroyed" (*Democracy in America*, I.I.5: 62–63). On the other hand, Tocqueville also claims that "it is only after a long existence in the laws that it [i.e., *la liberté communale*] can be thus amalgamated" (*Democracy in America*, I.I.5: 63). In other words, participatory structures require the support of the mores appropriate to a politically active people and, simultaneously, reinforce those very mores through their continued operation. Participation in voluntary associations continually revives in a citizenry the taste and habit of self-rule.

The Montesquieuian-Tocquevillian picture of reciprocal causality is more complex than the monocausal models more commonly found in the contemporary social sciences (which, undoubtedly, have the advantage of being much simpler conceptually and easier to operationalize in a quantitative sense). When nuanced, complex approaches like those of Montesquieu and Tocqueville are discussed in the contemporary literature, they tend to be interpreted in the more familiar terms of the monocausal framework. The notion of *mœurs*, for example, is usually understood to mean "values," "ideas," or, following Talcott Parsons, "orientations" of an affective, cognitive, or evaluative nature that are said to exist in our minds and exert their influence monocausally on our practice (see Parsons, 1951; see also Taylor, 1991b: 194–95). Seen through this Parsonian lens, Montesquieu and Tocqueville's work is often understood as part of a social psychological approach to politics that allegedly explains the nature of the social and the political by reference to the shared "values" (or "political culture") of society. Seymour Martin Lipset, for example, interprets Tocqueville's discussion of voluntary associations as an account of the mechanisms required "for creating and maintaining value consensus" and links his work with that of twentieth-century Parsonian theories of mass society, like that of William Kornhauser (Lipset, 1981: 7, 52).

Although some social scientists follow Parsons and Lipset in seeing Montesquieu and Tocqueville as concerned exclusively with subjective "values," others claim to read a structuralist logic into their account. Theda Skocpol, for example, asserts that in the Tocquevillian approach, the state "affect[s] political culture, encourage[s] some kinds of group formation and collective political actions (but not others), and make[s] possible the raising of certain political issues (but not others)" (Skocpol, 1985: 21). It is undoubtedly true that Tocqueville devoted much attention to the composition of state structures and thought them greatly influential, but Skocpol's reading, like Lipset's, treats only one element of a complex, nuanced picture of the social and political world.[10]

Fortunately, there is some sign in the contemporary literature that the legacy of Montesquieu and Tocqueville has not been lost altogether. Katzenstein, for example, in reflecting on the para-public spheres of the small and medium-sized countries of post-war Western Europe and in comparing these models of democratic corporatism with the very different American context, has brought out how the public and private spheres—indeed, the entire public-private distinction—are constituted differently in different cultural contexts. His account of the nature of his own *démarche* suggests the manner in which all such inquiries should be assessed:

Analyses like this one . . . cannot meet the exacting standards of a social scientific test that asks for a distinction between necessary and sufficient conditions, a weighting of the relative importance of variables and, if possible, a proof of causality. . . . I am concerned less with proof than with increasing the plausibility of the argument. (Katzenstein, 1985:138)

The emphasis here is less on universal, monocausal laws than on an impressionistic account that can make sense of and do justice to the particularities involved in each case.

The modern-day United States, argues Katzenstein, has emerged out of a cultural and historical context characterized in part by the absence of feudal or aristocratic elements (with the exception of the manorial enclaves of eighteenth- and early nineteenth-century Virginia). The lack of countervailing social forces allowed for the victory of business interests early on, which encouraged and reinforced both a decentralized business structure and a deep hostility in the business community toward any coordinating role for the state (Katzenstein, 1978:325; see also Beard, 1960).[11] Moreover, the overwhelming influence of business interests on early American culture crippled efforts at organizing the working class into an independent political force in its own right (Katzenstein, 1985:172), setting the stage for an imbalance of power that further discouraged the development of a "culture of compromise" between the major players of American industrial society. The result was a conflict-ridden (and often bloody) history of industrial relations, and a winner-take-all mentality in the workplace and the political arena.

Business interests in continental Europe, by contrast, had to adapt to a very different cultural setting. In countries like Switzerland, the Netherlands, Sweden, and Denmark, the cultural landscape was shaped in large part not by the dearth of an aristocracy, as in America, but by its political weakness relative to the well-organized groups and parties representing the burghers, the peasantry, and the nascent working class. The landed gentries of these regions were obliged to come to terms with a plurality of social forces, thereby contributing to a climate of political accommodation and compromise that made possible the bargains and compromises of the 1930s and 1940s. These bargains and compromises, of course, led to the establishment of the formal and informal structures of mediation and coordination associated with contemporary democratic corporatism (Katzenstein, 1985: Ch. 4).[12]

Although the development of corporatist structures of accommodation and compromise in these countries was far from preordained, in Germany the context proved to be even more problematic. Unlike the smaller European countries, with their decentralized civil societies and politically weakened aristocracies, Imperial Germany of the eighteenth and nineteenth centuries seemed to be dominated by the all-pervasive ethos of the Prussian Junker class.[13] However, two important ingredients to a successful democratic corporatist mix were already present, mitigating to some degree Junker hegemony: an independent working-class movement that, in spite of Bismarckian repression, possessed considerable political clout, and a tradition of state activism in industrial development and social welfare.[14] Moreover, federalist practices of municipal self-government, the presence of occupational associations or guilds (*vereine*), and the vibrant university communities that developed before the period of Prussian hegemony, during and after the time of the decentralized Holy Roman Empire, served to nurture German pluralist traditions (Maier, 1988:104–15; Orlow, 1986: *passim*). These heterogeneous and interlocking public-private linkages, savaged during the national-socialist reign of total state power between 1933 and 1945, re-emerged during the post-war period. With the reactionary Junker class dissolved, the remaining conservative forces adopted a more pragmatic, conciliatory attitude toward the workers' movement; and once again numerous non-state institutions reclaimed important policy functions under public law. As Katzenstein suggests, the trade unions, employer associations, churches, municipal government councils, factory councils, and other para-public groups in the Federal Republic of Germany might be seen as "a West Ger-

man version of the intermediary institutions that Tocqueville 150 years ago
saw as so important to American democracy" (Katzenstein, 1987: 80).

In discussing the environmental policy arena in Germany and the United
States, Katzenstein touches on an important reason why the para-public
sphere in America is unlikely to evolve in the direction of the Federal
Republic of Germany. Whereas German environmental groups have formed
their own political parties to voice environmental concerns (in part because
of their limited chances of obtaining satisfaction in the German courts),
American groups are able to launch environmental class-action suits and
engage in other litigation in pursuit of their political ends. German civil
courts grant hearings only to claimants with a direct and tangible interest in
a particular matter, whereas in the United States access to the courts is much
broader (Katzenstein, 1987: 375). Here Katzenstein uncovers an important
feature of contemporary American political culture: a litigious style of politics focused on rights retrieval through the judicial system, which tends to
steer policy issues away from the political arena and into the courts, which
have become, in turn, a (perhaps *the*) major focus of interest group activity
(Sandel, 1984).

As we have noted, much of the interest in and controversy over intermediary bodies today, at least in the literature on corporatism, is centered
around questions of instrumental rationality, that is, the perceived economic
efficacy or inefficacy of particular organizational arrangements in the para-
public realm. By contrast, the discussions of intermediary bodies in the work
of Montesquieu and Tocqueville were set against the backdrop of a clear
normative affirmation of a mode of collective life characterized by participatory freedom and self-government. Indeed, an important source of theoretical continuity between Montesquieu's *Spirit of the Laws* and Tocqueville's
Democracy in America and *The Old Regime and the Revolution* is the crucial conceptual linkage between the intermediary bodies of the para-public
sphere on the one hand and social pluralism and political freedom on the
other.[15]

In their view, the intermediary structures that serve as foci for commu-
nity-based or regionally based religious, juridical, commercial, and political
practice also protect the liberty and group identities of citizens who otherwise might be subject to the homogenizing effects of the state's bureaucratic
machinery. These intermediary bodies, it is argued, stand as a buffer between
the expanding power of the central government and individual citizens.[16]
These structures can only be effective, however, if they are infused with the
spirit of participation. In Montesquieu's time, this spirit came in part from
the wholehearted attachment of the European aristocratic classes to the principle of *honneur*, that is, an acute sensitivity to and lively defense of one's
own rights and privileges in the face of royal encroachment (*Spirit of the*

Laws, 3.6–8, 4.4; see also Taylor, 1991a: 126). Without a strong class of nobles imbued with this *honneur*, monarchy can fall into despotism, an immoderate form of government that can tolerate no intermediary power whatsoever (*Spirit of the Laws*, 2.4).

One of Tocqueville's most important contributions lay in his fine-tuning of Montesquieu's analysis for the democratic age. Whereas Montesquieu's *corps intermédiaires* were for the most part bastions of aristocratic privilege, in Tocqueville's account of the American polity they are transformed into the voluntary, self-governing associations characteristic of a democratic society. Whereas Montesquieu saw aristocratic *honneur* as a crucial factor in motivating widespread participation in intermediary bodies, Tocqueville, writing about the most post-aristocratic society of his time, saw *l'intérêt bien-entendu* (enlightened self-interest, or interest rightly understood) as a key factor that ensured citizen participation in America.

Through their healthy possession of *l'intérêt bien-entendu* (which Tocqueville contrasted with a narrower, short-sighted, "free-riding" form of self-interest), the Americans of the early nineteenth century understood the connection between their long-term individual interests and participation in public life.[17] Moreover, participation in deliberative structures nurtured and increased their appreciation of this connectedness; an apolitical public, Tocqueville maintained, could not easily grasp how public policy can redound to one's benefit or harm one's interests (*Democracy in America*, 1.1.6). For Tocqueville, only a network of intermediary bodies animated by this modern mix of long-term self-interest and concern for the common good could serve as the guarantor of social differentiation and pluralism and stave off what he darkly described as the "soft despotism" of a paternalistic, all-controlling state, which can arise if an apathetic citizenry neglects public life and succumbs to the short-term "petty and vulgar pleasures" of a materialistic existence focused solely on the intimate circle of family and friends (*Democracy in America*, 2.4.6).[18]

As a means of combating the "petty and vulgar pleasures" of materialistic democratic life, Tocqueville insisted upon the cultivation of a lively civic spirit, which he believed to be both nurtured by participatory structures and responsible for the constant regeneration of these structures. "Town meetings are to liberty what primary schools are to science; they bring it within people's reach, they teach men how to use and how to enjoy it" (*Democracy in America*, 1.1.5: 61). He understood what the constitution builders of nineteenth-century Latin America and the peoples of Eastern Europe after World War II discovered the hard way: the existence of a constitution guaranteeing the formal right to organize does not, by itself, suffice. Clubs and associations with apathetic memberships and town-hall meetings that no one attends are mere empty shells rather than sites of self-government. They cannot generate the spontaneous coming together that is necessary to discuss public matters and act together.

For Tocqueville, "democracy" (a term he often used as a synonym for equality, or the equalization of social conditions) was a world-historical inevitability; henceforth, he declared, if the agenda of freedom was to move forward at all, it would have to move in concert with the equally pressing agenda of equality. This insight was the *point de départ* for Tocqueville's well-known analysis of the French Revolution. Although he was sympathetic to the liberal spirit of 1789, Tocqueville blamed the cataclysmic events of the post-1793 period for the demise of the vestiges of political pluralism in the French para-public realm. Whereas in early nineteenth-century America the agendas of freedom and equality were interwoven from the start, in France all the warring parties unintentionally conspired to ensure the continued mutual antagonism of these agendas.

On the one hand, the Legitimists, clinging anachronistically to premodern notions of aristocratic privilege, refused to recognize the reality of the societal (and, indeed, epochal) move toward equality, a move that had begun long before the Revolution, during the monarchy's campaign of centralization and usurpation of regional aristocratic structures. On the other hand, almost all self-proclaimed progressive political forces, while ardent partisans of equality, dealt freedom a severe blow by moving to abolish intermediary bodies (which had degenerated in the last years of the *ancien régime* and had come to be seen as irretrievably reactionary). "The Revolution declared itself the enemy at once of royalty and of provincial institutions; it confounded in indiscriminate hatred all that had preceded it, despotic power and the checks to its abuses; and its tendency was at once to republicanize and to centralize" (*Democracy in America*, I.I.5: 100; see also *The Old Regime and the French Revolution: passim*).

In the emerging Jacobin notion of a free democracy, the citizenry is truly free only when it coalesces into one, common, sovereign will that cannot, as a matter of principle, tolerate opposition; for if the unitary general cannot carry the day in all respects, the freedom of the people is frustrated. Any differentiation within society is looked upon with suspicion, since partial social groupings (e.g., political parties, occupationally based interest groups, etc.) that exclude the majority of citizens on the basis of religious, occupational, ideological, or other affiliations represent cordoned-off areas of social life untouched by the general will, areas of potential privilege in which relations of domination and alienation may arise (Taylor, 1975: Ch. 15; Taylor, 1991a: 133). Ironically, by sweeping away the remaining impediments to a homogeneous general will, the Jacobins accelerated the push toward social uniformity and created a despotism much more draconian than the one that had existed under the Bourbons.

In our century, this Jacobin hostility toward intermediate bodies, accompanied by the urge to bring all semi-autonomous groups under the control of an undifferentiated public realm of equality, remains alive in the left-wing criticisms of corporatist arrangements that we mentioned earlier. Governments that initiate corporatist arrangements are accused of creating new hierarchies by excluding certain kinds of interests from the process of consensus-building while favoring others, thereby undermining the possibility of "universal participation" (Cohen, 1982: 196–203; Offe, 1981, 1985). Meanwhile, juxtaposed to the absolutist picture of democratic freedom is a rival model of society that, while de-emphasizing the idea of collective, political freedom, champions both individual liberty and the efficiency of the supposedly self-adjusting market. The market is posited as a zone of "private" transactions that must remain separate from the public realm of the state. Any call for a rethinking of the dichotomy is said to carry fascist or Leninist implications (Krauss, 1984).

For over a century, these two compelling visions have remained at loggerheads, and the passions generated by their struggle have succeeded to a large degree in deflecting attention away from a third option suggested by Montesquieu and Tocqueville (and, in different ways, by contemporary authors like Taylor and Katzenstein). This option focuses attention on the important economic and political role of a realm either ignored or denigrated in much contemporary left-wing and right-wing discourse, a realm in which the public and the private meet but that is neither wholly public (in the sense of state-directed) nor private. The sphere of mediation that is the para-public can serve to "accommodate . . . the logic of the market by compensating for it, and . . . tolerate . . . the power of the state by circumscribing it" (Katzenstein, 1985: 38).

It would be foolish to suggest that any move toward corporatist consensus-building is preordained for any particular country in the industrialized world. Indeed, nothing guarantees an eternal life for the corporatist structures in place in Europe. In the face of evermore intense international economic pressures, and the lobbying of governments by business interests to move toward neoliberal economic arrangements or by unions in favor of pure state intervention, the temptations to scuttle existing corporatist arrangements may become overwhelming (Katzenstein, 1985: 193). Moreover, for countries with a predilection for market-driven strategies (like the United States, with its weak and declining labor movement), any move toward corporatist bargaining on a "macro" scale would be difficult indeed. For others, such a move could be less painful (like Quebec, given its tradition of state activism and its almost European-style manner of economic management). However, corporatism can make a more modest appearance at the sectoral level, and even in the United States some movement toward meso-corporatism has been detected between interest groups and state agencies at the state and municipal levels of government (Cawson, 1985: 222; for the Scandinavian experience, see Hernes and Selvik, 1981).[19]

As we have suggested, some mix of market mechanisms and state coordination appears likely to continue to characterize the most prosperous industrial democracies of the late twentieth and twenty-first centuries. The crucial (and difficult) question that remains, then, is what mix suits each society (Taylor, 1991a: 119). Structuralist theories claiming cultural neutrality, of either a neo-Marxist or non-Marxist bent, cannot help us here. What we need, as Evans and colleagues have suggested, are "thoroughly dialectical analyses that allow for non-zero-sum processes and complex interactions between state and society" (Evans, Rueschemeyer, and Skocpol, 1985: 355). We have tried to argue that a return to the culturally sensitive thinking of the sort evinced by Montesquieu and Tocqueville would greatly help future research in this area.

ACKNOWLEDGMENTS

Many thanks to Lance Dadey, Erica Brown, Ruth Abbey, and Jeremy Moon for their helpful comments and criticisms.

NOTES

1. For a discussion of policy communities, see Coleman and Skogstad, 1990. On civil society and the new social movements, see Cohen, 1985; and Keane, 1988. The literature on corporatism is vast; see, for example, Schmitter, 1974; Panitch, 1980; Schmitter and Lehmbruch, 1982; and Cawson, 1985.

2. The fact that the term originated in fascist Italy and was associated at one time with what is widely regarded as the backward, liberal social doctrines of the Catholic Church in Europe and Quebec (Panitch, 1979; Archibald, 1984) has served only to reinforce the sustained attack on corporatist models from across the political spectrum. As Katzenstein indicates, many contemporary interpretations of "corporatist tendencies" around the world have this authoritarian variant as their implicit benchmark (Katzenstein, 1985: 30).

3. Right-wing critics of corporatism would of course deny that the post-war structural changes in the world economy call for anything like corporatist mediation and negotiations, because they continue to place their faith in the "invisible hand" adjustment mechanisms of the market.

4. We are simplifying matters somewhat for the purposes of exposition, and we must add the following nuance: although the recent left-leaning literature on corporatism is not wholly averse to the goal of growth, it also tends to emphasize other, more "expressivist" concerns stemming from its close relationship to early nineteenth-century European romanticism. For a discussion of expressivism, see Taylor, 1975.

5. The notion of culture invoked here is the broad sense often found in anthropology, referring to ways of life that incorporate all manner of belief and practice.

6. Most contributors to the literature on corporatism make little or no reference to work predating the 1950s, leaving the impression that the recent focus on the para-public sphere is without precedent in political science. A notable exception is the work on new social movements. There the concept of civil society is traced back to Hegel (see Cohen, 1985; Keane, 1988), and reference is often made to historical studies tracing its development in early modern Europe and America. Of these, one of the earliest and perhaps most influential has been Jurgen Habermas's *The Structural Transformation of the Public Sphere*, translated by Thomas Burger (Cambridge, MA: MIT Press, 1991).

7. Criticism of this one-sidedness has become commonplace in the social science community. See, for example, Kenneth Dyson's (1980: 18) recent expression of dissatisfaction with contemporary theories of the state: "[The state] represents not only a particular manner of arranging political and administrative affairs and regulating relationships of authority but also a cultural phenomenon which binds people together in terms of a common mode of interpreting the world." As we shall see, contemporary treatments of cultural variables in a Montesquieuian or Tocquevillian spirit can still be found, albeit at the margins of the social sciences.

8. The skeptical strain in the French intellectual tradition, with its suspicion of ambitious theoretical enterprises and its emphasis on the particular nature of knowledge, can be traced back at least to Montaigne (1533–1592). Consider the following pensée from his essay "On Cannibals" (l. 31): "One man, who otherwise knows only what everyone else knows, may have some special knowledge at first-hand about the character of a river or a spring. Yet to give currency to this shred of information, he will undertake to write on the whole science of physics. From this fault many great troubles spring" (Montaigne, 1958: 108. Translation modified).

9. This insight has been put to good use in recent work in anthropology. See, for example, Clifford Geertz, *Local Knowledge: Further Essays in Interpretive Anthropology* (New York: Basic Books, 1983).

10. Skocpol, as one of the best theorists in the structuralist tradition, has occasionally demonstrated an openness to forms of analysis other than structuralism. Consider this example: "[the presence or absence] of specific organizational structures . . . seems critical to the ability of state authorities to undertake given tasks. In turn, the presence or absence of organizational structures is connected to past state policies, thus underlining the need for historical as well as structural analysis if specific state capacities and incapacities are to be understood" (Evans, Rueschemeyer, and Skocpol, 1985: 351).

11. Tocqueville's observations of these aspects of early American culture formed an important part of *Democracy in America*, particularly Volume 1. He was also sensitive to the initial religious (puritan) foundation of American business activity, an insight later developed at length in Max Weber's justly famous *Protestant Ethic* and the *Spirit of Capitalism* (1904–1905).

12. Katzenstein, like Montesquieu and Tocqueville, does give some weight to acultural factors. He suggests, for example, that the dependence of these small European states on world markets has impelled them to develop efficient economic units through corporatist cooperative efforts. However, the nature of the corporatist accommodation varies from country to country. For his comparative analysis of the various forms that corporatism takes across Western and Central Europe, see Katzenstein, 1985.

13. See Weber's insightful discussion in his essay "Capitalism and Rural Society in Germany," *From Max Weber: Essays in Sociology*, eds. H.H. Gerth and C. Wright Mills (New York: Oxford University Press, 1958), pp. 363–85.

14. In Germany, Katzenstein explains, the state never emerged in the public consciousness simply as a neutral arbiter and enforcer of law, an artificial entity existing apart from

and potentially hostile to an independent civil society, but rather as an entity intimately related to and overlapping with civil society, involved in processes of coordination and reaching consensus (Katzenstein, 1987: 382).

15. With their emphasis on political freedom, Montesquieu and Tocqueville may be placed within the context of what has been variously termed the "civic humanist" or "classical republican" tradition, associated with such thinkers as Aristotle, Cicero, Machiavelli, and Rousseau. For an insightful historical account of the civic humanist tradition, see Pocock, 1975.

16. Montesquieu and Tocqueville claimed to have found the healthiest and most dynamic networks of intermediary bodies in the Anglo-Saxon world of their respective eras. This association of political liberty with the "English model" greatly influenced later Anglo-Saxon writers of the nineteenth and twentieth centuries and served directly or indirectly to reinforce their own Anglophile tendencies. See, for example, the English Canadian political scientist Alexander Brady's analysis of social and political life in the British Empire and its former colonies (1958: 8, 11):

> Colonial society in the nineteenth century was a projection of British voluntary society, composed of spontaneous associations, zealous to act apart from the state with a purpose and *élan* of their own. Such associations could flourish only where democracy was interpreted in the British sense as something beyond mere majority rule or the coercion of absolute numbers; where, in other words, it was associated with tolerance towards individual and group diversity. . . . Thus democracy in the Dominions showed no leaning to the political cult fathered by the French Revolution of maximizing the role of the state and minimizing that of free associations.

Brady the Anglophile was steeped in the British intellectual tradition of pluralism, which arose in part as a reaction against more monistic views of state and society emerging on the Continent as well as in England. F.W. Maitland and Harold Laski were among the tradition's luminaries. See the interesting discussion in Dyson, 1980, Ch. 7.

17. See *Democracy in America*, 2.2.14. As Richter has pointed out, Tocqueville's notion of enlightened self-interest was foreshadowed in Books 11 and 19 of the *Spirit of the Laws*, in which Montesquieu suggested how the self-interest characteristic of English commercial society was compatible with the maintenance of the general good (Richter, 1970: 95). This notion plays an important role in Katzenstein's discussion of democratic corporatism as well. In the small European states, he claims, all major social groups understand that in light of the intense pressures of economic competition emanating from abroad, "all members of society are in the same small boat, that the waves are high, and that everyone must help pull the oars." In other words, they have learned to link their own interests "with shared interpretations of the collective good" (Katzenstein, 1985: 35, 32).

18. Tocqueville's dark portrayal of "soft despotism" as a possible future for America and other modern mass democracies in Volume 2 of *Democracy in America* was later developed in the social sciences of the late nineteenth and early twentieth centuries, as authors like Moisei Ostrogorski and Max Weber analyzed the oligarchic and bureaucratic tendencies of modern mass political parties and the atrophying of public-spirited participation in the politics of liberal democracies. For certain later "elite theorists" of democracy, like Joseph

Schumpeter, mass political apathy comes to be seen as a virtue, not a vice, of modern political systems. See Ostrogorski (1902), Weber (1958), and Schumpeter (1962).

19. With the recent election of Bill Clinton and the entry into his Cabinet of pro-corporatist analysts such as Robert Reich (1983, 1991), we may see in the coming years some tentative moves toward federal involvement in meso-corporatist practice in the United States.

2

Policy Networks and State Autonomy

Martin J. Smith

The notion of policy networks has almost become the dominant paradigm for understanding the relationships between the state and interest groups (see Marsh and Rhodes, 1992; Jordan and Schubert, 1992). Although the approach has paid much attention to the role of groups and the nature of interactions between the state and groups, it has paid relatively little attention to the nature of the state. Most writers adopt, implicitly or explicitly, pluralist definitions of the state (Jordan and Richardson, 1987; Rhodes and Marsh, 1992; Richardson and Jordan, 1979). Consequently, they emphasize the role of groups in the policy process. Pluralists believe that groups wield a "significant amount of power" and are therefore important in determining policy outcomes (Easton, 1965; Truman, 1951).

Almond (1988) claims that contrary to the views of many of its critics, pluralism does pay a great deal of attention to the role of state actors. However, it cannot be denied that the central tenet of pluralism is the dispersal of power throughout society. Therefore, the basis of pluralist democracy is that the people ultimately control the government (Nordlinger, 1988). Despite Almond's protestation, pluralist approaches to pressure groups have concentrated on the activities, interests, and resources of groups in understanding their impact on policy outcomes. They see policy networks as a mechanism for allowing particular groups to achieve access to the policy process. The pluralist approach to policy networks and policy communities regards them as fragmented subsystems that involve a large number of groups in the policy process (Richardson and Jordan, 1979).

Pluralists counterpose themselves to the state autonomy approach, which sees state actors as the key determinants of policy outcomes (Jordan, 1990). State-centered theorists suggest that state actors have their own organizational and individual interests, which may have a major impact on policy. Both perspectives accept that groups and the state are important, but each emphasizes one particular set of institutions. Hence, most advocates of the policy network perspective see them as a constraint on state autonomy.

This chapter suggests that the concept of policy networks is compatible with a notion of the state that emphasizes the interests of state actors and, indeed, can help to provide the state theory that is missing in most accounts of policy networks. We argue that the autonomy of state actors is dependent on the types of relationships that exist between pressure groups and government agencies. If we are to understand properly the role of groups, we need to examine the context within which they operate. The impact of pressure groups on policy depends on the interest of state actors, the historical development of the policy arena, and the organization of group-government relations (Smith, 1990a). Likewise, the ability of state actors to achieve goals is dependent on developing relationships with groups that can create the mechanisms for implementing desired policy outcomes. Therefore, in this chapter we assess the concepts of policy networks and state autonomy and argue that policy networks can increase autonomy. The approach is applied to a number of case studies in Britain and the United States.

POLICY NETWORKS AND STATE AUTONOMY

Policy networks are a means of categorizing the interactions between groups and government. They exist where there is an exchange of resources between a group or groups and a part of government (Rhodes, 1990). This exchange can range from providing information to a group on a consultation list (Jordan and Richardson, 1987) to delivering a policy in return for support from a group. Consequently, there is a continuum of networks from a closed policy community to an open issue network (Marsh and Rhodes, 1992).

In a closed policy community there is usually a single decision-making center. One department or one section of a department is responsible for making decisions within a particular policy area. The policy community also includes a limited number of groups. Moreover, the groups and government actors have shared values on the parameters of policy, such as what problems exist and the range of solutions that are available. The groups involved accept the rules of the game laid down by government. Groups that do not submit to the dominant values of the community are excluded because they are operating outside of the game.

In an issue network the policy arena involves multiple decision-making centers, a wide range of frequently changing groups, an absence of shared values, and very little exclusion. Nevertheless, an issue network is not completely open. Within the network there is a degree of shared identity; the actors recognize that a specific policy sector exists. There is a particular range of groups involved in the policy process. Although there are low perimeter fences and groups have fairly easy access, there is still some exclusion (see Campbell et al., 1989: 94).

Therefore, as Rhodes and Marsh (1992) have outlined, the nature of the relationship between groups and government can vary according to the number of participants, the frequency of interaction, the degree of continuity, the degree of value consensus, the level of resource dependency, and the nature of bargaining. Changes in any of these variables can affect the nature of the policy network. Hence, group-government relations can be characterized by a variety of networks ranging from closed policy communities to open issue networks.

Policy networks can develop around departments, policy areas, or issues. They also operate at various levels (Grant, Paterson, and Whitson, 1988; Wilks and Wright, 1987). At the macro-level is the policy arena—for example, chemical policy. Within the policy arena are various subsectors such as pharmaceuticals and agricultural chemicals; there could even be microsectors concerned with a particular drug or regulation (see Grant et al., 1988). A policy arena may contain a range of policy networks with overlapping membership that shift according to the particular issues being discussed. Thus, policy networks can exist within certain areas like agricultural policy, but a new policy network can still form around a distinct issue such as salmonella poisoning in food (Smith, 1991).

Policy networks provide a stable means of representing interests in the policy process, particularly if they are well integrated. The range of groups, issues, and problems faced by policymakers causes the policy process to become increasingly complex. Establishment of policy communities by policymakers is a means of simplifying the policy process in order to make issues and policy areas manageable (Jordan and Richardson, 1982). Policy communities limit the number of actors involved in a policy area and, by establishing a degree of consensus, can limit the policy options that are available. The policy agenda of a community defines the issues and groups that have access to the policy process, and this allows certain problems and difficulties to be excluded.

Policymakers have an incentive to institutionalize relationships with particular groups. These institutions ensure particular patterns of behavior by restraining the policy options that are available (Hall, 1986; Ikenberry, 1988). Once these institutions have been established, they are difficult to change. As Ikenberry (1988: 224) outlines,

Particular institutional arrangements create privileged positions for individuals and groups who work to perpetuate those arrangements. At the microscopic level individuals within organisations seek to preserve and protect their missions and responsibilities even when specific circumstances that brought the organisation into existence have changed. At the macroscopic level, institutional reform is carried out within an existing array of organisations and structures that shape and constrain any efforts at change.

Policy networks are usually seen as limiting the actions of state actors. Where policy-making takes place within the closed circle of a subgovernment, the distinctions between government and governed are blurred. Thus, "a subgovernment is the most effective form of access for private interests. Provided that the participants are prepared to compromise and can avoid controversy, they can run their policy area for a long time" (Rhodes, 1990: 207). Many authors believe that policy networks provide institutional access for pressure groups to government departments and agencies; this enables the groups to "capture" the policy process or at least become highly influential (Jordan and Richardson, 1987; Heclo, 1978).

However, this view results largely from an overconcentration on groups and a failure to conceptualize the role of state actors. State-centered theorists maintain that the state is not captured by groups but that state actors have interests of their own and, on occasion, the ability to transform these interests into policy. Nordlinger (1981: 1) asserts that in determining public policy, "the preferences of the state are at least as important as those of civil society." Often the state actors follow their own interests, "even when [their] preferences diverge from the demands of the most powerful groups in civil society."

The interests are many and varied. The state is not a unified actor (Jessop, 1990) but is divided between many departments, agencies, and individuals. In particular, interests vary between bureaucrats and politicians (Weir and Skocpol, 1985). Politicians have interests in their own re-election, their careers, their departments, and their own ideological goals. Bureaucrats have interests in developing their careers (which might conflict with the career interests of politicians), increasing their power vis-à-vis other departments and politicians, and reducing the problems and surprises of policy-making. State actors also have general interests in maintaining internal order, external security, and economic growth. But there can be conflict over how to achieve these goals. There is no reason why the state must act in the interests of groups or classes in society. However, if state actors take autonomous actions, they must have the resources to act independently of society.

The ability of the state to act autonomously depends on its capabilities— the extent to which it can intervene in society—to achieve its policy goals without the support of societal actors. If the state structures do not provide policy instruments for a particular policy, then that policy is unlikely to be proposed. Mann (1984) distinguishes between the state's *despotic* and *infrastructural* power.[1] Despotic power involves the state acting "without routine, institutionalised negotiations with groups in civil society" (Mann, 1984: 188). This occurs when state actors move directly to achieve their own goals without taking account of the interests of groups within society. Despotic power usually occurs within ancient empires or authoritarian regimes. However, even within liberal democratic regimes, state actors have the ability—through their authority, their control over legislation, and their control over coercive apparatus—to act without negotiation. In a democratic regime, the cost of such an approach might be very high in terms of vocal/physical opposition, difficulty of implementing the policy, or loss of an election. Nevertheless, it is an approach that governments are occasionally prepared to use. In particular, presidents and prime ministers can use their political authority and their formal (if not actual) control over governmental machinery to use despotic power and attempt to adopt policies without consultation. In this way they can break up or bypass traditional state-group relationships.

However, in liberal democracies it is more usual for states to use infrastructural power. This is "the capacity of the state to actually penetrate civil society, and to implement logistically political decisions throughout the realm" (Mann, 1984: 189). The state is able to intervene in society through its administrative machinery and its relationship with social groups. The state has developed these capabilities because its resources and functions are necessary for society and the groups within it (Mann, 1984).

If the state is to act autonomously, it needs both the ability to intervene and the resources to be exchanged with groups in society (Rhodes, 1981). The process of exchange and the building of capabilities depends on the existence of policy networks. Policy networks are relationships that allow groups and state actors to exchange resources in order to increase state capabilities in policy intervention.

This suggests a break from the position of state-centered theory. State interests and actions do not occur in a vacuum, sealed off from civil society—state autonomy is not a zero-sum. Rather, the development and implementation of state interests depend on building relationships with particular groups. Therefore, networks are not essentially a constraint on state autonomy—the two concepts are not mutually incompatible. It is possible that policy networks provide a mechanism for exchanging the resources necessary for state actors to exercise infrastructural power.

Policy communities, in particular, increase state autonomy by establishing the means through which state actors can intervene in society without using force. By integrating state and societal actors, policy communities increase the capabilities of the state to make and implement policy. They create state powers by providing resources of legitimacy, information, and the means for implementation. In doing so they increase the autonomy of actors in a policy area by excluding other actors from the policy process. In a policy community, state and societal actors work together to increase their autonomy in relation to other groups. Hence, autonomy is not something that the state has in relation to society. Instead, particular state and societal actors develop autonomy in relation to other actors and networks. Policy communities do not necessarily imply that state actors are captured by groups. This depends on the nature of the policy area, the external circumstances at the time of decision-making, and the resources of various actors within the community.

In a less well integrated network, even though the pressures on government actors to adopt a particular policy might not be very great, the autonomy of government actors is limited. In an issue network, state actors lack infrastructural power because the mechanisms to intervene in society do not exist. When several government actors are involved in the policy community, no single agency or government department will have the ability to act on its own. Likewise, the existence of many conflicting groups within the arena means that the policy area is likely to be highly political, so state actors will be unable to make decisions unobserved by the public, legislature, or media.

Policy does not develop as a result of the state reacting to group pressure. Both state actors and groups have resources, and in order to exchange resources they develop relationships that have a particular organizational form. This organization—the policy network—affects not only the interests of the actors involved but also the ability of the state actors to take and implement decisions.

It is frequently the case that policy networks affect the degree to which state actors achieve their goals. Rather than preventing autonomy, policy communities can (in particular circumstances) increase the infrastructural power of state actors. Both state actors and interest groups have resources and could be dependent on each other, according to the nature of those resources and the particular policy area. Interest groups need government in order to influence policy, and government needs interest groups in order to make and implement policy. Government can ignore interest groups and develop alternative machinery for making and implementing policy. But the costs of this action could be high in terms of creating confrontation and developing alternative administrative machinery. Therefore, state autonomy and policy networks are interacting but in different dimensions that have a relationship that varies according to the circumstances. Figure 2.1 illustrates the various relationships.

Figure 2.1
Policy Networks and State Autonomy

Level of Autonomy	Policy Network	
	Policy Community	*Issue Network*
High Autonomy	1. Closed relationship producing infrastructural power	2. Many actors, high state freedom
Low Autonomy	3. Closed relationship, pressure group capture	4. Many actors, limited state control of policy

In situation 1 of Figure 2.1, a policy community increases the infrastructural power of state actors by establishing the means for policy-making and intervention. Although there is a policy community, there is also high state autonomy. In situation 2, an issue network exists. Here, although state actors might lack infrastructural power because they do not have the ability to intervene with a large number of actors, they could still have a high level of autonomy because the various societal interests involved do not have the organization or resources to prevent the state from adopting certain policies. If there is confusion and conflict between pressure groups within the policy arena, then state actors can impose their own solutions without high costs. In situation 3, a policy community exists that is dominated by the groups rather than state actors, and it is the group that determines the interests of the policy community. This policy community is rare in Britain but more common in other European states and in the United States. Finally, in situation 4 an issue network reduces the infrastructural power of the state by making the policy process difficult and by reducing the control of state actors over policy implementation. This chapter suggests that although all these situations do occur, the most likely relationships between networks and autonomy are situations 1 and 4 because networks affect infrastructural power.

Therefore, state actors are not always dominant. In particular circumstances, networks can be dominated by groups with high resources in terms of knowledge, control over implementation, economic power, or ideology. Yet it must be remembered that it is state actors who determine the rules of the game. The matrix does not include actors who are outside the policy networks changing the rules of the game. State actors have the resources to select which actors are included in a policy arena and what issues and policies are appropriate to a policy community. Even in a captured policy community it is possible for state actors—probably outside the community—to change the rules of the game and remove the dominating group. In Britain the former secretary of state for education, Kenneth Clarke, simply ignored the teachers in the development of education policy and radically changed aspects of education policy without any consultation. Evidently political actors can change the rules of the game if they are prepared to bear the political costs in terms of creating new relationships and developing alternative administrative machinery.

In understanding policy outcomes it is necessary to examine the relationships that exist between groups and government and the impact of these relationships on state autonomy. If a policy community exists, the infrastructural power of state actors will likely be greater (although this is not always the case), so there is a probability of state intervention and stability of policy. In an issue network the policy outcomes are likely to be much more varied, as there is no agreement on the available options and no single decisionmaker; but it will be much more difficult for the policy decision to be implemented.

In the remainder of this chapter, we examine the relationship between state autonomy and policy networks in specific cases. We examine policy networks in Britain and the United States in order to compare the types of relationships that exist in different types of states and the impact of these relationships on state autonomy.

POLICY NETWORKS IN THE UNITED STATES: HEALTH POLICY AND TRADE POLICY

The United States has been described as a weak state or even a stateless society (Dyson, 1980; Nettl, 1968; van Waarden, 1992). However, as Atkinson and Coleman (1989a) point out, it is difficult to make generalizations about the nature of states because the strength of the state in terms of its control over policy can vary from one policy area to another. Case studies of trade and health policy in the United States indicate that the level of autonomy of state actors varies and to a certain extent depends on the nature of the policy network. In health policy, where there has been a relatively loose policy network, state actors have had limited control over policy; in trade policy, where a policy community existed during the 1950s and 1960s, state actors have had greater autonomy.

U.S. Health Policy

The development of health policy in the United States has been on the basis of conflict rather than consensus. There has long been disagreement between doctors, Congress, and the chief executive over how health care should be provided. This conflict has prevented the development of a closed health policy community and has limited the control of state actors— whether officials, Congress, or president—over the development of policy.

One key area of conflict has been the issue of national health insurance. After World War II, President Harry Truman made health insurance central to his domestic agenda (Peon, 1979). The main doctors' organization, the American Medical Association (AMA), saw national insurance as an attack on their autonomy and so responded immediately. They initiated a fierce campaign, using professional lobbyists, contacts with the public, and politicians to oppose health insurance. They contacted thousands of groups to convince them that "the voluntary approach to health insurance was desirable" (Campion, 1984: 162). Truman was unable to get his proposals for health insurance through Congress, and with the election of Eisenhower the issue of health insurance was removed from the agenda (Peon, 1979). Hence, unlike the situation in Britain, there was little agreement on the direction of health policy and in particular there was conflict between the chief executive and Congress over the issue.

As a consequence the supporters of health insurance realized that it was better to follow a gradualist approach, so they aimed to obtain health insurance for the aged. Although such a bill had little chance of passing under President Eisenhower, President Kennedy strongly supported coverage for pensioners. However, the AMA was still strongly opposed, seeing it as the first step toward socialized medicine. The AMA again launched a massive campaign of opposition and the legislation was defeated in the Senate (Marmor, 1970). Nevertheless, President Johnson used the swell of public opinion after the assassination of Kennedy and the new Democratic influx into Congress to make Medicare a central part of his Great Society program. With the changes in Congress, the final legislation widened health coverage to include the indigent in addition to the aged.

The central features of U.S. health policy developed in an atmosphere of conflict rather than cooperation. Throughout the period 1920–1965 there was almost no agreement between federal government and the doctors, or within Congress, over the nature of health policy. Consequently, during the post-war period doctors failed to establish close and institutionalized relations with government. It was relatively difficult for government to make health policy because it did not have the support of the doctors. Without a policy community, state actors lacked the infrastructural power to make health policy. Nor did they have the resources or political will to use despotic power. The U.S. government's autonomy in making health policy was greatly limited.

Nevertheless, the U.S. government is highly involved in health policy: there is a broad range of government schemes and at least $60 billion being spent on the uninsured alone (Havighurst et al., 1988). However, the lack of consensus on health policy and the range of activities means that there are a large number of government agencies involved in the health process. There is no single coordinating authority, so the network is very loose.

Laumann and Knoke (1987) maintain that despite the lack of integration, the network does have a core with the Department of Health and Human Services (DHHS) at its center. However, the core includes the "White House Office, the OMB, the Health Resource Administration, the HCFA, the FDA Commissioner, one Senate subcommittee, and four private sector groups" (Laumann and Knoke, 1987: 245). Close to the core are specialist organizations like the AMA, the American Hospital Association, and the main insurance organizations, plus most of the federal health agencies. Many core actors—like the Office of Management and Budget (OMB) and the Food and Drug Administration (FDA)—have the authority and resources to make their own health policy; the president has access to the arena through the OMB and the White House Office, making it difficult for policy to be made autonomously from the president. Even the core organizations are highly fractured when it comes to making policy. The DHHS contains a large number of relatively independent agencies, each with its own priorities. In order to strengthen their position relative to other government bodies, these agencies all encourage interest groups to be active within the health arena. Whereas in Britain there is one department largely responsible for health policy and a limited number of interest groups, in the United States there are many departments and numerous interest groups.

Further disaggregation occurs because there are a number of congressional committees involved in health policy. In addition, states have a considerable role and discretion in certain aspects of health policy. Consequently, U.S. health policy involves literally hundreds of interest groups and government agencies. Laumann and Knoke (1987) have suggested that there are 151 organizations involved in the health policy domain. As a result of this large and loose network, it has been very difficult for any government actor to control U.S. health policy. Any significant changes in health policy have required substantial presidential support, but even presidents have been constrained in what they could achieve. As a result it is relatively easy for parts of the network to prevent change. There is now a health service crisis in the United States, with costs rising and the quality of treatment for a large number of people falling. Despite the very high costs of the U.S. system, a large and increasing number of people receive little or no health care (Feldstein, 1988; Marmor, Mashaw, and Harvey, 1990).

The loose network is partly a result, and partly a cause, of U.S. health policy. The network takes a loose form because in the absence of consensus, U.S. health policy has always been highly conflictual. Key developments in U.S. health policy have been subject to highly political debate and overt lobbying. The policy process has occurred within Congress in addition to the executive branch. Politicization of the issue has prevented health policy from being carried out in routinized and obscure subgovernments, so it has been relatively easy for large numbers of actors to achieve access. With politicization, numerous group and state actors, and a lack of consensus, state-group relationships have not become highly institutionalized and an issue network has continued to exist.

The issue network has affected policy outcomes. Lacking infrastructural power, the executive branch has not been able to determine the direction of health policy and as a consequence the AMA has been able to prevent many proposed changes in health policy. Moreover, because of lack of consensus between state actors, no single organization has been able to dominate policy. The existence of an issue network has enabled many groups to enter the policy process; this has increased the politicization of the arena and emphasized the difficulty of getting new ideas accepted within it.

U.S. Trade Policy

Despite the openness of the U.S. political system and a history of demands for protection, the executive branch did manage to establish a relatively closed community in trade policy during the 1950s and 1960s. After World War II the United States had the resources to establish itself as a hegemonic power, whereby "one state is powerful enough to maintain the essential rules governing interstate relations and is willing to do so" (Keohane, 1984: 34). Because of its economic strength and the post-war weakness of its competitors, the fear of a return to the inter-war depression, and the strength of liberal ideology within the country, the United States wanted to create a liberal world order. The Marshall Plan, GATT, and Bretton Woods were established to provide the institutional framework for this policy (Krasner, 1978). The United States aimed to ensure its own economic prosperity and to appear as a benevolent power helping Western Europe recover from war. European recovery entailed access to U.S. markets (Destler, 1986). Free trade suited both the economic interests and the political goals of the U.S. government. Consequently, a consensus could be established over the direction that trade policy could take: "The ideological consensus proclaimed that foreign trade was a good thing, that high tariffs were to be avoided, that we should be helping or drawing closer to our free world allies, and that we should not sell abroad without buying abroad. Protectionists, on the defensive, rarely denied these principles" (Bauer, DeSola Pool, and Dexter, 1972: 465). In order to achieve the free trade policy, it was important for the executive branch to establish a policy community that excluded the interest groups and members of Congress that demanded protection.

In a congressionally dominated system, how was the executive branch able to reassert its control over trade policy? First, it was clear, even to Congress, that the legislature could not make trade policy in the national interest. If there was to be liberal trade—which many members of Congress, the executive branch, and business believed to be desirable—the policy process had to be controlled by the administration. Second, because various interests had historically lobbied hard for protection, the executive branch was prepared to buy off certain industries with special concessions (Krasner, 1978). Third, there was little public opposition to such a policy. Trade policy was not a salient issue among voters; and most business people, whatever their direct material interests, preferred a liberal trade policy to protection (Bauer, DeSola Pool, and Dexter, 1972). Fourth, during the post-war period, liberal trade was promoted as necessary for the fight against communism and so became part of a wider Cold War ideology, which made it even more difficult to question (Krasner, 1978). Finally, Congress was not cut out of the policy process. Trade policy was still based on negotiation between White House and Congress, and channels for congressional influence remained. Through the House Ways and Means Committee and the Senate Finance Committee, Congress had controlled access to the policy community.

The trade policy community had two important components: the widely accepted liberal trade ideology, and the leadership of the State Department. The spectre of the inter-war depression, the rise of communism and its closed trading bloc, and the domestic tradition of liberalism in the United States made a belief in liberal trade widely accepted—if not by the general public and particular industries, then by the governing elite. This had the important effect of depoliticizing trade policy. The ideology meant that the only policy option within the community was liberal trade (Destler, 1986). This ideology made it difficult for the issues of protection to be discussed; therefore, groups that wanted protection had little access to the policy process. The issue of protection was not completely ignored. There were a number of special cases—for example, textiles, steel, and agriculture. By making these exceptions, the policy community managed to depoliticize even the areas in which controversy was almost endemic. Safeguards were built into the legislation (e.g., escape clauses and anti-dumping regulations) in order to protect constituents who could not compete on the world market. More important, Congress protected itself from interest group demands for concessions by creating legislation whereby "interest groups could go to bureaucratic agencies whose legal task was to placate potential congressional clients" (Goldstein, 1988: 188).

At the executive level a large number of actors were involved in the policy community. The central actor was the State Department, and within that was the Bureau of Economic and Business Affairs. An important role was also played by the Treasury and, within the Treasury, the Office of the Assistant Secretary for International Affairs. "With a staff of over 200 professional economists and access to economists in other Treasury Bureaus, OASIA has the resources to weigh in on any governmental exercises involving international economics" (Cohen, 1988: 45). Increasingly important was the Special Representative for Trade Negotiation, who was largely responsible for conducting negotiation for GATT. Other organizations like the United States Department of Agriculture (USDA), the Department of Commerce, the OMB, and even bodies like the Central Intelligence Agency (CIA) and National Security Council (NSC) played a role on a more ad hoc basis (Cohen, 1988).

Despite the number of government actors, the policy community had numerous mechanisms that allowed it to remain relatively closed. First, the degree of consensus on a liberal trade policy was such that none of the concerned groups were actually trying to pursue a different policy. Consequently, throughout the 1950s and 1960s all those involved in the community were prepared to accept the leadership of the State Department. This was helped by strong presidential support for the trade policy and the State Department's leadership role. Through the president, the State Department had an important resource for ensuring its dominance and for making certain that the liberal trade policy was widely accepted.

In addition to State's strength, the department likely to support industries wanting protection, Commerce, was relatively weak. It did not have the resources or capabilities to make an effective impact on trade policy (Cohen, 1988). Finally, the unity of the community was maintained by the limited role of interest groups. Industry had little institutional access to the policy community and was generally committed to the liberal trade policy. Moreover, the industries with special demands were provided with safety valves. Hence, there were few interest groups pressing agencies within the community to pursue a different policy.

By ensuring that trade policy was contained within an executive-dominated policy community, the trade policy community could ensure a policy of liberal trade. In particular, by allowing State rather than Commerce to dominate, the policy could be directed toward foreign policy goals rather than purely economic goals. The policy community had a major impact on policy by excluding the interests that would have supported a policy of protection. By excluding Congress and limiting the role of Commerce, the community closed access to the majority of protectionist interests. By making steel, textiles, and agriculture special cases and allowing some degree of protection through quotas or voluntary restraint agreements, the policy community was ensuring that these sectors were satisfied and did not become subject to widespread debate—in effect, the policy community had its own "pressure diverting management system" (Destler, 1986: 36).

Through exclusion, its own ideology, and the key institutions like State and the International Trade Commission, the policy community ensured that a free trade policy continued. It was able to exclude the interests of many business organizations by closing off their demands for particular forms of protection and by developing the trade policy it believed was in the best interest of the United States.

In two policy areas within the United States, there are different types of networks. This had important implications for the autonomy of state actors. In health policy there was an issue network with many interests and a lack of consensus over the direction of policy. This made it very difficult for state actors to control the direction of policy. They did not have the infrastructural power to make health policy because Congress, the doctors, and the insurance companies controlled different parts of the health policy process and thus could prevent changes in policy. In a sense, the power of all groups within the network was negative. They could prevent change, so any change that did occur had to be incremental as a coalition developed around policies of the lowest common denominator.

In trade policy, the policy community provided state actors with the infrastructural power to intervene. Although a range of actors were involved within the community, by excluding protectionist interests and shifting the locus of decision-making from Congress to the executive branch, the community managed to develop a consensus on trade policy. Thus, state actors rather than pressure groups controlled the policy process.

POLICY NETWORKS AND STATE AUTONOMY IN BRITAIN: AGRICULTURAL AND INDUSTRIAL POLICY

In Britain there is an interesting contrast between the networks in industrial policy and agricultural policy. Despite the fact that Britain is an industrial country with long-term economic problems, the relationships within the industrial policy arena have been relatively loose and industrial policy has tended to be ad hoc and incoherent. The degree of state intervention has been limited relative to other industrial countries such as France, Germany, and Japan. However, despite the fact that agriculture accounts for less than 4 percent of gross domestic product (GDP), a very close and closed policy community has developed between the farmers and the Ministry of Agriculture and the state has followed a policy of high intervention and high subsidies. Part of the explanation for these differential policies is the nature of the policy networks and the level of state autonomy.

British Agricultural Policy

The agricultural policy community in Britain was, at least until the 1980s, the archetypal closed policy community. Before World War II, agricultural policy was made within a fairly loose network that involved a number of interest groups, the Treasury, the Board of Trade, the Foreign Office, and the Ministry of Agriculture (Smith, 1990b). However, a number of events led to the establishment of an interventionist agricultural policy and a closed policy community. First, the inter-war agricultural depression undermined faith in the laissez-faire solution to the problems of agriculture. Second, initially with the approach of war and then with the actual war, the government realized the need to increase agricultural production and was prepared to provide agricultural support and involve the farmers in the policy process. Third, the National Farmers Union (NFU) established itself as the monopoly representative of the farmers.

The requirements of the war placed the farmers in a strong position. Government could not afford to lose their confidence, so it promised them fixed prices for their produce. In order to prevent conflict over price fixing, the government announced that it would set up "a better machinery for fixing prices" (House of Commons, c.726). Hence, the Annual Review was established whereby the Ministry of Agriculture and the NFU would annually review the conditions of agriculture and the goals of agricultural policy. Subsequently, the Ministry would determine what price increase the farmers would receive (Smith, 1989). This arrangement established the institutional basis of the policy community. Agricultural policy-making was effectively removed from government and placed in the hands of the Ministry of Agriculture and the NFU, who were guaranteed consultation through the 1947 Agriculture Act. This effectively excluded all other agricultural groups from the process. Moreover, the economic and financial crisis that hit Britain after the war caused the government to commit itself to supporting agriculture in the long term as a means of saving imports and dollars.

In this way, the policies established during the war were strengthened in the post-war period. It was accepted that the farmers would have a privileged position in policy-making and that they would receive a high level of state subsidy in order to substantially increase production. As a Treasury official informed a MAF official, "we are now in the position where agriculture will be under fire for not expanding enough. . . . In these circumstances the time may come when certain advances which have hitherto been regarded as visionary may become practical politics" (Cab 124/572).

As a consequence a very closed policy community was established. It had two important internal structures: the ideological and the institutional. The ideological structure was the dominant set of beliefs shared by members of the agricultural policy community. All those involved in agricultural policy-making between 1945 and the late 1970s (and to a large extent during the 1980s) held a common view of the goals of agricultural policy. Governments, officials, ministers of agriculture, and NFU representatives believed that the state should intervene in agriculture, provide price support, and increase production. Therefore, the issue faced by those within the agricultural community was not whether prices and production should be increased but by how much they should be increased. Groups or individuals who raised questions about subsidies or production were not given access to the policy-making process.

The institutional structures were the second means of excluding unwelcome groups from the agricultural policy community. There were four important institutional structures. First was the Ministry of Agriculture, Fisheries, and Food (MAFF). MAFF provided the community with a single decision-making center with the authority to make agricultural policy. It had an interest in maintaining good relations with farmers and in increasing agricultural expenditure. Second, until Britain joined the European Community (EC), the Annual Review surveyed the state of agriculture and determined agricultural prices for the coming year. It gave the farmers a statutory right to consultation and excluded other groups from the process. Moreover, the goal of the Annual Review machinery was to see the extent to which prices should increase. It therefore lacked a mechanism for changing agricultural policy or creating new goals (Smith, 1989). Third, "the rules of the game" (Saunders, 1975) determined how groups should act in order to obtain access to the community. Fourth, an institutional structure was created with Britain's membership in the European Community that until the 1990s privileged the interests of farmers.

Again, this policy community can be seen to have had a substantial impact on policy. The community had an ideology of high prices and high production, and any group that disagreed with its agenda was excluded from the policy process. Hence, environmental groups and consumer groups that might have suggested policies to favor their interests had almost no access. In addition, the main policy machinery of the community—the Annual Review—was concerned solely with increasing subsidies and production. It did not have the ability to change the direction of agricultural policy. Through the strength of its ideology, institutions, and technical barriers, the community was also very effective at excluding other government actors. Most other departments saw agricultural issues as technical rather than political because of the strength of the consensus on agricultural policy. Even the Treasury, the traditional bastion against public expenditure, was prepared to support agricultural production because the policy was seen in terms of Britain's economic survival. Consequently, the agricultural policy community established a high level of capability in terms of agricultural policy and a high level of autonomy in relation both to other government actors and to non-farm groups in civil society.

This case study highlights the problems of the notion of state autonomy. The policy community was established in order for the state to achieve its goals during and immediately after the war. The government needed to increase agricultural production and could only do so with the assistance of the farmers. Establishment of the agricultural policy community was a means of increasing infrastructural power in agriculture. It was the government that determined the direction of agricultural policy during and after the war, albeit not in a direction that the farmers opposed.

However, the policies and interests became enstructured (Giddens, 1986). The policy community developed institutional structures, ideology, and rules of the game, which made it difficult to change the policy when circumstances changed. Consequently, autonomy shifted from the governmental level to the network level. The policy community managed to seal off the agricultural policy process. This was not because of pressure group capture but because the NFU and MAFF had mutual interests in maintaining the community and autonomy. The farmers were ensured high prices and the Ministry had control over a simplified policy process because it did not have to adjudicate between conflicting interests or deal with other departments (Smith, 1993). This highlights the fact that there are layers of autonomy. A section within the state might have autonomy at the expense of a higher authority. It also demonstrates that autonomy can be increased by state actor/group interaction rather than being limited by groups. The fact that the Ministry of Agriculture had such a close relationship with the farmers increased their infrastructural power and their control over agricultural policy.

British Industrial Policy

The history of post-war industrial policy in Britain has seen a range of interventionist policies. Yet these policies have tended to be ad hoc, incoherent, and, in the sense that Britain's industrial base has declined, unsuccessful. The failure of state intervention is due to the lack of capability to intervene effectively. The state has not managed to build the institutions that would allow cooperation to develop between industry and government. Although there have been a range of networks and tripartite and bilateral organizations, these have not been very well integrated, they have been unstable, and they have lacked the capability to direct policy.

The networks that were established usually lacked consensus. Industry was generally hostile to government intervention (Hall, 1986). There were major differences between government, industry, and the unions over the form and degree of intervention that was acceptable. Even the unions opposed any planning that would limit their rights to free collective bargaining, and they preferred a voluntaristic framework to legalistic industrial relations (Coates, 1989). In addition, union power tended to be negative, concentrating on preventing the rationalization of industry rather than being involved in a state-led program of modernization. Consequently, the networks were very unstable; membership changed according to particular political circumstances (e.g., which party was in government and which policy was being introduced). There was little consensus between parties and a lack of any long-term policy. In addition, perceptions of the importance of various groups constantly changed.

Among state actors there was little agreement on industrial policy, and no single organization could either lead or organize industrial policy. The strongest potential leader of a policy community was the Treasury, but it generally preferred macro-level intervention in the economy and was not prepared to support detailed industrial policy. Therefore, within and outside government, industrial policy remained political and a set of shared values failed to develop.

A number of factors account for the failure to develop a coherent industrial policy and a closed policy community. First, the international orientation of the British economy has caused the value of sterling to be a constant concern of policymakers. A fall in the value of the pound could have resulted in the widespread selling of sterling, which would have presented Britain with liabilities that it could not meet (Stones, 1990). Faced with a balance-of-payments deficit, the government has been forced to deflate; so the demands of the City have taken priority over those of industry.

Second, economic policy has been dominated by the Treasury. Thus, within the inner core of the economic bureaucracy "there were no spokesmen for industry" (Zysman, 1983: 201). As a consequence "industrial policy decisions and the administration of industrially orientated programmes are unusually fragmented" (Grant and Wilks, 1983: 22). Third, the Civil Service has little experience of industry and little knowledge of how it works, so "interventionist policies run against the training and traditions of the bureaucracy" (Zysman, 1983: 202).

Fourth, the dominant ideology within the British state, despite increased intervention and collectivism, is one of liberalism and the free market. "Britain industrialised under a laissez-faire regime and prospered in circumstances which confirmed for capital and the state that the business of government was to keep well clear of business." As a result, "The laissez-faire compulsion has proved astonishingly powerful" (Grant and Wilks, 1983: 25–26). Industrial policy has lacked an essential feature of a policy community: an ideology that could hold the community together by setting the agenda, defining the consensus, and determining the potential actors and policy problems.

Finally, the nature of groups has made it difficult to establish an integrated network. On one hand, economic actors—both capital and labor—are very strong, especially at the plant level, and have been able to resist government attempts to coopt them into reorganization policies (Hall, 1986). On the other, they have substantial weakness. They lack strong peak organizations; they are often divided; and although they are economically strong in a negative way, they are weak politically, which has made it difficult to establish constructive relationships within government. They have often been concerned with short-term economic goals rather than being involved in long-term policy-making, and this has made any possibility of depoliticization extremely remote.

Hall has outlined how the organization of the state, capital, and labor has affected the way in which economic policy is made and the nature of the policy. In Britain these factors have led to the failure to develop a closed community in industrial policy or a coherent interventionist industrial policy. As Zysman (1983: 225) makes clear,

In Britain the efforts to expand the interventionist capacity of the state simply drove the parties and producer groups apart, for each policy introduced to promote industry was also viewed as a challenge to the position of business and finance. Each political cycle has exacerbated the free-market-versus-nationalisation dichotomy, leaving no intellectual or political space in which to build a strategy by which the state could nurture private enterprise.

The ideology of the state, capital, and labor, as well as the political parties, has made it very difficult to establish the consensus necessary to build a policy community. In addition, the City and finance have been privileged and the central economic policy-making organization has paid little attention to the demands of industry. Consequently, the state has failed consistently to develop the capabilities to intervene in industrial policy.

The key impact of the differing networks on industrial and agricultural policy is on the ability of the state to intervene. In agriculture, the policy community gave the state the infrastructural power to develop an interventionist agricultural policy that increased agricultural production and the prices received by farmers. In industry, the lack of consensus, the conflict between actors, and the unwillingness of interest groups to become integrated in a network meant that the government was unable to intervene effectively in industrial policy. This had a direct impact on policy. First, attempts at intervention were half-hearted. Often, planning took a very weak form of indicative planning. The National Economic Development Council, which was established as part of an industrial strategy, was purely advisory. Second, intervention was ad hoc and occurred at a time of crisis rather than as part of a long-term coherent strategy. Third, policies were subject to frequent change because of the lack of agreement within and outside government. Fourth, even when a policy was developed, government lacked the means to implement it because it had neither the cooperation of peak interest groups nor the key economic ministry—the Treasury.

We see significant differences between the agricultural policy community and the industrial policy network. In agricultural policy there was consensus on the nature of policy; this allowed the building of a policy community that excluded groups that accepted the rules of the game. Thus, in agriculture the key actors agreed on the direction of policy and they dominated the policy process, whereas in the industrial sector the key actors seldom agreed on the direction of, and no single state actor was able to develop a central role in, the policy process. The network remained open to the conflicting interests of different unions, competing industries, and various ministries. All had access to the policy process. Consequently, in agriculture the state had the capabilities to develop the policy it favored, whereas in industrial policy state actors lacked infrastructural power and attempts at a coherent industrial policy ended in failure.

CONCLUSION

This chapter has demonstrated that close relationships between groups and government actors through policy communities are not necessarily incompatible with state-centered approaches. One must acknowledge that in policy-making both interest groups and state actors have resources and interests. However, interests sometimes derive from the nature of state/interest group relations, and the use of resources often depends on mutual support. In addition, levels of state autonomy and the ability of groups to influence policy depend on the nature of the policy network within an arena. The existence of an open issue network might not only reduce the power of groups but also could diminish the ability of state actors to achieve policy goals. Likewise, the existence of policy communities does not always mean that state actors are captured by pressure groups. It can increase the ability of state actors to achieve their policy goals by increasing their infrastructural power.

The problem with state-centered approaches is that they draw the distinction between the state and society too strongly. State actors develop their interests within the context of societal relationships. The interests of state actors and of groups develop within policy networks through negotiation and mutual dependence. Consequently, state autonomy is not something that exists vis-à-vis society but something that exists vis-à-vis other policy networks. Policy networks increase autonomy by creating mechanisms of infrastructural power and by sealing off sectors of policy from wider interests within government and society. Policy networks are organized relationships that enable state actors and particular societal interests to obtain control over a policy area.

Why are networks more integrated in some areas than others? There are clear advantages to government in developing a closed community: it simplifies the policy process; it reduces the problem of overload; and it increases the autonomy of the actors within the network. Highly integrated networks develop when state actors have clear policy goals. In both examples of trade and agricultural policy, state actors desired to intervene in a particular way and needed certain mechanisms to do so.

However, the desire to intervene is not a sufficient explanation. Government wanted to intervene in U.S. health policy and British industrial policy. States also need the ability to establish mechanisms for intervention. Intervention could occur through despotic power, but that would involve very high costs. The most effective means of intervention is infrastructural power. This involves the ability to establish an integrated relationship with a pressure group that has the resources to use in intervention. Establishing such a relationship involves developing some sort of consensus. This consensus fosters a close relationship between a group and government; it provides the framework of the policy problems and solution, and it is a mechanism for excluding other groups that might complicate and politicize the policy process.

The development of an integrated network is easier where there are well-organized interest groups. These groups can provide the community with legitimation by making it seem representative and authoritative. More important, they can increase infrastructural power by winning the cooperation and assistance of societal groups. Nevertheless, not all policy communities depend on pressure groups. We saw in the trade policy community that the exclusion of interest groups was essential for establishing a free trade policy. Through organizations of international political economy—GATT, the International Monetary Fund (IMF), and fixed currencies—the United States had the means for implementing the policy. It had to ensure that the community was free from societal pressure in order to develop a free trade policy at home.

Why did integrated networks fail to develop in U.S. health policy and British industrial policy? In both cases, state actors at particular times wished to intervene. However, various state actors within the arenas disagreed on how to intervene, and interest groups were not prepared to cooperate in the intervention. In addition, there was no dominant state agency, institution, or department solely responsible for decision-making. In both cases a range of state actors were involved in the policy process, and each state actor gave access to a different set of interest groups. This increased the difficulty of achieving agreement. Each state actor and pressure group introduced particular ideas on how to treat the policy sector, which made it very difficult to develop cooperation in implementation. This was particularly the case with the Treasury and British industrial policy. For example, during the 1960s the Labour government created the Department of Economic Affairs in order to develop a coherent industrial policy. However, the Treasury undermined the new department by failing to coordinate economic and industrial policy and by refusing to give any of its economic powers to the new department.

Policy networks depend on ideology, groups, and institutions. For a policy community to exist, it is essential to have defined groups with established interests and resources they can exchange. There also has to be an ideology to define the policy problems and solutions. Policy communities need formal or informal institutions to provide a forum for the community and to enable inclusion, exclusion, and mechanisms for implementation. In some policy communities where there are many groups (e.g., trade policy), ideology is especially important as a means of binding the various actors. In British agricultural policy, the existence of policy-making institutions that excluded a range of actors was most important in maintaining the community. So communities depend on ideology and institutional structures, but which is the most important varies according to the policy area.

The difference between U.S. health policy and U.S. trade policy demonstrates that it is not the nature of the U.S. state that prevents the development of closed policy communities. In U.S. trade policy, a community could develop because there were a limited number of state actors who accepted a consensus on the general direction of trade policy, and they managed to exclude actors who were liable to raise issues that threatened this agenda. In health policy there was no consensus and a wide range of governmental and pressure group actors. It was consequently very difficult to exclude groups and to keep issues off the agenda.

Policy develops from the interaction of groups and state actors within particular types of policy networks. State actors clearly have superior resources, but the use of those resources may have very high costs. Therefore, rather than using despotic power, state actors prefer to develop mechanisms for infrastructural power. These mechanisms create dependency between the groups and the state. This increases the ability of state actors to intervene in society, but they have to give groups a role in the policy process. Hence, the relationship between groups and the state is highly complex and not simply state- or society-centered. State actors need groups in order to increase, not restrict, their autonomy.

ACKNOWLEDGMENTS

I would like to thank Fiona Devine, Andrew Gamble, Wyn Grant, and David Marsh for comments on earlier drafts of this chapter. I would particularly like to acknowledge Andrew Gamble's role in suggesting that Mann's notion of infrastructural power could be linked to the concept of policy networks.

NOTE

1. When Mann uses the notion of despotic power, he is generally referring to autocratic kings who can literally use despotic power through force to achieve their goals. However, the range over which they can use this power is restricted to the range of force. Nevertheless, I think the notion of power is useful in liberal democratic regimes, where it refers to the exercise of power by governments without negotiation. For instance, when a state actor directs the state machinery to take a particular measure despite the opposition of officials and pressure groups, he or she is using direct "despotic" power rather than negotiated "infrastructural" power. In this situation the state actor is dependent on his or her ability to use the state machinery. Perhaps this is a form of power that exists between what Mann sees as despotic and infrastructural power.

3

New Social Movements and Routes to Representation: Science versus Politics

Susan D. Phillips

If the social sciences are taken as the theater of moral debate in modern society, the problem facing modern liberal democrats is not a lack of moral guidelines but a plenitude.

(Wolfe, 1989: 7)

At the heart of politics is a struggle over meaning. Science and social science are both creative forces in the construction of meaning. They are also an integral aspect of political control because it is through the opportunity to create and impose intellectual paradigms and ways of seeing the world that governments and other actors gain and maintain political and social domination. Over the past two decades, the terrain of political struggles over meaning has shifted significantly from parliaments and parties to bureaucracies and civil society. New social movements (NSMs) have become important forces in opening new political spaces, shaping alternative discourses, and locating multiple sites of struggle.

Although considerable scholarly attention has been paid to the study of NSMs, relatively little analysis has been directed toward consideration of social movements as producers and consumers of knowledge. As producers of knowledge, social movements forge collective identities, give meaning to social problems, engage in the imaginative process of connecting issues, and translate social science into popular beliefs and moral obligations. As consumers of knowledge, they gather, select, and use scientific and technological information as a commodity in lobbying governments on specific policy issues and in persuading the public to understand issues in particular ways.[1]

However, a different logic applies to social movements than to other types of interest groups, business, or the state in the ways in which they can create and consume knowledge.

Social movements are characterized by their engagement in the politics of identity—which, in contrast to the politics of interests, demands a process of individualization as well as collectivization (Melucci, 1989: 6). Identity politics involves the definition and representation of self through participation in a collective identity that is tried on and worn reflexively.[2] From an individual's perspective, this process is more intrusive and enveloping than the pursuit of or identification with a single, external interest (such as opposing Sunday shopping or supporting better health care) because it requires people to name themselves, not simply to articulate an interest. Therefore, the practice of identity politics involves a process of individualization—"the attribution of a sense of social action to potentially every individual" (Melucci, 1988: 256). But it also necessitates collectivization through which participants socially construct a "we" that becomes part of the definition of self (Gamson, 1991: 258), and this process requires participation, solidarity, and the creation of identity communities. As Jenson (1992b: 6) argues, the implication of identity politics is that a dual process of representation must take place: "the representation of interests via state institutions as well as those of civil society *and* the constitution of the identities of the represented, through political mobilisation and policy innovation."

This dynamic affects the meaning, action, and structure of social movement politics. In terms of meaning, social movement actors must be both imaginative and specific (Magnusson and Walker, 1988: 61–62). That is, they need to engage in the imaginative process of rethinking basic relationships (e.g., consumer to the environment) and connecting disparate themes and issues into a coherent discourse (e.g., linking feminism and peace, or environment and community). But they also pursue specific interests and policy issues. Social movements, therefore, need the capacity to use knowledge as both a creative force in constructing meaning systems and a vehicle for refuting or defending a particular policy option.

The action repertoires of social movements are also influenced by the individualization/collectivization of identity politics. Both representation of the identity and its specific interests *and* participation through direct personal and collective expressive action are essential. But as Melucci (1988: 258) notes, belonging to and participating in an identity are not the same as, and in some ways may be the opposite of, being represented. Representation is indirect, usually involves deferred satisfaction of goals, and may be carried out by third parties, whereas participation is immediate, personal, and a much greater investment of an individual's time and effort. Representation and participation require different resources, types of knowledge, and organizational practices.

Finally, the structures and organizations of social movements operate differently than other types of organizations. First, the organizations must be able to accommodate and balance representation and participation, passion and pragmatism, imagination and specificity—a task that can be exceedingly difficult. Within social movement organizations, this balancing act often generates a natural caution about becoming institutionalized, a situation that other types of interest groups might welcome, and a fear of the leadership becoming isolated from the grassroots. Second, the structures of social movements are composed of networks of organizations and individuals through which flow information and resources. The configuration of the movement network, as well as the structure and action of individual organizations within that network, influences the construction of the collective identity, its capacity to use information, and its ability to balance representation and participation (Phillips, 1991b: 756–57).

Naturally, social movements do not act independently and autonomously. Rather, the struggle for meaning, the possibilities for action, and the routes to representation are shaped by the political opportunity structure of state institutions and other players (Tarrow, 1989). At some periods of history, legislatures, parties, and bureaucracies may be more open to representation by certain movements or groups and may be more receptive to certain discourses than others. In many post-industrial countries, a significant change in the opportunities for representation has taken place in recent years due to a "double democratization" of both civil society and the state (Held, 1991: 24). Since the late 1960s, a "democratization" of everyday life (Melucci, 1988: 245) has taken place by the very fact that the NSMs have created new identities and definitions of the political that did not exist previously. Thus, there simply is greater competition for the space to form meaning systems— and more freedom to do so—than ever before.

But there also have been significant changes on the part of states to enhance democratic governance. By the term "democratic governance" I refer to the means—constitutional, institutional, and uncodified practices— through which the relationship between the state and citizen is mediated or bridged.[3] Not all states have changed their practices of democratic governance benevolently or even willingly; in many cases they have been pushed by citizens who have become highly disillusioned with the effectiveness and legitimacy of representation through traditional channels of parties, elections, and legislatures. Citizens and their organizations are demanding and expecting to be more directly involved in the formulation and implementation of public policy. For their part, governments recognize that the old interventionist and spending methods no longer seem to work or no longer are regarded as legitimate for many complex policy problems. Yet governments now, as much as ever, need to promote economic and social restructuring.

Therefore, they are seeking new forms of relations with both the market and society.

There is a paradox in the current unfolding of enhanced democratic governance that, I argue, will disadvantage the representatives of identity politics. Although there may be more opportunities and more channels of representation for citizen interests (e.g., advisory councils, regulatory hearings, royal commissions, task forces, legislative committees, "multi-stakeholder" consultations, and, ultimately, "partnerships"), the *mode* or practice of representation by social movements and other groups is becoming increasingly constrained. Offe (1980: 8) makes the case that increasingly the "location of major political conflicts and struggles and the institutional location at which state policies are formed shift away from those institutions which democratic theory assigns to these functions." In other words, representation increasingly is being channeled through the para-parliamentary routes of the bureaucracy, the judiciary, and neo-corporatist partnerships with the consequent diminution in importance of the democratic institutions of parliament and parties (Paltiel, 1989: 348; Jenson, 1992a: 27–28). As a result of both greater competition among more actors for representation and the location of policy-making in these non-partisan forums, there is a growing emphasis on scientific advice and technical expertise. Paradoxically, as social movement organizations gain greater access to the policy-making process, there is greater pressure to behave in conventional, institutional ways with an emphasis on representation over participation and with reduced tolerance for the expressive actions that are essential to identity politics. Thus, as "partners," NSMs run the risk of undermining the very essence of their politics.

Although NSMs as political actors can be distinguished from other interest groups, there is considerable variation in the meaning, action, and structure of the same movement across countries and across different movements in the same country. The capacity to use science and the tradeoffs between representation and participation that social movements make, therefore, can be expected to vary considerably across movements. The purpose of this chapter is to compare the women's and environmental movements in Canada with a focus on their ability to be both producers and consumers of knowledge and on their strategies regarding institutionalization in the face of a changing locus of politics.

KNOWLEDGE, INTERESTS, AND SOCIAL MOVEMENTS

Studies of social movements of the post-1968 era have been dominated by two perspectives. The resource mobilization approach has concentrated on how, rather than why, social movements develop; in this approach the analysis has centered on organizational resources and structures (Jenkins,

1983; Tarrow, 1989). The NSM perspective, in contrast, has been focused on analysis of the meaning and values inherent in movements in the context of post-industrial societies, but it has paid relatively little attention to the processes by which this meaning is constituted (Cohen, 1985; Klandermans and Tarrow, 1988). In an attempt to link the how with the why of social movements, Eyerman and Jamison (1991) develop a perspective that they term "cognitive praxis," which focuses on the concept of knowledge interests.

The cognitive praxis of social movements is not just social drama; it is, we might say, the social action from where new knowledge originates. It is from, among other places, the cognitive praxis of social movements that science and ideology— as well as everyday knowledge—develop new perspectives. (1991: 48)

Knowledge in this perspective is not only or even primarily the systematized, formalized knowledge of the academic world, nor (merely) the scientific knowledge produced by sanctioned professionals. It is rather the broader cognitive praxis that informs all social activity. It is thus both formal and informal, objective and subjective, moral and immoral, and, most importantly, professional and popular. (1991: 49)

Drawing heavily on the notion of "knowledge constituting interests" developed by Habermas (1972), Eyerman and Jamison delineate three types of knowledge interests: (1) cosmological, (2) technological, and (3) organizational. Cosmological knowledge interests involve the production of a worldview that offers explanations and counter-explanations of basic relations of individuals to nature, society, and the state; it also provides a movement with its utopian mission or "emancipatory aims" (Habermas, 1972; Eyerman and Jamison, 1991: 68). This cosmology is the intellectual core of the collective identity and the fundamental basis that gives rise to all other forms of knowledge interests. For example, the concept of patriarchy offers an explanation of oppression for the women's movement and a focus of struggle for emancipation, just as colonization is the explanation and sovereignty the mission for movements of aboriginal peoples. This articulation of meaning through a worldview is the most social of all knowledge interests and thus relies heavily upon networks of individuals and organizations; expressive, often spontaneous action; and a conception of an identity community that differentiates "us" from "them."

Intellectuals play an important part in the creation and communication of a worldview. Gramsci (1971: 121) makes a distinction between two types of intellectuals: traditional or established intellectuals who are involved in the production or manipulation of cultural symbols and language from established institutions, such as universities, versus organic or movement intellectuals—in Eyerman and Jamison's (1991: 95) terms—who are primarily communicators and activists. For instance, Betty Friedan and her book *The Feminine Mystique* (1963) provided an important intellectual spark to the women's movement; and Rachel Carson (1962) and Barry Commoner (1966, 1972), among others, issued a challenge to human behavior based on a fresh perspective derived from the principles of ecology. Although the established intellectuals, using science and social science, are crucial in formulating the worldview and society's moral obligations as a result of it, the articulation of new knowledge alone cannot carry a movement's development. This depends on the "organic" intellectuals: artists, orators, and activists who communicate, rally, and inspire people—as Martin Luther King, Jr., did for the civil rights movement in the United States or as Chief Dan George and Mary Two Axe Early have done for aboriginal peoples in Canada.

Although the cosmological base of a movement is likely to provide it with a relatively stable core, it is by no means immutable. Indeed, as it comes under attack by counter-movements and opposing interests, or as a movement matures and specialized organizations pursue their own interests, the worldview may become fragmented and may even split apart. Alternatively, if it is widely acceptable to other constituencies, the worldview may be absorbed into the dominant political culture and state institutions.

Technological knowledge interests are the conceptual equivalent of a child's taunt to a playmate: "Oh yeah? Prove it!" The pressure to concentrate on technological knowledge follows as a natural response to the challenges by competing claims on the political space of a movement's newly established identity. In contrast to the imaginative, defining aspect of the cosmological dimension, the technological relates to the specificity of the identity and the particular objects of critique (Eyerman and Jamison, 1991: 75). It defines the "means of intervention: the scope and methods, as well as the proper means through which the human and natural worlds interact" (Jamison et al., 1991: 6).

It is through the technological dimension that social movements encounter the power and the politics of science. In attempting to support their worldview on specific issues, social movement representatives must be able to substantiate their claims against counter-claims. The intellectuals of this stage are not those who can manipulate symbols and mesmerize crowds with their rhetoric; they are the counter-experts who can amass and massage data. As Aronowitz (1992: 131) argues, "science, far from its claim to social neutrality, becomes a master discourse and confers legitimate power upon its agents." In the face of counter-claims and disputed expertise, "those ideas which cannot pass muster as scientific are merely consigned to the margins of public discussion. They may be valued in other terms (as poetry, myth, or opinion), but they are not taken seriously as knowledge which contributes to the collective goal of progress or state policy" (Aronowitz, 1992: 131).

The power of science arises, in part, from the image of ideal science that presents itself as value-free, its conclusions independent of their ultimate use, and its process public, open to debate, peer review, and refutation. Although this is the apparent strength of ideal science, Salter (1988: 315) argues that "mandated" science—scientific activity conducted with a mandate or objective to reach conclusions that will lead to public policy or government regulation—conforms to none of the goals of ideal science. Disputes over the results generated by mandated science are seldom resolved by further studies. Scientists and policymakers can demur from addressing the larger political, value-laden questions that gave rise to the scientific study in the first place precisely because they have narrowly defined the specific issues at hand as scientific, not political. Thus, science is a powerful tool for politics because it allows the scope of conflict to be restricted by defining the issues as technological ones, the range of legitimate parties to be reduced, and norms of professional conduct to dominate (Offe, 1980: 9; Pross, 1986: 227).

The third aspect of cognitive praxis Eyerman and Jamison (1991: 69) call organization or communicative interests: the practice or modes of organizing the production and dissemination of knowledge. The ways in which organizations get their meaning across and the organizational forms in which cosmological and technological interests unfold may be as important as the worldview itself. Although people may share beliefs and ideas at a distance, it is through organizations that they become connected as a political community, build solidarity, and develop a sense of agency and empowerment. Organizational practice matters as both medium and message: "movements that take seriously the goal of enhancing the capacity of people for collective action must make sure that their practices do in fact promote and encourage participants to be active and collaborative" (Gamson, 1991: 50).

One of the oldest themes in the study of democratic organizations, beginning with Michels's classical work of 1911, addresses the issue of who imposes (and how they impose) cosmological interests and determines political strategies. Although not all students of social movements see the law of oligarchy as iron-clad, there is a recognition that social movements are ill-equipped to deal with the problems of time (Offe, 1991: 237). Their organizations usually face a distinctive tension between fundamentalism and pragmatism—a tension between remaining committed to fundamental social change based on the movement's worldview and adapting to the exigencies of competitive politics (Kitschelt, 1990: 85; Kuechler and Dalton, 1991: 288–89). By their very nature, movements value participation, spontaneity, and expressive action. However, once a movement's identity must be defended by technological knowledge, the pressures for institutionalization grow. There are pressures for organizations to specialize in order to devote more attention to their particular interest, employ professionals, produce

expertise, and act in a conventional manner so that their representatives will
be invited to join councils of other experts explaining positions and statistics, rather than staging parades or sit-ins. To compete, they must be able to
tell governments what they know, not what they feel, and this usually signals
a shift in the intellectual life and identity of the movement (Eyerman and
Jamison, 1991: 100). The fact that social movements are not in themselves
institutions or organizations, but networks of organizations, may work to
their advantage. Specialization and professionalization may occur among
selected organizations that represent specific interests or aspects of the collective identity. These specialists can compete in conventional politics based
on expertise and then share their technological knowledge with the other
organizations whose emphasis remains focused on participation and spontaneity.

I argue that the ways in which a social movement produces and uses
knowledge are central to how it conceptualizes itself as a community, the
political strategies that are feasible, the organizations it can support, and
claims it is likely to make. The capacity of a movement to use knowledge
and construct meaning systems, in turn, is shaped by the structure of its
organizations and networks and by its action repertoires. This has three
implications for empirical analysis. First, analysis must not treat a movement
as a unitary and univocal actor—such as *the* women's movement or *the*
peace movement—but must explore the convergence and differentiation of
the elements within it (Melucci, 1988: 338). Second, it should be sensitive to
the historical specificity of the movement under study. At certain times, a
consensus may exist around a particular language of politics that encourages
movements to express themselves in ways that go relatively unchallenged,
whereas in times of greater political competition or crisis, movements must
struggle to defend themselves and their worldview assumptions (Jenson,
1992b: 8–9). Finally, analysis should take into consideration the life stage of
a movement because movements, like organizations, are rarely static. Over
time, the shared beliefs may shift focus, expand, or contract; the demands
for technological information may vary and organizational forms evolve in
response to changing times. Although institutionalization is by no means
inevitable, the character of a movement in its fledgling youthful stages is
likely to be very different from the same movement once it has experienced
political challenge for three decades. The following sketch of two movements—the environmental and the women's movement in Canada—illustrates that the knowledge interests and routes to representation vary greatly
across movements at the same life stage and historical period within a single
country.

THE ENVIRONMENTAL MOVEMENT IN CANADA

The names that movements give themselves reflect their worldview and influence the discourses they create and political strategies they pursue (Jenson, 1992b: 1–6). It is significant that the environmental movement in Canada has named itself "environmental" rather than "ecological," as many of its European counterparts have done.[4] This name mirrors a discourse that is shaped by at least three distinct philosophical strands within the movement, which is composed of over 2,000 organizations at the local and national levels (Doern, 1992b: Ch. 5; Macdonald, 1991: 30–38; Rucht, 1991: 173; Toner, 1991). The "conservation" groups allied informally as the Group of Eight—consisting of the Canadian Wildlife Federation, Canadian Nature Federation, World Wildlife Fund, Parks and Wilderness Society, Wildlife Habitat Canada, Nature Conservancy, Canadian Arctic Resources Committee, and Ducks Unlimited—are rooted in the late nineteenth-century ethic of "wise use" (see Nash, 1968) and are focused overwhelmingly on nature and wildlife issues. They are a strong force within the movement because they have well-developed financial bases and tend to have institutionalized access to government (Faulkner, 1982; Toner, 1990; Wilson, 1992: 119). Consequently, their organizational form and capacity to use technological information has influenced the expectations of the public servants and politicians with whom they interact and, thus, has exerted considerable pressure on other groups to behave in similar conventional ways.

The second philosophical stream, which probably in numbers comprises the majority of the movement, has been termed "reform environmentalism" (Macdonald, 1991: 36). Groups such as the Sierra Club, Pollution Probe, and Friends of the Earth are concerned with both pure preservation and prudent management. Although many were willing to be confrontational in their heady youth of the 1970s, most are now more likely to use conventional lobbying and litigation tactics.[5] By comparison, the biocentric "deep ecology" groups, like Earth First, which are local rather than national in scale and are prepared to use more radical tactics of civil disobedience and direct action, are a minuscule part of the movement (Kaulbars, 1992: 4; Macdonald, 1991: 37).

The greatest strength of the environmental movement has been its ability to produce credible technological knowledge and to use this expertise as a commodity in the political process. Even Greenpeace, master of the high-seas campaign and attention-grabbing stunt, has been built on this strategy. On the occasion of its twentieth anniversary, Jim Bohlen, one of the founders of Greenpeace in Canada, stated that "part of what makes it work is the fact that Greenpeace does a lot of good science . . . so that credibility is always at a high level" (Wilson, 1991: A2). It is also a technologically sophisticated, hierarchical organization with worldwide computer link-ups that provide instantaneous communication and information-sharing with its international counterpart organizations on a daily basis. In part, the emphasis on technological knowledge has been facilitated by the fact that (1) ecological issues lend themselves to debates over the measurable impact of environmental damage from a megaproject, for example, or the quantifiable extent of ozone depletion, and (2) regulatory hearings and environmental assessment panels have been important forums for resolving disputes.

The capacity to produce good science has also been supported by specialized professional organizations, international organizational linkages, and innovative fundraising tactics. The philosophical differences have reinforced organization and interest specialization; thus, environmental groups have carved up the field into niches: groups for wildlife and wildlife only, ozone specialists, pollution, and so on. The logic in this approach is that there are so many complex issues that a single group could not possibly cover them all adequately. However, the risk is that the imaginative processes of connectivity become lost so that individuals, as potential supporters, no longer see the bigger picture on environmental issues and sometimes feel deluged by requests for money.[6]

Compared to other social movements in Canada, environmental groups have become money-making machines: they entered the direct mail market early and vigorously; they have devised innovative fundraising schemes, such as the sale of wildlife stamps and bonds; and their expert staffs of biologists, hydrologists, and lawyers regularly undertake consulting or legal advisory contracts and use the revenue to fund other research or advocacy activities. This strategy of expertise fueled by extensive fundraising has meant that their knowledge is often sought out by governments and that they can be persuasive adversaries in litigation or regulatory hearings, as well as important counter-sources of information for the public. Alternatively, some groups have been able to buy out the problem, literally—as the Nature Conservancy and others have done in purchasing endangered habitats and thereby protecting them through private ownership.[7] Most environmental groups have cultivated good relations with an interested and responsive media, which allows them to get their messages out to a wide audience effectively (Toner, 1991: 11–14). International collaboration through their organizational counterparts in other countries also provides global linkages.

The result has been that most national environmental groups have moved in a relatively short space of time—from the early 1970s to the early 1980s—from being on the outside to being on the inside by being cooperative, although not uncritical. The tension between pragmatism and passion—that is, between a strategy of institutionalization versus loyalty to a fundamental ideology that is not coopted through overly cosy relationships with the very institutions that are part of the problem—has been hotly debated within many of the reform environmental groups founded in the 1970s (see

Kuechler and Dalton, 1991: 286–89). However, most eventually moved in a professionalized direction and a rapprochement with industry and government. As Michael Perley of the Canadian Acid Rain Coalition notes, conventional politics are the norm in the 1990s: "an anti-authority mentality really doesn't have any place any more. Sometimes you have to go up against authority, but that must be a deliberately chosen tactic, not just acting out of hostility" (quoted in Toner, 1991: 21).

This strategy, albeit successful in enhancing groups' ability to be strong advocates, has had its costs.[8] Participation of individuals in national-level organizations has atrophied, if it ever truly existed. Although national organizations claim large numbers of members—as, for example, the Canadian Wildlife Federation, which has a "membership" of 36,000, or Friends of the Earth with 25,000 (Wilson, 1991: 111)—in almost all cases these individuals give only money, not time, and there is no mechanism for them to be involved in decision-making. Few national groups have local chapters any longer, although many like Pollution Probe did have relatively autonomous local branches until the early 1980s. National environmental groups tend to be staff-led and they seldom hold general policy-making meetings, celebrations, or demonstrations through which sympathetic supporters can partake of and affirm a collective identity as environmentalists. Eyerman and Jamison (1991: 107–8) note that this is typical of most highly successful environmental groups in the United States and Europe, and they lament the distance this has created between the intellectuals and supporters in Greenpeace—a large but typical organization:

Greenpeace is centrally steered and hierarchically organized, run by administrative professionals who hire technical and specialist help on a short-term basis and who radically restrict supporters to the role of temporary office help and anonymous financial donor. Its relations to its public and its opponents is also highly mediated and professional. Campaigns are carefully planned and run with militarylike efficiency to achieve the most effect and visibility in the mass media. The object of such campaigns, however, is mostly publicity that is fundraising efforts for the real work, which is pressure on governments and private corporations. Direct mailing follows such campaigns and potential support is tapped. There is thus little direct contact between activists and the public or their opponents. This is certainly a long remove from the leaflet and the newspaper which has served a means of direct contact or communication between the activist and the public. The public is also tapped through opinion polls and surveys and the sale of articles like T-shirts and pins. Such activity not only creates a different type of relation to public and opponent alike but a different kind of intellectual: the highly effective manager and highly organized professional activist.

Given this professionalism, the locus for participation in the environmental movement resides almost exclusively at the local level with few connections between the local and national organizations.[9] Indeed, local activists often lament that it is difficult to get the national organizations interested in or supportive in any way of community concerns (personal communication). Because local groups usually are resource-starved, they can provide the means for participation but not for effective representation, except through collective action that attracts media attention.

In part, rationalism and specialization have been feasible because concern over the environment has permeated such an expansive segment of the population. In general, citizens are sympathetic to the movement's goals; give tacit support, if not dollars, to the organizations; and want environment to become part of the dominant, as opposed to the movement, culture. The movement's worldview has become the world's view (at least in post-industrial countries). The dilemma is that because of this support and the organizations' concentration on representation over participation, the environmental *movement's* identity has begun to dissipate. In fact, Jamison and colleagues (1991: 60) claim that in Europe its identity has all but disappeared (compare Adkin, 1992: 136–37). Without a movement identity to sustain both participation and representation, environmental activism becomes a responsibility of the individual to act as an individual consumer. Therefore, interest in environmental issues is more likely to be at the mercy of other pressures or self-interests; in fact, during the current recession we have seen environmental concerns sacrificed to those of the economy.[10] Without a movement that is part of one's everyday life to encourage self-sacrifice, people are not willing to take more than the small steps. However, "[o]nce you get beyond recycling and changing your showerhead you face fundamental issues involving big institutions . . . and piecemeal gestures are no longer enough" (David Kraft of Greenpeace, quoted in Heinrich, 1992: 8).

THE WOMEN'S MOVEMENT IN CANADA

In many superficial respects, the contemporary women's movement is quite similar to the environmental movement: both have experienced longevity of more than two decades, have a diversity and strength in their organizations, tend to be dominated by the white middle class, and have had some degree of success in policy outcomes and in changing public attitudes. However, there are significant differences in the capacity and preferences of the two movements to pursue knowledge interests. Whereas the environmental movement is focused on representation to the state and is highly skilled in employing technological knowledge, the women's movement has greater capacity for participation and is still very much engaged in political struggles over discourse.

Women's organizing is generally recognized to have occurred in two waves, one beginning in the late 1800s and the second in the late 1960s, although organizations of the first wave continue and co-exist with the younger feminist groups. Partly as a result of this inter-generational aspect and partly as an outflow of the feminist sensitivity to difference, the movement has attempted to encourage the connectivity of women with dual identities (visible minority, disabled, and poor women), and groups of both the first and second wave have often taken up the same issues (Phillips, 1991a: 766–77).[11] In terms of structure, most national women's groups tend to be umbrella organizations composed of local chapters or affiliates, although some have individual memberships, but both forms are based on actual participating members rather than donors.[12] Thus, the structures aid in connecting the national organizations to individuals and issues at the local level, and they allow some concerns developed in grassroots groups to filter up to the national executive, even if the intertwining of the two spheres is by no means intimate or complete. The attention given to mechanisms of democracy within the national organizations, ironically through procedures of representative democracy more than through feminist consensual practices (Vickers, 1988), allows individuals to participate in their organizations through annual general meetings and regional conferences. Participation is also achieved in women's groups through celebrations, such as International Women's Day, or demonstrations and parades, such as "Take Back the Night." This encourages individuals to wear the collective identity as part of their definition of self with the support of others who share that identity.

The movement organizations, however, have been less successful at the task of representation as a result of both structural factors and strategic choices. For example, women's organizations tend to be led by a president whose position is often full-time in terms of time demands but unpaid in compensation, and they usually have a small staff that is not encouraged to act as voices for the organization. Because even the president usually is required to consult the membership before speaking out on policy issues, the movement's leaders often have been unable to respond immediately after a political event in a thirty-second news clip. Furthermore, the media have seized on one leader, the president of the National Action Committee on the Status of Women (NAC), as the voice of the movement with the result that a sense of the diversity and breadth of the movement is not well transmitted to the public.

The difficulties of fundraising have exacerbated the problem of representation. Comparisons of size and budget of national organizations are illuminating: for example, the World Wildlife Federation Canada had a budget of $5.5 million and a staff of 28 in November 1991 (although four staff were to be laid off and donations were down 20 percent due to the recession), and Friends of the Earth had a budget of $1.2 million and a staff of 14. In comparison, the largest women's group, NAC, which is composed of approximately 500 member organizations representing roughly three million women, controlled a budget of approximately $700,000 and had a staff of 7 in 1991.[13] Fundraising traditionally has been undertaken with little enthusiasm in women's organizations, perhaps because women have little money to give and corporations little inclination to do so or because many women came from gendered roles in other organizations in which they ran bake sales or canvased door-to-door; in women's groups they want to be involved in developing policy, not relegated to asking for money.

The majority of women's groups receive a substantial portion of their funding from the federal government through the Department of Secretary of State Women's Program.[14] Although government financial assistance may have been a factor in the slow development of direct mail and corporate fundraising, the task of filling out grant forms or developing projects for funding is equally disliked by the volunteer board; and few women's groups have a paid fundraiser, as do most environmental groups (Phillips, 1992: 20). The problem of fundraising is getting worse because the federal government is cutting back on its sustaining funding to women's groups or is offering only project money, the pursuit of which can distort an organization's priorities (Phillips, 1991a: 200–205). As a consequence of limited and shrinking financial resources, women's groups are less able to buy expertise; rather, it tends to be offered on a voluntary basis by sympathizers who are expert or interested in a particular topic. Moreover, most women's organizations are still engaged in struggles over worldview; theirs is still a political fight over values, as well as the how and who of representation.

These struggles are illustrated by two issues that have been the main initiatives related to women's issues of the Conservative government in its second term beginning in 1988. However, both have been characterized by bitter battles over values and approaches. In May 1991, a nine-member panel was established by the federal government, with the support and encouragement of NAC and other women's groups, to examine the issue of violence against women. However, concerns over the inadequate representation of women who are also members of visible minorities boiled up. Four months later NAC, joined by the Congress of Black Women, the DisAbled Women's Network, and the Canadian Association of Sexual Assault Centres, decided to boycott the panel over the issue of who is being represented and, by extension, over the appropriate discourse on the issue of violence (*Ottawa Citizen,* 1991: A5). Similarly, the Royal Commission on Reproductive Technology, established in 1989 to address the science and ethics of reproductive technology, was torn apart two years later over an ideological division between commissioners on how far technology should be allowed to go and whether women should have the sole right to determine those limits (Howard, 1991: A1). The nine commissioners divided between a rational science-medical perspective and a feminist one. The federal government intervened by conferring exclusive authority to run the Commission and determine its priorities and research to its chair, a female professor of medical genetics, and by adding two new members to put the feminist side in a clear minority. In November 1991, the dissident feminist members launched a lawsuit against the Commission and the federal government challenging the chair's authority over the Commission. As a result, the substantive work of the Commission was stalled for a long period, although it has resumed and the Commission's report was published in the autumn of 1993.

One consequence of the movement's unwillingness to let issues be defined in technological terms is that many groups, especially NAC, are often portrayed as quirky, even cranky, by the media and are seen to be uncooperative and unprofessional by the public service (Gray, 1988: 240). But in the face of a neo-conservative government that shared few values or policy preferences with NAC—or most other women's groups, for that matter—protest was one of the few means of access available. For instance, when the federal government decided to cut funding to 76 women's shelters and centers in 1990, national and grassroots groups protested with sit-ins at government offices, by jamming the department's phone and fax machines, and by holding "wiener" roasts in which the minister responsible for the cuts, Gerry Wiener, was symbolically roasted. The strength of this protest, supported by a sympathetic media and public opinion, succeeded in forcing the government to reverse the cutbacks (*Lobby Digest*, 1990: 5).

The dilemma for the women's movement in the 1990s will be to enhance its ability at representation while providing appropriate opportunities for participation by younger women who do not have strong gender-collective identities (and for whom the doors opened by the women's movement seem invisible). It will also be imperative to maintain the inclusion of minority and disadvantaged women. The fact that the current president of NAC (who assumed office in June 1993) and almost one-third of its executive board are minority women is read by many as a signal that this imperative is being taken seriously.

ROUTES TO REPRESENTATION:
GREEN LIGHTS IN ENVIRONMENTAL POLICY

The styles of public policy advocacy are a product not only of knowledge interests and organizational forms but of the political opportunity structure—the routes and resources provided by the state for making citizen claims. Of course, the available channels of representation are not consistent for all identities and interests. Organizations in some movements may prefer or create certain modes of representation that are different from those in other movements. The state, through legislation or organizational practice, may open channels for some claims and interests that remain closed to others. Over the past decade, there has been an apparent enhancement of democratic practice in environmental policy that has been undertaken by the federal Department of Environment (DOE), aided by the courts, Cabinet, and provincial governments. The result has been to open government to more voices, as well as new and alternative routes for representation. In this short time span, environmental groups have moved from being marginalized contenders in the process to being stakeholders and partners. However, most of the new routes to representation are para-parliamentary: representation through the traditional apparatus of democracy—legislatures, elections, and parties—has been superseded by representation through the bureaucracy, a more activist judiciary, and international bodies. To some degree, conflict has been supplanted by consensus. Specifically, four new routes of representation have been created since the mid-1980s for environmental interests: (1) "multi-stakeholder" consultations, affiliated with the concept of sustainable development; (2) partnerships, often linked to a principle of stewardship; (3) a legalistic approach based on a rights discourse; and (4) supranational routes premised on a global definition of citizenship.

During the 1960s and 1970s the federal government's relationship with its constituency was characterized by closed, cooperative, bipartite bargaining with business, which was seen to be *the* constituency, while environmental groups railed against the process through the media (Hoberg, 1993: Ch. 10; Doern, 1992b: Ch. 5; Schrecker, 1984: Ch. 1). This cosy relationship began to change significantly during the mid-1980s, in part because the environmental groups had proven themselves to be capable of credible science, and in part because the Department of Environment had begun to see the conflict between business, the environmental movement, and government as unproductive. A renewed concern for environmental issues following major disasters, such as Bhopal and the Love Canal, was wedded with a new public philosophy, "sustainable development," that emerged from the World Commission on Environment and Development (the Brundtland Commission) in 1987. Canada had participated extensively in the Commission, and it had a significant impact upon the environmental policy community in this country. The concept of sustainable development, defined as development that meets the needs of the present without compromising the ability of future generations to meet their own needs (World Commission on Environment and Development, 1987: 8), was sufficiently vague that it satisfied both industry with its promise of continued economic development and the environmental movement (although never completely satisfied) with its notion of sustainability. Implicit in the concept was the premise that business, government, and environmental interests could be reconciled and that they would have to find ways of working together to achieve both ends.

At about the same time, a process of resolving differences that had a natural affinity with the idea of sustainable development—called multi-stakeholder consultation, or the Niagara process—was being developed and touted by DOE. The Niagara process evolved out of a 1984 meeting of representatives of business, labor, environmental groups, and the Department that was facilitated by the Niagara Institute (a firm specializing in negotiation). The representatives were trying to grapple with the issue of "plant modernization," a euphemism for integrating the economy and environment, but they found that they had difficulties with language and coming to a common understanding of the problems (Toner, 1990: 9; Doern, 1992a: 363). Over the course of the next year, a process called multi-stakeholder consultation emerged to deal with such differences. The process involves the following:

An ongoing dialogue among affected stakeholders, including government, aimed at obtaining all the relevant information, evaluating the available options and their related consequences, and providing an objectively balanced perspective to each stakeholder's decision making. A prime objective is to obtain consensus at each stage of the process. (Niagara Institute, 1985; quoted in Hoberg, 1993: 317)

This process was soon adopted by the Department of Environment as its official vehicle for conflict resolution when the government began in 1985 to develop legislation, now the Canadian Environmental Protection Act (CEPA), governing the management of toxic chemicals. Multi-stakeholder consultations have been used extensively since, including the creation of federal and provincial Round Tables on the Environment and Economy, which were formed as a response to Brundtland, the development of the Green Plan, and the process of pesticide review conducted by the Department of Agriculture (Hoberg, 1993: 319; Toner, 1990: 11). The significance of multipartite bargaining for democratic practice is that the government becomes merely another stakeholder, if its role is certain at all, but without any formal delegation of authority to a corporatist structure. As Hoberg (1993: 334) notes, the process appears to be more open and, therefore, more representative of a range of environmental interests; but in reality it may serve as a means for the state to mobilize consent or provide legitimation for its own policies.

But it retains the informal and co-operative aspects of the traditional [bipartite] style. Proposals are developed in face to face meetings, under the auspices of professional facilitators who attempt to guide the participants towards consensus. The product of such forums typically is a report representing the consensus of the participants. The reasons for particular decisions are not necessarily given, and as a result the essentially political nature of the process is obfuscated. The winners and losers, concessions made, and bargains struck are not revealed to non-participants in the end. (Hoberg, 1993: 334)

In the Department's enthusiasm for the process, its consequences have not been fully debated. One possible implication is that because the process is relatively invisible to the public, the professional staff–led environmental groups become even more distanced from their constituencies and the public in general.

Partnerships have become the natural extension of power-sharing involved in multi-stakeholder consultation and, indeed, have become the buzzword of the 1990s. For example, the Environmental Green Plan announced in 1990 is replete with the language of partnership, positing the strengthening or forging of government partnerships with the provinces, aboriginal peoples, industry, local communities, other nations, environmental groups, and consumers. In its proper sense, partnership differs from consultation (an exchange of information) because it involves collaborative joint action in an effort to solve a problem that requires an ongoing commitment, acceptance of shared contributions, and recognition of mutual needs and benefits. Participants not only have their views represented by having a place at the table, but they have a direct role in the implementation and administration of policy. It is supposed to entail a decentralization of power, responsibility, and accountability from government to the partnership (Waddock, 1988: 17–23; Phillips, 1991b: 206–12). In some cases, governments may not be involved at all or may maintain only ex officio status.

The concept of partnership as a mode of representation is highly compatible with (but not limited to) the notion of stewardship over the environment in which individuals and groups within civil society are seen to have direct responsibility for the management, as opposed to merely the representation of interests and opinions to government and industry about the management of environments. Numerous successful stewardship arrangements have been undertaken as contracts between DOE and national environmental groups or local communities. For example, the Canadian Nature Federation and the Nature Conservancy of Canada have established a partnership with the Canadian Parks Service to raise money to support the purchase of lands to complete Grasslands National Park in Saskatchewan (Toner, 1991: 17). Similarly, the Canadian Wildlife Service has entered into joint ventures with national and local environmental groups to conserve, restore, and enhance waterfowl habitat (Doern, 1992b: 25–27). In addition, some groups have begun to bypass government altogether by working directly with the polluting industries, as in the "New Directions" partnership in which selected environmental and corporate representatives are directly and voluntarily negotiating emission standards with no intervention by governments at all (*Ottawa Citizen,* 1991: A4). The long-term implications of partnerships have yet to be determined. Although they may provide secure funding and institutionalized access for particular groups, it is very difficult to be critical of government policy from within a partnership. The long-run effect on public policy may be to truncate, obscure, or silence the range of representation and degree of citizen participation and to push environmental organizations further into the role of professional managers, rather than representatives or vehicles for participation by "amateur" citizens.

The third route for representation, which increasingly has been sought out by the environmental movement, is the judicial one. A legalistic approach depends on three elements: (1) formal administrative procedures that include access to information and participation; (2) pro-regulatory interest groups with access to the courts; and (3) non-discretionary duties imposed on government that are enforceable in court (Hoberg, 1993: 337–38). It is rooted in a rights discourse that, as Cairns (1991: 173–74) argues, has become more prevalent in Canada since the introduction of the Charter of Rights and Freedoms in 1982. The Charter has enhanced the notion that citizens not only are entitled to substantive rights but also hold procedural rights to be part of the public policy process or to act as watchdogs to ensure that the process has been conducted fairly. In contrast to the United States, where the National Environmental Policy Act (NEPA) of 1972 has long provided access to the courts to ensure proper procedures for environmental assessment, legislation in Canada had not opened similar doors to the judiciary. However, decisions by Canadian courts in 1989 and 1990, which were brought by environmental groups on the construction of two dams (the Rafferty-Alameda dam in Saskatchewan and the Old Man River dam in Alberta), gave a legal basis to the existing federal environmental impact assessment guidelines (Doern, 1992b: Ch. 12; Schrecker, 1992: 95–98). The judicial activism of the courts had the effect of granting to citizens enforceable rights that are not subject to negotiation with the bureaucracy or Cabinet. In Ontario, legalism has been taken one step further by the New Democratic government's public commitment to an Environmental Bill of Rights,[15] which would confer on citizens positive rights to a healthy environment, and by the Class Proceeding Act, which was given royal assent in June 1992. This legislation will further facilitate and encourage class actions that previously had been possible theoretically, but actually were difficult to execute because of legal rules and economic realities.

As a way of making claims, a legal route is a sharp contrast to consultation or partnerships: it is more formal and thus more open; it is adversarial and premised on distrust of administrative actions; it both limits government's autonomy to a greater degree and is a riskier prospect because if the plaintiffs lose in the highest court, there is little scope for reverting back to a bargaining mode with a government that is on the opposite side of the issue (Hoberg, 1993: 42). Legalism also accelerates the need on the part of claimants to produce credible information that can be publicly defended and scrutinized, and to raise sufficient funds to be able to sustain court challenges. Social movements using this route are thus propelled into being even more professionalized.

Finally, the evolving idea of a global community has extended the concept of citizenship beyond the borders of any particular nation-state. Thus, supranational strategies—such as appeals to international bodies to develop codified and enforceable standards, pass motions of censure, or impose the force of moral suasion in order to embarrass governments in changing their policies—increasingly have become legitimate and powerful tools for social movements (Jhappan, 1992). The Canadian environmental movement appears to be following the lead of aboriginal peoples who have been highly effective in reinforcing a concept of global citizenship and have achieved considerable success in their appeals to international bodies. For instance, in 1984 the Council of the Haida Nation was one of the first groups to appeal to the United Nations (UN) when they claimed that Canada was inappropriately using the Law of the Sea Treaty to undermine the Haida's title to territorial waters (Jhappan, 1992: 21). Although the UN took no action, the Haida achieved their goals by embarrassing the Canadian government and opening the question of Canada's claim to sovereignty over aboriginal peoples and their traditional lands. More recently, in the aftermath of the armed standoff between Mohawk warriors and the Canadian army over disputed territory at Oka in 1990, the UN Human Rights Commission unanimously criticized Canada's record on native rights.

Not all international appeals are made to other nation-states or international institutions. Groups have also discovered that the threat of withdrawal of trade by corporations or other states can have considerable influence on domestic behavior. The James Bay Cree with the help of environmentalists won an important victory in 1991: through their direct lobbying of power authorities in Vermont and New York states, which were to be important customers of the second phase of the James Bay hydroelectric project, they precipitated the cancellation of these major contracts.[16] Because environmental issues increasingly are defined as global problems, environmental groups, too, recognize the importance of supranational institutions and forums for setting and enforcing policy at the international level for the local level. The environmental organizations that participated in the 1992 United Nations Conference on Environment and Development (UNCED) in Rio de Janeiro were anticipating, or at least hoping, that the conference would produce substantial international agreements and institutions (see also Boardman, 1992: 40–41).

Taken together, the impact of these multiple routes for representation has been, as Offe argues (1980), to further separate the form from the content of democratic politics and to depoliticize some of the issues by narrowing their scope to technological terms and restricting the range of legitimate players.

REPRESENTATION AND THE WOMEN'S MOVEMENT: POLITICS CLOSES DOORS

The opportunities and paths for representation by women's groups vary considerably from those taken by environmental organizations, and it is less clear that the policy process has opened to women's groups as much as to the environmental movement. In part, this is due to the nature of the claims made by women that rely to a greater degree on spending, regulation, or the direct provision of services by the state, an approach that is antithetical to the philosophy of fiscal restraint and free markets espoused by neoconservative governments. But closure to women's groups also relates to the fact that lobbying by most interests has become more professionalized and more dependent on technological knowledge in recent years. In the para-parliamentary forums it is science, not politics, that matters. However, women's groups are still engaged fundamentally in a struggle over values and definitions.

There is no doubt that over the past five years, women's organizations have been invited to an ever greater number of consultations with the governments, including consultations relating to the federal budget and constitutional renewal. However, many women feel that consultation with them is often a token effort and an exercise in legitimation—to allow government to say that it has consulted widely—but that their views, which tend to be contrary to the Conservative government's approach to social issues, are ignored completely. Many groups complain that they are being consulted by government beyond their ability to participate, and some are even beginning to charge governments a per diem fee to be part of a consultation exercise (personal communication). Indeed, there is little evidence that increased consultation on women's issues has had any significant impact on public policy. In addition, many women's groups are leery of participation in partnerships, and there have been comparatively few invitations to be part of such joint ventures, with the exception of the Labour Force Development Board established in 1990. The national board, which is an independent agency reporting to Parliament, is composed of 22 members, including one representative of women's interests, and has considerable autonomy to decide upon and fund training programs.

Since the equality provisions of the Charter of Rights came into force in 1985, litigation has been an important strategy. One organization, the Women's Legal Education and Action Fund (LEAF), is dedicated to taking court cases that will apply the law in favor of women, especially "doubly disadvantaged" women (e.g., immigrant, visible minority, or disabled women). However, the number of court cases under the equality provision of the Charter (Section 15) that benefit or even directly relate to women are few, and many women argue that the Charter appears to be working as a vehicle for the advantaged. Of the 600 court cases involving Section 15 that were litigated from 1985 to 1988, only 7 percent (44 cases) involved sexual equality and only 7 were initiated by or on behalf of women (Canadian Advisory Council on the Status of Women, 1989; Razack, 1991: 134). However, since 1988 there have been some encouraging signs that the courts are interpreting equality in ways that will be of greater positive benefit to women.[17] The major limitation on litigation for the women's movement is the availability of funding. This was restricted even further in 1991 when the federal government axed the Court Challenges program that had provided $9 million to LEAF and other intervenors representing disadvantaged interests to take Charter cases.

There are two striking similarities between the women's and the environmental movements in their representational modes. First, in Canada neither has made the transition from movement to party on a permanent or highly successful basis, as the Greens have done in Europe or the feminists in Iceland. Although a Green party was established at the national and provincial levels in Ontario and British Columbia in 1983 and has contested the federal elections of 1984, 1988, and 1993, as well as several provincial elections, it has captured on average only .2 percent of the popular vote (Macdonald, 1991: 39).[18] A national feminist party was created in 1979 and fought two federal elections in its first year, but it was short-lived and had little direct impact on women's participation in election politics, party platforms, or on party alliances with the movement (Bashevkin, 1985: 31).

The second similarity is that very different activities are taking place at the national and local levels of the movements. While many national organizations have been lobbying or litigating, a great many local groups have turned their attention to civil society rather than the state by providing services directly to individual citizens, such as shelters for battered women or urban "re-leaf" tree-planting projects. Thus, in both movements the grassroots appear to be growing even further disconnected from organization and action at the national level.

CONCLUSIONS

Changes in both civil society and the state are driving a fundamental restructuring of relations between governments and publics. With the rise of the NSMs, there has been a democratization of everyday life because their politics of identity necessitate both representation of interests through state institutions and direct participation in organizations and events that help to mold and affirm a collective identity. The state, too, is undergoing a transition to enhanced democratic governance through experiments in direct democracy, increased consultations, and power-sharing through partnership arrangements. However, there are still many tensions, inequities, and contradictions to be resolved.

The contemporary waves of the women's and environmental movements in Canada have had over two decades of campaigning. Although both have been successful in creating strong national organizations, to the point of becoming institutionalized, they vary markedly in the strategies employed for the production and consumption of knowledge. Whereas the women's movement has had some difficulty in achieving representation based on specialized technical knowledge, the environmental movement has been superb at knowledge acquisition and dissemination, facilitated by highly innovative fundraising and professionalized organizations. However, this strategy has been achieved to the detriment of participation by supporters, at least in the national organizations. In part the success of the environmental movement in getting its worldview absorbed into popular political culture has been its own undoing as a movement and has propelled it further into institutional forms. For the women's movement, the dilemma is one of improving research capacity and representation; for the environmental movement, it is one of enhancing participation.

The two movements encounter very different channels and limitations imposed by the state on how they make claims. The routes to representation in environmental issues have placed greater reliance on more closed, consensus-based para-parliamentary mechanisms that have had the effect of constricting the scope of political conflict, making managers out of representatives, and cloistering the professionals in organizations from their constituencies. For the women's movement, many doors remain closed, as their struggle is one of values and discourses that cannot be resolved by a stronger show of expertise or more data. Ironically, the Canadian political system is at once more open due to more routes of representation and more closed to certain identities whose representatives do not possess sufficient technological expertise or do not conform to the professional norms of conduct.

ACKNOWLEDGMENTS

The financial assistance of the Social Sciences and Humanities Research Council (Grant No. 410-91-0758) is gratefully acknowledged. I would also like to thank Sylvia Bashevkin, Grace Skogstad, and Paul Pross for their helpful comments on an earlier version of this chapter, and Benham Behnia for his research assistance.

NOTES

1. The term "science" is used throughout this chapter as a generic label that includes both the physical sciences and social science.

2. Of course, all social movements create collective identities and forge solidarity. NSMs differ from other types of movements in three principal ways: they are post-modern and (primarily) post-material in their orientations; their constituencies are composed mainly of the new middle class, but they are not in themselves class projects; and, finally, the action repertoires rely heavily on expressive, non-conventional tactics. For a general discussion of the characteristics of NSMs, see Diani (1992); Kriesi (1988); Rucht (1988); and Tarrow (1989).

3. Offe (1980: 5–6) develops the metaphor of a bridge to describe democratic politics. The functions of the bridge are twofold. From the perspective of the individual, the bridge is the opportunity to articulate interests, engage in conflicts over those interests, and eventually determine public policy. From the perspective of the state, the bridge is a means of resolving conflict. "Thus, political forms are at the same time generators of conflict and peacemakers. Their logic is to organize diversity *and* unity—thereby providing a continuous link between the individual and the state" (Offe, 1980: 6). However, Offe differs from liberal scholars in that for him, the relationship between citizen and state cannot be explained by reference solely to political and institutional dynamics; rather, he emphasizes that their base lies in the economic power and values that exist beyond the level of political institutions.

4. The analysis presented in this chapter is based on key informant interviews with the representatives of the national and some local organizations of the two movements, and on review of the structures and resources of the organizations as obtained through annual reports and other literature produced by the groups themselves. Interviews were conducted with the presidents and/or executive directors of 33 national women's groups in 1988, some of which were updated in 1992, and with the executive directors of 14 national environmental groups as well as several local activists in the Ottawa area in 1992.

5. See Pross (1992: 198–200) for a discussion of the evolution of Pollution Probe.

6. Although the Canadian Environmental Network (CEN) was created with considerable federal government support to have the express purpose of being a communication link between the national and local levels and among national groups, it seems not to be used effectively or be taken seriously by other major environmental groups.

7. Because environmental groups in the United States were a few years ahead in their experimentation with tactics, many Canadian groups—like the Nature Conservancy and the Sierra Club, among others—either had direct counterparts or simply were able to imitate strategies that seemed to work south of the border.

8. For a scathing critique of the professionalization of the movement, see Kaulbars (1992: 2, 4).

9. Eyerman and Jamison (1991: 107) note that a similar fragmentation of the national and local levels has occurred in the American environmental movement.

10. The recession of the early 1990s has hit Canadian environmental groups hard and has forced them to retrench after a boom period of the late 1980s. According to Larry Solomon of Energy Probe, "The bubble has burst on the environmental movement. . . . It wasn't based on anything lasting. [Most environmental groups] had a lot of support a mile wide and an inch thick" (Heinrich, 1992: 8). Public opinion regarding the environment is also affected by the recession. A 1991 CBC/Globe and Mail poll showed that the percentage of the Canadian public who view environmental problems as the most important issue facing

the country has declined from 17 percent in 1989 to 4 percent by April 1991 (Hoberg, 1993: 307–42).

11. The degree of success in being able to make the movement truly a movement for all women is hotly contested. My point is simply that the question of *who* the movement represents is an important one in its internal politics.

12. The few exceptions are groups of aboriginal women, such as Pauktuutit (the Inuit Women's Association), for which the problems of distance and communication impede development of formal organizational memberships or groups, such as LEAF, which were formed to fill a highly specialized niche (legal action under the Charter) and only later began to develop memberships and local chapters.

13. NAC's revenues have also declined as a result of the federal government's cutbacks in funding and the recession, but federal transfers are a decreasing portion of its budget.

14. Women's groups tend to rely heavily on state funding. In a study of national women's groups conducted in 1988 for which budget data were available for 29 organizations, the following facts are significant: 38 percent (11 groups) received less than 25 percent of their budgets from the federal government; 19 percent (4 groups) obtained 25 to 50 percent from the state; and 48 percent (14 groups) were 75 to 100 percent funded by the government. See S.D. Phillips, "Projects, Pressure and Perceptions of Effectiveness: An Organizational Analysis of National Canadian Women's Groups," unpublished Ph.D. dissertation, Carleton University, 1990: 238.

15. In July 1992, the provincial environment minister released a draft "Environmental Bill of Rights" for public review. See Ontario Ministry of the Environment, *Ontario's Proposed Environmental Bill of Rights: An Overview* (Queen's Printer, 1992).

16. In announcing the cancellation of a $17 billion contract to buy power from Quebec, Governor Cuomo of New York justified the decision on economic terms (that the state no longer needed the power because of the success of conservation measures), but it seems highly probable that political concern over destruction of the Cree's territory had a significant influence (Jhappan, 1992: 35).

17. Perhaps the most significant of these was the Andrews case; see Razack (1991: 100–107).

18. The largest percentage of the vote captured was in Quebec in 1989, when the Greens ran 46 candidates and received 2 percent of the popular vote. In contrast to the European Greens, Canada's Green parties have not made strong connections with labor, women, or the left (Adkin, 1992: 148–49).

4

Ideas, Institutions, and Innovation: Economic Policy in Canada and Sweden

Neil Bradford

> Not ideas but material and ideal interests govern human conduct. Yet very frequently the "world images" that have been created by "ideas" have, like switchmen, determined the tracks along which action has been pushed by the dynamic of interests.
>
> Max Weber[1]

This chapter addresses two important issues in recent debates about the state and public policy: strategic choice and historical change. It argues that renewed attention to the role of economic ideas in shaping political behavior and policy formation can enrich understandings of choice and change. We begin with a theoretical discussion suggesting a way to conceptualize the political power of economic ideas within an institutionalist analysis of state-society relations. The focus is on the process of political representation, exploring how patterns of conflict and compromise are shaped by the organizational expression of ideas. The concept of learning network is introduced to facilitate cross-national study of how policy discourses are created and acquire influence in different national settings. The chapter offers a comparative-historical review of the dissemination of Keynesian economic ideas in Canada and Sweden. It then considers the significance of learning networks as historically evolved configurations of "discourse definers" within postwar Swedish and Canadian economic policy communities.

BRINGING IDEAS BACK IN

Policy Communities and Learning Networks

Under what circumstances can human agency change systems of social relations, and in what direction is such change likely to proceed? This question has been at the heart of recent controversies within state theory, triggered by the demise of once popular structuralist formulations. Various functionalist traditions described the process by which "objective interests" rooted in structures of production were politically expressed in ways conforming to long-term systemic needs. Statist writers first disputed the reductionism inherent in such society-centered theories of politics, arguing that country-specific factors, ranging from the predispositions of officials to the organization of government institutions, intervene between social structure and political choice with significant effects on historical outcomes (Skocpol, 1985). The statist corrective to functionalism and pluralism usefully shifted the analytical focus to actors and institutions, rekindling theoretical interest in historical contingency and cross-national variation in policy processes and outcomes.

However, this sensitivity to divergence and openness has not yet produced fully adequate accounts of state behavior.[2] Hollow statist notions of the "national interest" or "bureaucratic politics" tell us little about why states act the way they do. Similarly, preoccupation with the weight of policy legacies and institutional rigidities in channeling political life reintroduces a structuralism into state theory that obscures recognition of critical conjunctures when human agents construct the interpretive categories ordering their world.

These explanations of the state's role in capitalist democracies remain partial because their assumptions about behavior and goals—the national interest, class interest, functional requirements, and so on—foreclose empirical engagement with ideological and political struggles constituting social relations and policy patterns. Still underspecified in both functionalist and statist models is the process by which agents attach meanings to material conditions and mobilize to embed such claims in the decision-making routines of the state. Dissatisfaction with arguments that states either pursue an autonomously formulated "national interest" or remain beholden to capitalism's structural imperatives has renewed concern with the creative role of ideas in political life. Relaxing structuralist assumptions about the organizing principles of politics without embracing an unsatisfactory state-level pluralism raises important questions about how decisionmakers come to recognize problems and conceptualize solutions (Hall, 1989, 1990).

Of course, this concern with thought and culture is not new.[3] Within political science much work has been done from the cultural values perspective, deducing explanations for action from the mix of values and beliefs congealing in societies. Critical variants of this approach isolate the ensemble of ideas, symbols, and meanings embedded in the dominant ideology, tracing the reproduction of class relations to legitimating cultural practices. Despite divergent worldviews, "political culture" and "dominant ideology" theories are deficient in their exploration of concrete historical settings where such influential notions are created, contested, and confirmed. In consequence, any argument relating politically significant idea systems to state action remains undeveloped. Recently, an attempt to bridge this gap has come from theorists stressing the autonomy of ideas within a broader claim about the "irreducibility of politics" (Block, 1987: 18–19; Laclau and Mouffe, 1985). Discourse theorists have described pluralistic competition— seemingly unmediated by any systematic relations of social or institutional power—between different discourses, relating political outcomes to the persuasiveness of certain "universalistic" visions articulated by social groupings. This approach highlights the human agency involved in the creation of culture and the formation of political identities. However, in its preoccupation with overturning past arguments about structure and determinacy in politics, it appears to endorse the equally dubious position that anything is possible in an unpredictable world driven by debate (Block, 1987).

In short, none of these approaches clears a path to the state and its decision-making environment beyond the limited horizons of an abstract materialism or idealism. Sweeping, "top-down" arguments about the primacy of culture (or the ideological imposition of consent) are as unconvincing as their opposite—the notion that the discursive formulations of any social group can be recognized and acted upon by policymakers.

In this chapter we argue that what is needed at this point is a middle-level analysis paying close attention to institutional settings in which state officials and societal forces create authoritative interpretations of so-called objective conditions (Bradford, 1994). In any policy sector certain ideas cohere as frameworks modeling the field of strategic action for decisionmakers. These integrative conceptions specify what is wrong, what can be done, and what technical and political instrumentalities are available to sustain or adapt policies. Such idea systems constitute a policy discourse structuring thought and action over time in particular areas (Ross, 1987; Brooks and Gagnon, 1990a: 58–59). Policy discourses are neither invented by the state nor dictated by social forces. They are historical constructions—interpretative frameworks created and maintained by political actors engaged in an on-going struggle to embed "official" understandings of complex situations.

Here, we can build on the observation that "certain conceptual vocabularies" acquire influence over the behavior of diverse political actors because of "the successful work of organized discourse definers . . . who conceive their strategic task to be that of defining the 'true meaning' of events and processes" (Ross, 1987: 57–58). Every political system contains a distinctive constellation of actors—party politicians, interest group representatives, civil servants, professional experts—channeling the flow of ideas and information between state and society. From this vantage point, policy formulation can be viewed as proceeding inside identifiable networks of discourse construction, housed within policy communities at the interface of state and society.[4] Across countries, specific relations of political forces have evolved to acquire legitimacy as deployers of strategic understandings about desirable policy development and the appropriate boundaries of state action. Therefore, substantial variation in both the actors and locales critical to policy learning may be observed, arising from differences in social structure and organizational patterns (Heclo, 1974). *Learning networks* can find their institutional base in a variety of policy-relevant settings, including the party and interest group systems, the bureaucracy, the judiciary, public inquiries, and commissions.

Accordingly, the internal properties of such configurations of organized discourse definers—their social base, patterns of interaction, intellectual traditions, modes of analysis—are important in policy analysis. These networks are not launching pads for the doctrinal breakthroughs of individual thinkers any more than they are transmission belts for objective interests. Rather, they express the "organizational intelligence" of a political system, crystallizing certain ideas and interests into operational discourses that clarify policy goals and map political alliances (Hall, 1986: 232–34; Hodgetts, 1968: 259–60; Pontusson, 1988: 40).[5]

There are moments when these collective deliberations are especially intense and their political impact particularly significant. Creative work in the realm of ideas during periods of great uncertainty can mobilize new partisan formations, recast social coalitions, and shift the orientations of policy elites (Gourevitch, 1986, 1989). Innovations in the goals and instruments animating the policy process find their origins in the productive activity of organized discourse definers in periods of crisis. Such episodes may fruitfully be considered turning points within a larger historical process of debate and struggle over political identities and policy projects.

To analyze the intellectual content and political logic of strategic policy choices, this chapter focuses on nationally specific learning networks within economic policy communities. For empirical reference it draws on Canadian and Swedish responses to the chaos of the Great Depression. During the 1930s, long-standing views of the economy and basic social accommodations were challenged by the combination of mass unemployment, skyrocketing debt, and collapsing trade. From the upheaval eventually came adjustments in relations between state and society, inspired by new economic ideas that offered both an intellectual rationale for policy departures and the ideological foundations for novel political mobilizations. Our aim is not to contrast outcomes between cases as a way to generalize about economic performance in these two very different political economies. The goal is to use "individualizing comparisons" to investigate how different political forces elaborated new policy understandings in a period of acute international economic pressure and domestic political contestation (Myles, 1989: 7). The varying processes by which similar era-defining discourses entered nationally specific patterns of state-society relations to overturn policy premises and practices are highlighted.

ECONOMIC IDEAS AND THEIR POLITICAL CONSEQUENCES: A CANADIAN-SWEDISH COMPARISON

Nineteenth-Century Legacies

Historical patterns of economic and political development create organizational contexts for discourse construction. From country to country distinctive combinations of parties, interest organizations, civil servants, and experts may cohere as creators and carriers of the ideas that shape relations between state and society in policy sectors. The Canadian and Swedish cases bring this variation into sharp focus, each constituting a kind of ideal typical expression of different forms of political organization. Swedish and Canadian paths to modernity, charted through nineteenth-century dynamics of industrialization and democratization, left in place very different templates for contemporary economic policy-making (Berger, 1981: 1–23).

Simplifying greatly, Canada emerged from this formative period a fragmented and dispersed political community. Salient organizational features included parochial forms of group formation and collective action corresponding to a divided constitutional structure, regionalized economy, and ethnic-cultural dualism. The national party system was dominated by basically indistinguishable cadre factions brokering ad hoc electoral coalitions disconnected from programmatic considerations or enduring policy principles. Regular channels of liberal democratic representation remained underdeveloped as first Conservative and then Liberal politicians, without deep roots or broad presence in civil society, engineered nation-building deals with business elites and provincial officials. In fact, many critical political functions involved in consolidating the nation were given over to a federal bureaucracy coordinating immigration, transportation, and tariff policies. The federal Department of the Interior, for example, was "handed a political mandate" in the 1870s that was "crucial in formulating and executing the policies of 'defensive expansionism'" (Wilson and Dwivedi, 1982: 9).

It follows that Canada entered the modern era with a peculiarly statist institutional-political configuration composed of a weighty federal bureau-

cracy, weakly organized societal interests, and limited forms of party competition. The state system was pivotal in the strategic organization of economic
development and political integration (Hardin, 1974).

Similar historical transformations in Sweden fashioned a political landscape and policy-making environment dominated by cohesive, nation-span-
ning, class-based interest organizations and programmatic political parties.
Sweden's particular pattern of centralized, late industrialization provided
fertile ground for the formation of a unified labor movement, politically
mobilized alongside equally comprehensive and centralized business peak
associations (Ingham, 1974). In this context, the early twentieth-
century struggle for parliamentary democracy and universal suffrage organized by the Social Democratic Party revealed an enduring and distinctive
feature of Swedish politics and policy-making: realignments generated from
the evolving strategic interaction of parties, interest groups, and popular
movements merging ideological appeals with organizational imperatives. As
G. Therborn concluded, the "popular movements of the founding period of
Swedish political modernity had a long-term and still enduring impact upon
twentieth-century politics in Sweden: its popular but not populist character,
based upon well-structured, resourceful mass organizations . . . and the
movement dynamic of these organizations" (Therborn, 1989: 201).

Thus, the making of modern Swedish politics was organized in civil
society where partisan channels of interest representation provided decisive
arenas for coalition formation among politically active groups challenging
conservative forces entrenched in the state. The party and interest group system was pivotal in organizing struggles for democratic reform and economic
policies for industrial take-off (Lash and Urry, 1987).

These fundamental patterns of state-society relations have conditioned
the evolution of national styles of economic policy-making in the modern
period. In particular, the ruptures and innovations associated with the twentieth century's great watershed of the 1930s and 1940s emerged out of these
preexisting forms of political mobilization and organization. They provided
the institutional matrix for the major reconstruction of economic policy constituting the Keynesian revolution. But these legacies were constraining
rather than determining. The challenges and changes shaping the "revolution" emerged from the dynamic interplay of ideas and interests during this
period of profound uncertainty in each country's history.

Policy Innovation and Post-War Settlement in Canada

The Great Depression in Canada exposed the regional and class
inequities rooted in Canada's first economic strategy and the institutional
rigidities imposed by outdated constitutional arrangements. The simultane-
ous appearance of destitute farmers, unemployed workers, business

bankruptcies, and debt-ridden subnational governments spawned a variety of new parties and movements expressing concern with the Dominion government's attitude toward capitalism and federalism. Unfamiliar pressures were placed on the state system in the early 1930s as deep-seated divisions in Canadian society suddenly became rallying points for rival organizations articulating radical alternatives.

As many writers have emphasized, however, for a variety of reasons these pluralistic currents of class and regional protest never acquired the political status of a heterodox interest coalition unified by a coherent policy discourse (Ehrensaft and Armstrong, 1981; Laxer, 1989; Simeon and Robinson, 1990). Indeed, at the height of this social turbulence, the 1935 election intervened only to effect a routine transfer of majority power from the Conservatives to the Liberals. Both governing parties were steadfast adherents to the classical fiscal-constitutional orthodoxy of "sound finance and responsible government" (Neatby, 1976). The disbelief registered in all quarters when Conservative Prime Minister R.B. Bennett suddenly announced a death-bed conversion to a "New Deal" was amply confirmed in the 1935 campaign when neither he nor his Liberal opponent Mackenzie King offered any support for such ideas. In fact, the 1935 election effectively closed down the possibility that party-led social movements would bring new solutions to a paralyzed state system. Throughout the 1930s the imbalance between society's popular discontent and the state's policy inertia remained largely unaddressed by national party politics (Underhill, 1975: 164–82, 192–202).

It was in this specific context of political representation at the national level in Canada, where long-term policy debates were not encased in the thought and strategy of governing parties or social coalitions, that a technocratic caste of policy intellectuals became critical agents of history, directing the changes necessary to meet the Depression crisis. Canada's federal party system was oriented toward personality politics and cultural accommodation; the interest group system was too fragmented to devise or build support for national-level policy projects. Consequently, policy intellectuals, mobilizing ideological and organizational resources in the expert world of state commissions and intra-bureaucratic committees, assumed key roles in the reshaping of Canadian state-society relations that occurred during the interwar and wartime periods. With successive Conservative and Liberal Cabinets floundering in the face of protracted fiscal and social crisis, the King government finally responded in the late 1930s by appointing two commissions of inquiry mandated broadly to explain the origins of the breakdown and clarify the path out of the impasse. The National Employment Commission (NEC) and the Royal Commission on Dominion-Provincial Relations (the Rowell-Sirois Commission) became institutional-political focal points for the mediation of popular struggles and for the creation of new constitutional-economic categories. In their wake, the discursive context for partisan and inter-governmental politics in Canada was transformed.

Appointed following the stalemated Dominion-Provincial conference in 1935, the NEC was initially viewed by the King Cabinet as a further line of defense for protecting the federal treasury in the face of deteriorating employment conditions (Struthers, 1983: Ch. 5). Savings would result from the commission's careful scrutiny of relief eligibility, grants-in-aid, and provincial and municipal administration. The reformist *Canadian Forum* accused the government of the "crudest kind of empiricism" in framing the commission's work outside of an analysis of the "axioms of capitalism in its present phase of restriction of production" (*Canadian Forum*, 1936: 3, 6).

However, to the dismay of the prime minister and critics alike, the NEC's 1937 *Final Report* did not simply pile up more statistics to buttress prevailing practices. It unveiled policy proposals suggesting a new course of action beyond the orthodoxies. Its economic analysis introduced new techniques of public finance into Canadian policy discussion, explicating how adjustment to international market conditions could be stabilized through timely measures from the federal government to offset business cycles. Successful implementation of these economic ideas was linked to a call for political leadership in transferring constitutional authority over employment policy to the federal government. Although the prime minister was outraged by such official presentation of these ideas, senior bureaucratic officials responded favorably and began to incorporate them into their fiscal thinking and budget preparations.[6]

These initial departures set the stage for three years of further debate, research, and deliberations carried out in the Royal Commission on Dominion-Provincial Relations. The Rowell-Sirois Commission fully elaborated the connection pointed out by the NEC between an altered conception of the state's role in society and greater federal power in economic policy (Owram, 1986: Ch. 9). Centralization of taxing capacity in Ottawa, the commission argued, would facilitate counter-cyclical budgeting to attack unemployment and would allow for coordinated fiscal transfers between provinces to counter the regional disparities historically associated with federal economic governance. The policy notions tabled by the NEC were forcefully integrated by the Rowell-Sirois Commission in its central argument relating the introduction of Keynesian economic and income stabilization doctrine to Canada's historic political preoccupation with national unity.

These two commissions brought into focus an alternative discourse (policy goals and means of implementation) beyond the polarized visions of a unitary state and planned economy peddled by radicals, or the classical federalism and budget balancing defended by politicians in power. The concept of state intervention was appropriated by the commission experts from the anti-capitalist planners (Scott, 1937–1938). Equally important, they also clarified for conservative advocates of "responsible government" the constitutional blockages and political obstacles to such fiscal balance and administrative efficiency in the modern industrial age. A reform agenda was unveiled that envisioned federal economic leadership but did not run roughshod over provincial sensibilities (Smiley, 1962). Its implementation could proceed through bureaucratic negotiation of new inter-governmental fiscal arrangements, potentially sparing Canada's risk-averse federal ministers from the political troubles associated with securing formal constitutional amendments to allow state action.

Keynesian ideas came to Canada through expert inquiries as part of an emerging regime of scientific policy management by economic professionals. This project laid the foundations for a governing partnership between techno-bureaucratic officials and an emerging progressive faction within the Liberal Cabinet led in the late 1930s by Labour Minister Norman Rogers. Of course, the ever-cautious prime minister, Mackenzie King, waited anxiously on the sidelines as the experts—hailed in the popular press as authors of a "Charter of Re-Confederation"—dissected the country's problems and developed solutions (Fowler, 1940). Yet eventually he revised his outlook. His government had quietly responded to the NEC proposals in their final budget statements of the 1930s, introducing a new form of public works expenditures into federal economic policy (Brecher, 1957: 215–19; Struthers, 1983). In 1941, the Cabinet followed this initial breach with formal support for the Rowell-Sirois package. Abruptly ending a decade's resistance to economic and constitutional change, King convened an intergovernmental conference to advertise his conversion and sell the Cabinet's new discoveries to the provincial premiers and the public.

Mackenzie King recognized that the commission discourse contained the intellectual reference points for a new era of "centrist" politics in Canada (Pickersgill, 1960: 161). His governing Liberal Party could resume brokering "rolling compromises" at each election, backed by the framework of ideas from the technocrats integrating national economic stabilization and regional income equalization. In all of this, Canada's process of policy innovation was organized through commissions rather than elections or inter-governmental conferences. They became the *switchpoint mechanism* for the political system. Political conflict rooted in social protest movements questioning capitalism's future and the country's balkanization was mediated in the late 1930s by commission-based policy intellectuals and their new concepts—counter-cyclical budgeting, national adjustment grants, income security programs, automatic stabilizers, and the like (Rice, 1985: 223–32).

In the end, it was wartime that completed the political movements necessary to institutionalize these policy ideas. Opposition from three provincial premiers to the fiscal plan was disregarded as the basic Keynesian framework for manipulating and monitoring investment and expenditure flows was rapidly introduced with the onset of the war. Many of the professional experts moved from the commission arena to administrative agencies and departments at the center of the wartime policy apparatus (Granatstein, 1982). The war became the crucial testing ground for the new techniques, and their success in organizing emergency production ensured that those responsible for their design would be well positioned to guide the post-war transition. In fact, the new era's benchmark statement, the 1945 White Paper on Employment and Income, was conceived and written by W.A. Mackintosh, the intellectual architect of the innovations contained in the commissions of the 1930s (Mackintosh, 1965). Similarly, the Green Book social policy proposals prepared for the Reconstruction Conference in 1945 repeated earlier commission-generated arguments merging claims for fiscal centralization, economic stabilization, and political unity (Mackintosh, 1953). These remarkable achievements in technocratic policy entrepreneurship were the logical culmination of a decade's worth of intensive mobilization by intellectuals within Canada's learning network.

Developed by economic professionals from strategic niches in an expanding bureaucracy, Canada's Keynesian discourse envisioned minimal institutional change beyond sustaining the fiscal momentum of the federal government secured through successful administration of the wartime economy. Beginning with the initial reflections on the crisis in the commissions of the 1930s to the White Paper and Green Book government declarations in 1944–1945, the goal was always to exercise general control over the economic environment by influencing aggregate components of national income. Federalism demanded the negotiation of complex inter-governmental fiscal arrangements to ensure the efficacy of such a national budgetary strategy; other more political forms of Keynesianism designed to modify economic ownership or plan national outcomes had been explicitly dismissed during the initial Rowell-Sirois deliberations on the crisis.

In post-war Canada, the politics of embedding the Keynesian revolution thus turned on renovating national administrative capacities to establish a more rational and efficient political economy. To stabilize the economy and rationalize the federation were goals demanding full post-war mobilization of the expertise of the new policy scientists (Lamontagne, 1954: 151–52). Here, the aim was to insulate policy formation from both the narrow, regional interests expressed through the decentralizing institutions of federalism, and the short-run factional and sectional interests expressed in the brokerage party and interest group systems. During the 1930s, these representative channels had only sustained what the technocrats saw as outdated constitutional understandings and unenlightened conceptions of the state's potential to achieve economic and social goals through "intelligent" monitoring of market activity (Mackintosh, 1948: 15–18).

Politicians in power eventually welcomed the new solutions from the technocrats because they involved minimal institutional-political change, comfortably incorporated within existing partisan practices and administrative procedures (Cairns, 1988: 168). This package mobilized a generation of policy intellectuals, conformed broadly to established state capacities, and satisfied pragmatic politicians searching to reassure electorates and business elites about markets and growth (Wolfe, 1984). Canada's pattern of "experts on top, not on tap" was consolidated as the "Ottawa men" deployed their resources, coordinating rapid expansion of the state's data-gathering capacity in relation to the new economic theory (Granatstein, 1982). They established inter-departmental mechanisms for integrating such scientific advances and consultative forums linking technocratic elites monitoring the results of policy measures (Daub, 1984–1985). There was, as Robert Campbell observed, "a willingness on the part of labour, capital and the politicians to allow the bureaucracy to get on with the job of managing the economy" (Campbell, 1987: 68). This peculiar technocratic embedding of economic ideas followed from the relationship between holders of scientific policy knowledge and representative institutions forged during the crisis period of the 1930s.

Policy Innovation and Post-War Settlement in Sweden

Economic policy-making in Sweden during the 1920s was dominated by classical assumptions of how self-regulating capitalist economies worked. Chronic unemployment throughout the decade did not occasion any sustained departure from restrictive budgetary practices, the gold standard, and free trade. After playing a key leadership role in the popular struggles for universal suffrage, the Social Democratic Party unexpectedly found its forward momentum stalled. The electoral benefits anticipated from political democratization failed to materialize. Liberal, Conservative, and Agrarian forces coalesced in opposition to Social Democratic policy initiatives, particularly in regard to taxation and industrial relations matters. There was no majority waiting to follow the Social Democrats along the parliamentary road to socialism. Confined largely to its bedrock working-class support in the elections of the 1920s, the Social Democrats were unable to exercise any decisive influence on government policy-making (Martin, 1984: 193–203).[7]

In fact, the political neutralization of the party was matched by limitations in its own analysis of the employment crisis and policy responses to the steadily deteriorating economic conditions. The Social Democrats explained the economic crisis as a consequence of capitalism's irrationality, but that theoretical critique deflected the party from exploring policy options short of the long-term goal of socialization. Even here the party temporized;

minimal attention had been given to the organizational and political requirements for implementing an economic program based on public ownership.
Accordingly, the Social Democratic leadership, when participating in Sweden's minority governments of the 1920s, deviated very little from the economic liberalism of other parties. By default the Social Democrats followed
the view that deflationary measures (including wage reduction) would facilitate the private investment necessary to provide relief to the unemployed
(Higgins, 1985: 215–16).

However, in 1930 the Social Democrats broke with the orthodoxies,
proposing in the Swedish Parliament a bill for greatly increased state spending on public works to stimulate the economy. Embracing these ideas effectively delivered the party from both its policy impasse and its political
dilemma. What factors led the party leadership to this dramatic shift in
thinking? The new policy emerged from learning dynamics driven by the
interplay of ideas and action within the political and industrial wings of the
labor movement. Theoretical innovation, electoral strategy, and organizational interest merged in the 1930s to generate and sustain this alternative
economic project.

In this context a series of developments between 1928 and 1930 proved
critical. In 1928, the Social Democrats suffered a significant electoral set-
back, with their share of the popular vote dropping by 4 percent. This defeat
triggered a far-reaching internal review of the party's economic policy and
its connection to electoral strategy (Hamilton, 1989: 166–68). From these
deliberations came the consensus that the party's future depended on its
capacity to attract the votes of small farmers and rural workers, unhinging
the Agrarian Party from its partnership with Liberal and Conservative parties. The positive experience with alliance politics from the earlier constitutional struggle could now be replayed by the labor movement, substituting
Agrarians for Liberals based on recognition of cross-cutting economic interests. Influential party intellectuals such as Gunnar Myrdal argued that the
1928 campaign run on the conventional, long-term socialist program had
only accelerated the movement of farmers over to the bourgeois parliamentary bloc. Consolidation of the strategic reorientation, however, presupposed
two departures: first, new economic thinking to specify common ground
between historically opposed labor-agrarian formations; and second, new
party leadership to link such policy ideas with political support (Gourevitch,
1989: 93). Here, Ernst Wigforss's theoretical work and Per Albin Hansson's
coalitional politics find their historical significance in Swedish public policy.

In 1928 Wigforss published the first of a series of pamphlets clarifying
an "action program" between liberal laissez-faire and Marxist breakdown
theory. In an original reformulation of underconsumptionist theory, Wigforss
provided an economic rationale for counter-cyclical budgetary policy in
times of less than full employment (Myrdal, 1973). This orientation accom-

modated the call in 1928 from the trade union leadership for the party to campaign for a new productive, public works program paid at market wages. Such a scheme would replace the existing system of below-market wage relief works that the state had used to undermine public sector unions and erode the movement's market power, rather than provide more employment. Expansionary measures could respond to the demands for economic stabilization from both urban industrial and rural agricultural workers.

The Social Democrats, of course, mobilized around this recovery program in the next election. In 1932, with the full effects of the Depression plunging Swedish export industries into crisis and causing unemployment to rise to over 20 percent, the Social Democrats won their greatest number of parliamentary seats. However, the party fell short of a governing majority and the spectre of a return to the failures of the 1920s persisted. Against this backdrop, the party used the new economic thinking to define the terms of a parliamentary deal with the formerly hostile Agrarians. The ideas gave substantive and strategic meaning to the social democratic concept of the "people's home" popularized by Per Albin Hansson. Armed with their unorthodox economic proposals, the Social Democratic leadership could now explore a new form of democratic political practice: forming an alliance around party policies with organized economic interests while also engaging voters in a dialogue over their merits.[8] In 1932, Hansson described the party's approach to group and electoral coalition building:

one has to seek to weave together interests, to get more and more people to integrate their special interests in the common interest. The latter is the same as getting the citizens to think and act democratically. It is possible that one can get the elite that presently dominates our economic life to act in this way. (Tilton, 1990: 139)

In 1932, the Social Democrats launched their loan-financed reflationary package. Between 1933 and 1936 legislation for public works, agricultural price supports, unemployment insurance, and pensions was passed through the "red-green" alliance. Moreover, each of these policies was institutionalized in the state's operating procedures through political rather than bureaucratic mechanisms. The theoretical rationale for this alternative administrative structure had been elaborated in the writings of party theoretician Nils Karleby (Tilton, 1990: Ch. 4). Karleby argued that social democratic progress depended on enhancing working-class capacities in civil society, not on placing reform-minded technocrats throughout the existing state apparatus. Under the leadership of Social Democratic Minister of Social Affairs Gustav Moller, Karleby's ideas about class power and public administration were put into practice. During the 1930s, responsibility for the design and implementation of many elements of Swedish social policy was assumed by the trade union movement itself. In this way the new programs reinforced the organizational strength and improved the policy competence of the Social Democratic Party's core electoral constituency (Rothstein, 1985).

For reasons largely unrelated to the economic effects of these policies, by 1935 the Depression began to subside. Rising external demand for Swedish products spurred by earlier currency devaluations, more than domestic stimulation, has been judged the critical force in the economic turnaround. Far more significant for the Social Democrats were the political consequences of their economic ideas, which extended beyond the partisan arena to facilitate a new accommodation between the labor movement and organized business. When a strike in the building trades jeopardized the party's parliamentary base in 1933, the trade union central took the unprecedented action of intervening to impose a settlement on the grounds that party control of the state altered the strategic context for achieving the overall goals of the working class (Swenson, 1989).

Similarly for business, the political success of the "red-green" alliance—reconfirmed in the 1936 election—forced reconsideration of its historic reliance on state policy to wage class struggle. Fearing hostile political intervention and with its domestically oriented sectors benefiting from demand stimulation, the employers' organization sought a compromise with the labor movement. The Social Democratic Party's economic ideas and political strategy had created innovative policies calling forth altered assessments of "class interests" by key private actors. Business and labor both reflected anew on their strategic positioning within the Swedish political economy in the wake of the 1932 and 1936 elections. These recalculations were confirmed in the 1938 Basic Agreement stipulating conditions for industrial peace and productivity; business recognized labor's dominance in the polity and labor recognized the economic power of business (Pontusson, 1987: 471–93).

At the height of the Great Depression, Swedish channels of political representation engineered three historic shifts: the recasting of parliamentary alliances, the renegotiation of relations between business and labor, and the reorganization of the state's place in the economy. In these interrelated breakthroughs the role of economic policy ideas loomed large. During the late 1920s, proto-Keynesian notions emerged within the labor movement as the party sought to overcome political isolation and the trade unions cast about for ways to arrest organizational decomposition. Resolution to these strategic dilemmas was not visible within prevailing policy discourses. Demand stimulation through government spending was an idea empowering the Swedish labor movement. It became the binding agent for a partisan mobilization and political realignment that gave the labor movement new and significant influence over public policy. The terms on which the state's economic role was debated by political actors changed in the mid-1930s from sound finance and wage deflation to employment creation and welfare provision. Keynesian ideas entered Swedish politics as a response to problems facing a politically neutralized yet structurally well positioned labor movement. They mapped the ground for a new cross-class coalition represented by parties and interest groups (Pontusson, 1988: Chs. 2, 3).

At the end of the war the labor movement collaborated to develop a new program departing substantially from the inter-war package. Drawing on the wartime experience with the regulation of production and anticipating that a return to Depression-like conditions was imminent, the union-party committee called for state investment planning and intervention in enterprise decision-making. However, these doctrinal changes were politically marginalized. First, the persistence of near full employment reduced greatly the persuasiveness of the new program's economic prescriptions. Second, the defection of the Agrarians signaled that these ideas could not sustain the cross-class coalition orchestrated during the 1930s. Indeed, they served to mobilize business and party opposition against the Social Democrats in the ideologically charged election campaigns of 1944 and 1948. Following successive electoral setbacks, the Social Democrats reconstituted the "red-green" alliance in 1951. The terms of the 1930s compromise were reintroduced in an altered strategic setting for economic policy formation and political mobilization—full employment and inflation. Organizational pressures and innovative thinking within the labor movement converged once again to introduce an economic policy framework sustaining Social Democratic governance through a new cross-class political compromise (Esping-Andersen, 1985).

Keynesian Revolutions Compared

The innovations common to Sweden and Canada were created and carried out by different political actors moving within system-specific networks of discourse construction and political representation. In Depression Sweden, national interest groups interacted with parties to debate novel policy ideas, promoting frameworks that became the basis for electoral conflict and coalition building. The elaboration of demand management ideas was linked to (and emerged from) the convergent strategic objectives of the political and industrial wings of the labor movement. Parties and interest groups faced the crisis of the 1930s with their own Keynesian-style policy ideas conceived in relation to political strategies for organizational survival.

As such, two decision-making arenas quite peripheral in the Canadian case—national elections and the internal dynamics of interest organization policy formulation—became significant locales of Swedish adjustment and innovation. In Canada, the policy shifts beginning in the late 1930s and continuing across the 1940s correlated weakly, if at all, to alterations in the partisan or ideological orientation of governing parties. Similarly, the successive conceptual breakthroughs (eclipsing the intertwined doctrines of sound finance and responsible government as the benchmark for state-economy relations) did not correspond in any substantive way to the political (or moral) victory of parties and social movements mobilizing around new economic ideas.

Instead, Keynesian ideas in Canada galvanized a previously inchoate community of technocrats—nonpartisan and formally apolitical—who exploited the policy space ceded to them in this political system to impose incrementally a new conception of state intervention on governing parties clinging to orthodoxy. Developing their theoretical notions into a macro-economic management paradigm across participation in successive Royal Commissions of Inquiry during the 1935–1940 period, these experts acquired political sponsorship for their ideas principally through personal communication with and participation in top echelons of the federal civil service.

In Sweden, of course, there was no shortage of state economic policy inquiries during the 1930s. However, in their composition and their discourse, Swedish commissions were fairly faithful reflections of partisan and ideological struggles anchored elsewhere.[9] In Canada, by contrast, commissions provided decisive institutional settings for interpreting the political meaning and policy implications of the chaos of the 1930s. Through their intellectual work and representational activities a new discourse was constructed. They launched Canada's version of Keynesianism, and with it many of the key actors in the bureaucratic mode of policy adjustment that came to characterize Canada's wartime realignments.

In both countries, the crystallization of new economic ideas triggered and shaped nationally specific processes of political and administrative adjustment. The result was the formation of distinctive styles of national economic governance for the post-war period (Pekkarinen, 1989).

THE ORGANIZATIONAL INTELLIGENCE OF POLITICAL SYSTEMS: ALTERNATIVE LEARNING REGIMES

The preceding analysis of the inter-war and wartime periods developed a number of points about the historical relationship between economic ideas, systems of political representation, and policy-making at moments of crisis in Canada and Sweden. Attention was drawn to cross-national variation in the relevant mechanisms of collective choice and in the learning networks that filtered options, selected policies, and therefore structured outcomes. In mapping such institutional configurations—in effect, the differing Canadian and Swedish divisions of labor within the network among parties, interest organizations, civil servants, and experts—the discussion showed how different elite formations at the interface of state and society coped with crisis and directed change.

These findings about cross-national variation in the institutional settings and social agents organizing departures during this critical watershed invite further consideration of patterns over time. Have the policy communities and associated learning networks underpinning different post-war settlements in Sweden and Canada created enduring centers of "organizational intelligence" in each political system? Here the historical record of subsequent responses to significant international economic changes is suggestive of such embedded country-specific networks. Across the post-war period, the Canadian and Swedish political systems have evolved characteristic ways of generating and confirming new policy understandings in the face of uncertainty (Bradford, 1994).

Beginning in the mid-1950s, intense pressures were placed on economic policymakers in both countries to supplement stabilization and demand management concerns with supply-side measures for growth and capital formation. In Sweden, as many writers have described, post-war economic strategies evolved as a "series of deals" originating in the thought and strategy of the labor movement (Gourevitch et al., 1984: 365). The Rehn-Meidner model launched Sweden's departure from Keynesian principles showing how restrictive fiscal policy could be combined with an egalitarian wage structure reinforcing trade union cohesion and promoting capital efficiency. In the place of incomes policy and general expansionary measures it called for selective spending on labor market adjustment. Budgetary surpluses would not only finance worker retraining and mobility but also provide a public capital fund to supplement private investment in the non-inflationary macro-environment.

Implementation of this economic framework was secured through party politics and interest group negotiation, against the backdrop of changes in Swedish class structure and corporate behavior. Specifically, in post-war Sweden farmers were losing their political significance to the new middle class, and the operations of industry were becoming increasingly internationalized. In this setting, the Social Democrats embraced active labor market policy and a supplementary public pension scheme to forge a new coalition of wage-earners and export-oriented industry behind the Rehn-Meidner structural change economic policy—a policy opposed by farmers and the generally less profitable home market firms. Core elements of the Rehn-Meidner model were confirmed administratively and politically in the late 1950s; first, the party greatly expanded the national labor market board and then cemented the new wage-earner coalition in the 1960 election, fought explicitly over the pension fund concept with its associated public investment strategy.

The latest chapter in this story would begin with the labor movement's third major economic policy initiative in the modern era—the wage-earner funds proposal, conceived by the blue collar trade unions in the context of the protracted economic problems of the 1970s and 1980s. The fate of that project poses complex questions about the historical and structural limits of Sweden's post-war learning regime rooted in labor movement innovations and policy-oriented mobilization. Indeed, the 1990s resemble the 1920s and the late 1940s as the Swedish labor movement grapples with the contradictions undermining familiar policy frameworks and gropes for new economic policy understandings responding to the organizational goals of both unions and party.

In Canada, the same post-war search for new economic perspectives was launched in 1955 through the Royal Commission on Canada's Economic Prospects (the Gordon Commission). This commission offered a multi-faceted re-evaluation of post-war practices, challenging established views of policy problems and goals, state-economy relations, and policy instruments (Kent, 1958). Questions raised by the commission about economic control and ownership, the spatial distribution of production, and the national economy's structural balance could not be formulated within Canada's Keynesian data-driven automatic stabilization framework. Answering them meant inventing a new mix of policy instruments for domestic capital formation: discretionary corporate taxation, relaxed anti-combines regulations, quid pro quo bargaining, and selective protection in foreign economic relations. In these fundamental areas beyond the boundaries of prevailing thought and action, the commission proposed a series of interconnected departures. The Gordon Commission set in motion an extended period of economic policy experimentation by successive Liberal and Progressive Conservative federal governments. Beginning in the 1960s, divisions over these commission-introduced ideas became institutionalized not in the party and interest group systems but in an expanding range of techno-bureaucratic agencies assuming key policy-making functions (French, 1984; Clarke et al., 1991). Although central issues of economic strategy in Canada were "banished from the arena of partisan political discussion," there continued a "fierce debate amongst Canada's intellectuals . . . reflected within the state and in the formation of state policy" (Williams, 1985: 666).

In fact, this latest round of technocratic policy formation culminated in the Royal Commission on the Economic Union and Development Prospects for Canada (the Macdonald Commission), appointed in 1982 (Brooks, 1990). Like earlier era-defining state inquiries, the Macdonald Commission was created when the regular channels of political representation were unable to devise, or build support for, credible solutions to serious economic problems. Using its "unbounded mandate to formulate a more detailed and sweeping blueprint for change than any Royal Commission in modern times," this inquiry became the crucial "policy event" in Canada's twenty-year search for a post-Keynesian framework (*Toronto Star*, 1985: 1).[10] It scripted a new policy era wherein supranational agreements on "market dictates" would overtake domestic politics in regulating the economy. Reporting in the wake of the 1984 election, its proposals for continental free trade and welfare reform gave direction to a sputtering new government rich in parliamentary seats but poor in policy ideas and governing strategy. At the same time, its public hearings brought into the policy system a range of popular forces that were subsequently galvanized into an oppositional political movement contesting the inquiry's final recommendations (Simeon, 1987; Cameron and Drache, 1988). Once again, the commission process in Canada both organized and materially affected an important debate over alternative economic futures (Clarke et al., 1991: Ch. 1). Not surprisingly, the 1988 federal election results confirmed policy choices and political alignments crystallized during the time of the Macdonald Commission.

CONCLUSION

This chapter has utilized the concept of learning network to describe country-specific processes of economic idea generation and public policy formation. In Canada, economic professionals and civil servants have dominated within a techno-bureaucratic learning network of Royal Commissions, task forces, advisory councils, and inter-departmental committees. Policy learning has been driven by various technocratic formations puzzling over the legacy of past policies. The generation of competing schools of thought by economic professionals—Keynesianism, industrial strategy, continentalism, and the like—and their search for political confirmation via ad hoc partisan-administrative factions has been central to learning dynamics and policy change in Canada (Clark-Jones, 1987: 222–24; Williams, 1986: Ch. 7).

In Sweden, such debates and processes have been anchored in party and interest group politics. Across the post-war period, learning has proceeded through organizational exchanges between parties and groups pursuing common interests made visible by the injection of new economic ideas. The generation of frameworks from within the political and industrial arms of the labor movement and their capacity to organize and sustain cross-class coalitions has been central to policy choice and change in Sweden.

This line of argument speaks directly to problems in recent neo-institutionalist attempts to introduce ideas into theoretical models of policy innovation. On the one hand, a decidedly state-centered approach has been developed by followers of Hugh Heclo's original formulation of the social learning argument (Heclo, 1974; Weir and Skocpol, 1985). These writers attach special significance in determining outcomes to civil servant and expert interpretations of past policies and existing administrative capacities. In countries where state structures facilitate engagement with policy intellectuals, innovative capacity is likely to be high. On the other hand, these same questions have been tackled from a society-centered perspective. Taking its cue from Samuel Beer's influential interpretation of political development stressing the modernizing role of ideological parties, this view assigns causal primacy to politicians (Beer, 1974: 135–52; Hall, 1986: 271–83; Gourevitch, 1986, 1989). Innovation flows from the vision of party leaders who create or package new policy ideas, merging them with established party doctrine to engineer political realignments.

This debate is off the mark because there is no single or stable division of labor between political forces mobilized to shape the orientations and perceptions of policymakers. The concept of the learning network accommodates such institutional-political variation. Imposing a statist analytical grid over the Swedish experience seriously underplays the importance of political parties and interest groups in driving the movement from one policy era to another. Far from simply ratifying choices based on expert findings, these actors have been integral to the generation of new ideas and the institutionalization of new policies. By the same token, the Canadian case reveals the limits of a society-centered model. There, policy intellectuals have been prime agents of change. Accounts of the inter-war crisis and wartime settlement that disregard the commission process—its mediation of competing societal claims and its doctrinal breakthroughs—in favor of a focus on conventional channels of political representation miss central elements in the specifically Canadian pattern of innovation. Royal Commission politics and their relationship to intra-bureaucratic forms of policy mobilization have been critical to Canadian transformations.

Further research is likely to uncover alternative institutional networks of discourse definers that persist for certain periods of time to encase particular regimes of policy learning. Comparative-historical examination of these networks traces the political effects of differing organizational intelligences, suggesting a new perspective on how states and societies create public policy.

NOTES

1. H. Gerth and C.W. Mills (eds.) (1958: 63–64).
2. Our position on "bringing the state back in" has been inspired by recent work highlighting organizational and ideational factors in politics. See in particular J. Jenson (1986, 1989) and P. Hall (1990) for applications of the concepts of political discourse and policy paradigms.
3. A classic statement of the cultural values perspective, familiar to all students of Canadian politics, is G. Horowitz's comparative essay (Horowitz, 1968) using Hartz's semi-

nal discussion of ideological traditions in new societies (Hartz, 1955). An equally paradigmatic statement of the neo-Marxist dominant ideology approach would be that of L. Althusser (1971).

4. Policy community is a useful organizing device for political analysis. However, this chapter argues that the concept of learning network has greater explanatory potential because it focuses on the "movement dynamics" of institutionalized political relations underpinning policy compromises (Therborn, 1989). Policy communities contain learning networks, and it is the latter that captures the interplay of ideas and interests between state and society.

5. Our use of "organizational intelligence" is somewhat different from Peter Hall's (1986) original formulation. Hall emphasizes how organization shapes interests and mediates policy design and implementation. In this chapter "organizational intelligence" refers to the ideologies and ideas—generated and disseminated within historically evolved institutional settings—that shape the definition of interests and strategic choice. Hall reveals much about the constraining dimensions of organizational life, whereas our interest is more with the creative capacities of political systems.

6. H.B. Neatby's political biography of Mackenzie King provides insight into the prime minister's strained relationship with the policy intellectuals converging on Ottawa in the late 1930s (Neatby, 1976: 246–47). King's own views are recorded in his personal diaries (Pickersgill and Forster, 1970: 207–15).

7. Background information for the Swedish case has been drawn from a variety of sources, including the following key texts: A. Martin (1984) and J. Pontusson (1988) on labor movement politics and strategy; T. Tilton on social democratic economic ideas (1990); M. Hamilton on the Social Democratic Party (1989); and B. Gustafsson on the "Stockholm" school of policy intellectuals (1973).

8. This capacity to mobilize support in the "private" world of organized economic interests and in the "public" world of elections has been the key to the remarkable political success and policy achievements of the post-war Swedish Social Democrats. See J. Pontusson (1988) and G. Esping-Andersen (1985) for an elaboration of the nature and limits of this governing project.

9. In Sweden, royal commissions are routine components of the highly organized consultation process that distinguishes Swedish public decision-making. In any given year hundreds of such inquiries may be at work. Far from being exceptional structures appointed at moments of deep policy confusion or uncertainty, they are very much part of normal politics and policy. Their membership is typically dominated by representatives from parliamentary parties and interest groups, narrowly charged to produce consensus around proposals originating in the political arena. In this light, the commission process in Sweden has been instrumental to the "Social Democrats' strategic ability to divide, wear down through continuous consultations, and periodically coopt factions of their opposition" (Heclo and Madsen, 1987: 29). Royal commissions operate within the distinctive organizational contexts of the Swedish and Canadian political systems. Their strategic significance in the economic policy learning network varies accordingly.

10. The *Toronto Star* (1985) offered further commentary on the process:

the commission may also prove to be a godsend for the Progressive Conservative government in Ottawa, which seems to have run out of ideas as to where to take the country. While in opposition, the Tories loudly denounced the establishment of the commission and the appointment of its head, former Liberal Minister Donald Macdonald. Now they may have to turn to it for an agenda.

PART II

THE ROLE OF INSTITUTES

5

Policy Research Institutes and Liberalized International Services Exchange

Stephen D. McDowell

INTRODUCTION

During the period 1945–1980, many service industries (i.e., transportation, communications, finance, health care, and education) were seen as national rather than international in scope. This was because services were of central importance to nations' political, economic, and social objectives. Foreign ownership and investment in key service sectors—such as finance or communications—would also reduce national autonomy and national sovereignty. In addition, the difficulties of delivering services from a distance meant that it was often technically impossible to trade them across borders. For these reasons services were not included in the international trade and investment institutions created after 1945. Many international agreements and organizations were arranged among nation-states covering services such as air transport, shipping, telecommunications, and finance. However, these institutions were guided by principles of cooperation, coordination, harmonization of policy approaches, the management of interdependence, or development assistance, rather than by liberal trade and investment disciplines.

Nationally, the welfare state consensus in market economy countries held that some services—such as education and communication—were necessary for the operation of liberal democratic institutions. These services, therefore, should be made universally accessible to all citizens regardless of their ability or desire to pay. Economically, some services were seen as infrastructural or support utilities that contributed to other productive and wealth-creating activities, rather than as producing value in themselves.

Theories of natural monopoly argued that given high infrastructural costs the duplication of transportation and communication networks was not feasible, and that competition among different service providers would be costly and inefficient. Problems of collective action and public good provision—the difficulties in charging for incremental individual use of services or excluding free-riders who did not pay—implied that a state monopoly was required to collect for public services through general taxation revenues.

These practices began to be questioned during the 1970s and early 1980s. The concepts and theoretical approaches used to understand the service sector, and the public policies and the role of the state in services, came under intense scrutiny and debate. Policies such as the liberalization of international trade and investment in service industries and the deregulation and privatization of national service industries gained adherents among academics, policy analysts, public affairs advocates, business groups, and state and international organization officials in a wide number of professional, organizational, and geographic sites. Liberalization includes institutional shifts: in the production and exchange of services (commodification of services, creation of service markets); in the role of states in service production (deregulation, privatization); and in international trade and investment in service industries using trade principles such as most-favored nation status, nondiscrimination, and progressive liberalization to shape international service transactions and investment (McDowell, 1991). Service policies are now under review and revision in a number of international organizations.[1] The importance placed by the United States on including trade in services in the Uruguay Round of negotiations in the General Agreement on Tariffs and Trade may best illustrate the emergence of these priorities.

This chapter examines the role that policy research institutes in North America and Western Europe played in the liberalization of institutions guiding international production and exchange of services, with specific focus on their influence in shaping the new arrangements for trade in services being negotiated in the General Agreement on Tariffs and Trade (GATT). The objectives of this chapter are to (1) relate the activities of national and international policy research institutes to research programs of states and international organizations; and (2) evaluate the significance of agency by individuals and groups involved in service policy research for broader institutional and structural change.

APPROACHES TO UNDERSTANDING POLICY
RESEARCH INSTITUTES

A variety of perspectives address questions about the role of social scientists in policy research and policy formation, or the importance of the activities of policy researchers and policy institutes. Some studies have treated independent (i.e., independent of government) policy research institutes as new forms of organizing and mobilizing political power, especially with regard to forming the concepts, knowledge, and information that modern bureaucratic states need to operate. Approaches focusing on the role of social scientists and their relationship to the state have emphasized their influence from differing perspectives: rationalistic (providing information that the policy process needs); enlightenment (improving slowly over time the sets of ideas and evidence with which policymakers work); or historical-comparative (Brooks and Gagnon, 1990b). As well as examining changes in the policies of state bureaucracies, we could examine the role of social scientists in electoral politics, class formation, "new social movements," or simple expert advocacy for clients. The stance of social scientists toward structural or institutional change could be explicitly addressed also. Do policy analysts "manage" change, "respond" to technological and economic change, or see themselves, in the context of their policy communities, as "agents" of historical change?

The types of organizations that engage in policy reflection and research—and their mandates, objectives, funding, and participation patterns—are also important parts of the story. Creative groups and individuals participate in public policy and politics in a variety of political and organizational mechanisms that are directed toward the formation of concepts and the creation of knowledge and information. These institutional forms vary from time to time and from country to country; they include organizations such as academic research centers, industry and professional associations, trade union research units, government-funded research institutes, lobbying firms, consultants, and privately funded independent policy research institutes and think tanks. Policy research institutes should therefore be seen in the context of other institutions and organizations involved in knowledge creation, and as being situated and participating in networks of individuals with shared and competing policy concerns, concepts, and directions (Peschek, 1987, 1989; Critchlow, 1984; Langille, 1987; Weaver, 1989). These organizations may engage in activities such as basic research, conference organization, public education and comment, policy advocacy in specific areas, and promotion of political and economic worldviews.

Borrowing from the comparative-historical perspective (which recognizes the differing characteristics and relationships of historical institutional forms), one could argue that the specific organizational forms and the purposes of policy research institutes are less important than the larger contextual connections between research institutes and other non-state, state, and inter-state organizations. Rather than idealizing a particular form of policy institute (e.g., the American privately funded think tank), one could view policy research institutes as another group of sites in which interactions among and within communities of policy analysts take place (with analytic priority being given to the groups rather than the organizational forms). We could therefore examine ways in which policy research institutes influence government policies *through* the formation and maintenance of "policy networks" or "policy communities" and how they have participated in those communities. To sort out these questions of emphasis and focus, it is useful to bring a larger theoretical perspective to bear on the relations between policy research institutes, research networks and communities, government and international organization research programs, and their role in structural and institutional change.

A Gramscian Interpretation of Intellectuals, Policy Communities, Social Classes, and the State

The linkage between policy research institutes, states, international organizations' research programs, and structural change in international political economy will be examined by drawing on applications of Gramscian approaches to the study of world politics. Antonio Gramsci's discussion of intellectuals (and their role in the formation of consensual sets of ideas) provides a unique perspective both on the role of individual actors and groups of intellectuals, and on how we can understand policy research institutes in the context of other state and societal bodies.

The place given consensually shared ideas in the Gramscian concept of hegemony, and the role of intellectuals and their ideas in the formation of historic blocs, situates policy knowledge and information in a historical and political context. The treatment of the role of intellectuals includes a broad definition of who intellectuals are (covering their organizational, connective, and articulating functions), their relationship to social classes and their role in the creation of social classes as historical agents, their part in linking the state to civil society, the connections between practical and economic activities and professional knowledge, and the formation of professional specialties and groups (Vacca, 1982; Brym, 1987).

According to Giuseppe Vacca, Gramsci opens a way to link the examination of intellectuals to the development of hegemonic or consensual social formations. The Gramscian use of hegemony signifies that one group has moral and intellectual leadership in addition to its control over the material aspects of power. The hegemonic group is granted this leadership position by other social classes because of concessions given to subdominant groups, and because it articulates the concerns of the entire society in "universal" language. There is, then, a consensual aspect to hegemonic power relations, in combination with the more coercive aspects of state power and production relations. A hegemonic arrangement between groups and classes could also be described as a historic bloc. The historical approach does not see these relationships as predetermined; the linkages and lines of historical causality run many ways. There is neither a necessary nor unique relationship between material forces and the policy approaches that may be appropriate for the management of power relations (this has been played out in history).

Intellectuals are not just specialists, researchers, and experts; they are also the managers, organizers, and technicians who organize production and participate in the formation of policy concepts in specific issue areas. This view of intellectuals is more holistic than views of intellectuals only as opinion leaders, as public policy analysts, or as those with expert knowledge in a small area of science or policy. Similarly, it does not exclude those who lack the broad perspectives that generalist managers or political analysts bring to the shaping of questions and policies.

Policy "networks" and "communities" are terms that complement this broader and more inclusive definition of intellectuals. They expand the scope of relevant participants wider than a circle of government policy analysts, academics, and writers. This terminology recognizes the need of the state (in policy formation) for consultations and connections with private sector institutions and experts. The state/civil society distinction allows (or directs) us to expand the relevant boundaries of groups involved in policy knowledge formation to a variety of institutional sites and groups outside of the state.

Intellectuals and their activities (i.e., the formation and dissemination of policy and cultural concepts) are seen as connected to social classes. Social groups and classes are based in economic and production patterns. The relationship between intellectuals and social classes is reciprocal: social classes can be the basis for intellectual activities, and the organizational and expressive roles of intellectuals can contribute to the formation and maintenance of social classes. Therefore, policy research is relevant not only to state policy and the relationships between states and civil societies. Because policy research contributes to the formation of shared ideas, concerns, and interests, it also serves to bring social groups together and to articulate their interests and identities. This definition of intellectuals challenges the views that (1) intellectuals serve the "whole" public by providing services to the state or to other public institutions like newspapers, publications, research bodies, or universities; or (2) intellectuals are totally disconnected from the narrow-interest articulation of political struggles.

Intellectuals and policy communities play an important role in linking states to the institutions of civil society. The connections between an enlarged notion of the state—including deliberative bodies—and the institutions of civil society are mediated in part by intellectuals. Policy research institutes may be seen as representative civil society bodies. Although they are independent, they do have important connections to the state, especially regarding the expert and advisory functions of managers and leaders in the private sector. Although policy research institutes are themselves situated within the network of state and civil society institutions, one opportunity for "agency" is to encourage and represent certain social groups in civil society and to facilitate the connections of some groups and their concerns to the state (to the possible exclusion of others). Similarly, the formation of knowledge embodied in research institutes and professional institutions is closely linked to practical and economic activities.[2]

The approach to shared ideas or ideology in the hegemony framework focuses on broad sets of ideas that bind together social groups and classes (i.e., in terms of their understandings of the world and their views of themselves and others). The hegemonic ideology or set of policy ideas not only is relevant to one social class but also encompasses the concerns and interests of other groups. Policy research networks—and their connective role between state analysts, those in civil society organizations, and so-called political intellectuals more involved with advocacy—could be seen as providing the loose but essential shaping of the communications and interactions required to create and manage consensual and hegemonic relations.

Attention is paid not only to the part that intellectuals play in the formation of social classes and in the connections and distinctions between the state and civil society; Gramsci also notes the dynamic and historical link between economic activities and the creation of professional specialties and organizations. Regarding the link between practical/economic activities and education, Gramsci argues that "each practical activity tends to create a new type of school for its own executives and specialists and hence to create a body of specialist intellectuals at a higher level to teach in those schools" (Gramsci, 1971: 26). In addition, these developments can be linked to the formation of professional associations: "every intellectual activity tends to create for itself cultural associations of its own; [which] take on the function of post-scholastic institutions, specialised in organising the conditions in which it is possible to keep abreast of whatever progress is being made in the given scientific field" (Gramsci, 1971: 27).

The Gramscian framework lays out a general indication of the possible connections among intellectuals and policy research institutes in civil society, social classes, and the research and negotiating programs of states. Political ideas and articulations (a rather broad interpretation of public policy) can be understood as arising in the context of the shared problems and concerns of social classes. Also, policy research and consultation are important parts of the links between states and the institutions of civil society. Hence, policy research programs connected to negotiations—by affecting and reflecting the shape and nature of consensus or dissension on policy ideologies—can contribute in part to the formation and nature of hegemonic social structures. As a way to participate in the policy debate, research programs can provide information about the nature of the economy and can point to priority areas for state action (e.g., inflation, unemployment, the deficit).

The Gramscian approach posits social classes as the agents of change (as opposed to viewing states as the champions of economic development or managed structural change, or viewing intellectuals either as "vanguards" or "philosopher kings" of rational public policy). Only social classes and their intellectual spokespersons can exercise leadership in forming historic blocs and hegemonic coalitions among classes; to depict the intellectual as operating in the context of a de-historicized absolute state—and intellectuals as absolute and pre-eminent—would be to miss the important historical dimensions of the Gramscian contribution.

The connection between intellectuals and social classes as the agents of historical change introduces a critical dimension to the theory. The critical approach recognizes that the purpose of research and theorizing is not to gain value-neutral knowledge but to contribute to the formation of a historic bloc among social classes that will change the social order. Therefore, historical research and the construction of concepts and questions are linked to questions and dialogues that evaluate and seek to change present policies and institutional orders. It is an approach that brings the questions of politics and social class into the analysis of policy, rather than accepting the mandates of existing public organizations and institutional structures as ahistorically given and working unreflectively within that framework.[3]

INTERNATIONAL INSTITUTIONS AND TRANSNATIONAL POLICY NETWORKS

Gramscian concepts and ideas address political, economic, social, and cultural orders and transformations, primarily within national societies and nation-states. However, policy research regarding international services liberalization is concerned with international political economy. Thus, we must examine the role of policy research institutions and policy communities in change in international organizations and in international trade and investment practices. The research question needs to be expanded to include the transnational linkages among national research communities. A body of theory and research in international relations literature has applied Gramscian concepts and approaches to the relations among states, among social groups in different nation-states, and among and within social groups that connect across national borders. I draw mainly on literature in the historical materialist approach to international institutions (Cox, 1983, 1986, 1987; Gill and Law, 1988; Augelli and Murphy, 1988).

Following Robert Cox's adaption of Gramscian concepts to international political economy and world order, hegemony is used to refer to a *fit* between (1) the relationship of material forces (productive and destructive forces) among various groups and states in world political economy, and (2) a shared set of ideas, methods, and approaches for dealing with problems (ideology, or intersubjective meanings shared among managers, intellectuals, and policymakers in international organizations and nation-states). A fit between ideologies (what I am calling policy research approaches and programs) and the relationship of material forces is necessary for the formation of international institutions (e.g., liberalized services institutions).[4] A fit between these three elements can be described as a hegemonic institutional order.

Effective international institutions (organizations, regimes, agreements, or conventions) are formed in a historical context, and their mandates and decision-making procedures tend to crystallize the relationship between material forces and shared ideologies at the time of their formation. An organization or agreement (the mandates often codify the priority of shared problems, common normative objectives, and the procedures for dealing with problems and reaching those objectives) tends to solidify the relationships between shared policy approaches and material power relationships among important groups. Institutional changes—such as services liberalization—can therefore reflect shifts in shared ideologies and the relationship of material forces. Policy research programs and negotiations in states and international organizations can contribute to creating and managing consensus among powerful groups and states in world political economy.

State/civil society complexes in dominant nation-states influence the characteristics of international institutional orders. The nature and objectives of states' participation in international politics is supported by the fit between forms of state and non-state civil societies (or productive and social forces) at the national level.

Therefore, a single state's power or dominance is not the only factor of importance in determining the shape of international order. For example, the characteristics of liberal institutions of Pax Britannia in the nineteenth century or the coordinated management of Keynesian demand and fiscal policies in the Pax Americana in the mid-twentieth century were shaped by the national institutions and social forces of Britain and the United States, respectively. This argument is of specific relevance for the questions at hand; the significance of research programs and policy directions in states playing major international roles are accentuated, and the linkages between national liberalization of services policies and institutional change in international services trade and investment are also highlighted.

The connections between national societies and world order are not only mediated through the foreign policies of states. What Robert Cox calls the "internationalization of the state" refers to the connections among policy-planning organizations and departments in different governments, patterns that have been institutionalized in bodies such as the Organization for Economic Cooperation and Development (OECD), the Group of Seven (G-7) economic summits, or bilateral and multilateral negotiations and commissions. The state/civil society linkage also occurs in international production. The globalization of production through trade—but mainly through foreign direct investment—in a period when the American state and U.S. corporations were dominant actors in shaping international institutions meant that American social, political, and economic forces and principles were also transmitted and externalized through the organization of production and the social relations of production (as well as through inter-state relations and formal international organizations).

This understanding of the nature of global production and institutional order is connected to a role for transnational civil society and specific transnational policy networks within that society. The groups of individuals who manage the external portfolios of states, international organizations, and global corporations could be referred to as a transnational managerial class. This group is not based only in the United States or other developed market economy countries. The successful formation of a transnationally hegemonic group incorporates economic, managerial, and policy elites from a number of other northern market economy countries, as well as counter-hegemonic groups and ideas from developing—and some formerly socialist—countries.

Similarly, Stephen Gill has argued that the transnational managerial class is connected not only with [North] American states and institutions but with groups, corporations, and states concentrated in other OECD states (specifically Japan and Western Europe) (Gill, 1990). His work focuses on the Trilateral Commission and the Group of Seven consultations on monetary policy. The original externalization of American institutions in the post-1945 Pax Americana has slowly been supplanted by the hegemonic leadership of a transnational managerial group, and the economic and financial institutions that attempt to manage world political economy. Shared policy approaches among policymakers, academics, and corporate officials in the mainly market-economy OECD countries do not arise naturally; they must be created and maintained through deliberate cooperative research and consultative mechanisms, such as the OECD or the Trilateral Commission (which deal with the management of economic interdependence).[5] The policy communities in newer or shorter-term issues may not be as institutionalized as the OECD or Trilateral Commission, but more informal contacts may emerge through research projects, conferences, or professional organizations.

The class linkages and relationships of these groups are most often not articulated, and the interlinked groups are said to speak for public interests or for interdependent interests and concerns shared among societies. Often, conflict management activities attract the greatest public and intellectual attention. However, there are commonalities of concerns and perspectives. For instance, the research problems and concepts of the huge professional network of international trade experts are aimed at promoting national prosperity and economic expansion through developing liberal institutions in global political economy. These perspectives are shared, even if there are differences of opinion on particular issues.

The Gramscian framework would link networks of analysts, government officials, and international organization officials to the perspective of a transnational managerial class (i.e., those sharing a global managerial perspective as opposed to a national perspective on economic issues). These actors and groups have a fairly consistent and shared view of problems facing the international economy, although they may view themselves as "competitors" with the national security and economic managers from other states or corporations. Similarly, they may see themselves as serving national interests rather than as adapting the state and its policies to fit with changes in the international political economy. The notion of a transnational policy network emphasizes the commonality of concerns or approaches. Consider Robert Cox's argument regarding the New International Economic Order analysis in the 1970s:

The intellectual participants who are politically active in the NIEO negotiations together with those academics who play a more indirect role can be seen as linked in a series of networks, each of which is mobilizing ideas around a certain partial consensus. There are, of course, disagreements among individuals within a particular network, but these disagreements are within a certain commonality of research or a basic common approach. (Cox, 1979)[6]

One objective of this chapter is to relate the activities of independent national and international policy research institutes to the research programs of states and international organizations. A second objective is to understand and evaluate the significance of agency by individuals and groups involved in service policy research for broader institutional and structural change. In the application of the Gramscian historical and critical approach to the understanding of international organizations and world politics, the activities of national and international policy research institutes could be significant in several ways:

by assisting in the creation and maintenance of transnational groups of policy analysts, professionals linked to an emerging "practical" activity, or "intellectuals" with shared purposes, questions, concepts, issues, and methodologies for solving problems; and by facilitating the development of common interests and concerns in these groups;

- by linking states and international institutions to national and transnational civil societies, through the provision of consultative and expert services not only to states but also to international organizations;

- by defining the activities of these groups in re-shaping national and international institutions not as narrow interest representation but as moral and intellectual leadership on behalf of—and in the interest of building consensus in—states, inter-state relations, and national and transnational civil societies;

- by providing places for dialogues to link the activities of policy communities to the formation and maintenance of social groups and their perspectives, and the practical and economic activities to which these social groups are linked. Social classes arising from production rather than policy networks are viewed as the main agents of change.

POLICY RESEARCH INSTITUTES, POLICY COMMUNITIES, AND THE LIBERALIZATION OF INTERNATIONAL TRADE IN SERVICES

How do these concepts and questions assist us in understanding the connections between service policy research and international institutional change? Given the tremendous volume of research reports and activities regarding international trade in services, I cannot provide here a comprehensive history of the development of the issue or of the policy research community built around international trade in services. Rather, I will attempt to show that by applying Gramscian concepts and arguments to the understanding of the activities and role of policy research institutes and policy networks dealing with international trade in services, we can develop important and useful insights about the changes taking place in international services institutions. The work undertaken in the General Agreement on Tariffs and Trade, given that its negotiations represent the most concerted effort to alter the shape of international services institutions, will serve as the focus for this study.

Before 1982: "Political Entrepreneurship" in the United States and the United Kingdom

In 1982 at the GATT ministerial meeting in Montreal, the U.S. representative suggested that services be included in a new round of trade talks. Although the Organization for Economic Cooperation and Development had codes on liberalization, the United States attempted to place the services issue on the agenda of the largest international trade body and indicated that it would be seriously pursued. The challenge for research is to understand why services was taken so seriously at this time, and how it was placed on state and international organization agendas. What role, if any, did policy research institutes or communities play?

Research on services was fairly minimal prior to the 1970s, although there were long-standing studies indicating the magnitude of service activities and employment in advanced economies. The research that was undertaken did not use "trade" language. The trade framework was applied to services and information issues only since the late 1970s (although the issue had been mentioned briefly in the U.S. Trade Act of 1974, and the U.S. delegation had brought up trade in services at the end of the Tokyo Round of GATT trade negotiations). Also, Harry Freeman of American Express argued in an OECD working group on transborder data flows in 1979 that information policy issues should be seen as trade issues (business and union representatives, as well as government representatives, are included in OECD working committees). Also, many economists and policy analysts wondered whether service activities actually produced value. This question was usually answered in the negative. However, there was a sense in some of the literature—usually that dealing with the information age or the information economy—that structural changes were taking place in advanced economies. In response, however, OECD studies in the 1970s argued that state-supported "information utilities" would be required to develop the use of information technologies, rather than markets or trade in information services.

It was from research on international insurance transactions in the 1970s that much of the initial interest in trade in services sprang. In Geneva, Professor Orio Giarini of the Geneva Association had been undertaking research on risk analysis and policies for insurance services. PROGRES, or the Research Programme on the Service Economy, published a newsletter (beginning in the 1980s) that provided information on research projects, conferences, and publication efforts regarding the service economy and trade in services. Raymond Krommenacker also conducted research in Geneva on the insurance industry, and his doctoral dissertation was one of the formative research efforts of this period (Krommenacker, 1984). Krommenacker was later an official at GATT, and like Giarini, he came to the examination of services as tradable from an initial examination of the insurance industry. In Britain, Gerard Dickinson and others at the City University Business School were also looking at the international aspects of insurance transactions in the mid-1970s. However, this work did not use trade language to a large extent, nor did it put the theoretical imperatives to liberalize ahead of empirical investigation of insurance transactions.

The situation began to shift in the late 1970s, when some businesspeople in the United States argued that many contentious international issues in information, finance, and telecommunications could be viewed as trade questions. National regulations prohibiting foreign supply of these services should be seen as barriers to trade. This can be described as a period of active but somewhat narrow coalition-building, when a small group of business analysts tried to get state officials and some international organization officials (mainly in the United States and Great Britain) to pay attention to (1) the importance of the services issue, and (2) the policy and regulatory shifts that, they argued, were required to respond to the transition to a services economy. Given the lack of empirical policy research or statistics on services activities, this early work was often very political in orientation, rather than being in the traditional form of empirical or rational public policy research. With little or no solid evidence regarding the results of liberalizing specific regulatory or trade regimes for services, many radical and ideological claims were based on micro-economic or trade theory (which also had not been applied to services).

In the United States and Britain, key financial and insurance companies championed the issue. Rather than being initiated by policy research institutes, it was business communities—and even specific entrepreneurs—that preceded policy research and academic groups. James Robinson, Harry Freeman, and Joan Spero of American Express made efforts to put the services issue on the U.S. state agenda as a trade issue, a strategy that has been described as "political entrepreneurship" (Yoffie and Bergenstein, 1985; Yoffie and Badaracco, 1983). Another influential study, arising from the work of Ronald Kent Shelp, vice-president of American International Group (AIG, an insurance company), was *Beyond Industrialization: Ascendancy of the Global Service Economy* (Shelp, 1981). Because of Shelp's work on services while he was at the U.S. Chamber of Commerce, according to one commentator, Hank Greenburg, the president of AIG, had hired Shelp and given him the "unofficial brief" of promoting the services issue. These individuals, along with Gordon Cloney, also made numerous interventions and representations before House and Senate committees throughout the early 1980s (two sets of hearings were held in May 1982, as well as others in April 1984 and June 1984). Geza Feketekuty of the United States Trade Representative's Office is one of the first government officials credited with taking an active interest in the issue (for a good history of the early period, see Feketekuty, 1988).

In Britain, Hugh Corbet of the Trade Policy Research Centre was seen to be of central importance in creating an international community of analysis and interest in international trade in services. Since 1977 the Centre has published *The World Economy,* a quarterly journal of international economic affairs. The November 1982 issue included an article by William Brock on negotiating trade in services agreements, just as the services were being proposed at the GATT ministerial meeting in November 1982 (Brock, 1982). Over the next seven years the journal became one of the best sources of theory and policy reflection on services, and it published articles from a wide variety of contributors in the field.[7]

The United Kingdom does not have direct representation in GATT (because it is part of the European Community, which is represented by the Commission of European Communities at trade negotiations). However, work by the Trade Policy Research Centre—and work by other British policy analysts, journalists, and businesspersons in organizations such as the British Invisible Exports Council (BIEC) and LOTIS (Liberalization of Trade in Services Committee of BIEC)—showed a much higher level of non-governmental policy activity than in other European countries. The European Community Services Committee was also coordinated largely by the same British participants (with a secretariat at the Bank of England). Later, LOTIS worked with the U.S. Coalition of Service Industries and Swedish policymakers in organizing Service Industries Conferences at Ditchley Park. This pattern of connecting with other national coalitions to develop a policy consensus is called "commercial diplomacy" by one American policy advocate.

Early in the 1980s, work on services also began in the Organization for Economic Cooperation and Development. Although this research did not lead to specific international agreements, the conceptual and theoretical questions encountered in the emerging push to liberalize trade in services were often posed first in the OECD, and the work that was completed there (and circulated formally or informally) was influential in many other organizations and throughout the research community.

In the United States, the private sector (American Express and American International) officials who worked along with public officials were more important than policy research institutes in raising the services issue as a government priority. Their major conceptual contribution was to phrase service liberalization as a "free trade" issue. Politically, this phrasing fit with the free market ideology of the Reagan and Thatcher administrations, which were receptive to non-governmental coalitions (from private business) seeking liberal solutions to political and economic problems. A small group of individuals engaged in an intense series of representations to committees of Congress and presented the services trade proposal as good for the postindustrial U.S. economy. Only later did more countervailing claims about the service economy emerge from the U.S. Congressional Research Service and the Office of Technology Assessment.

We can see these early efforts as an emerging but partial bid for the restructuring of services institutions. The financial and insurance firms championing trade in services claimed that they spoke not only for their own interests but for the interests of the entire U.S. post-industrial service economy. The theory of comparative advantage in international trade, it was argued, meant that liberalized trade in services would also be good for other countries that were not as strong in service exports. I call this a partial bid because even though part of the strategy of obtaining national and international attention for the issue was to build support in various corporations and government departments, and there was a broad effort to educate and convince the rest of the corporate and government community, it was based on claims that were not widely shared. To deliver on the promise of policy and structural transformation, it would be necessary (1) to go beyond the unsupported theoretic platitudes; (2) to create a new and more solid "normal" and empirically based public policy theory of services; (3) to develop concepts and measures to produce evidence backing up claims of the importance of services and services liberalization for the entire U.S. economy (even those in manufacturing industries); and (4) to demonstrate the supposed benefits of liberalized international trade in services for other social groups and countries. To accomplish these things, I will argue, required the building of a transnational services policy community.

Policy Research and Debate from 1982 to 1986: Getting to GATT

The pace and volume of research activities on services in a large number of countries outside the United States and Britain expanded greatly from 1982 to 1984, after which it became frenetic. Julian Arkell compiled a listing in February 1990 of over 100 "service centers" or policy research programs. Agreement was reached at the GATT ministerial meeting in November 1982 that member countries would examine services, exchange information, and review the results at a 1984 session. The exchange of information was to be informal, given the strong opposition to discussion of services by both developing and some developed countries. Nevertheless, approximately 18 country case studies of service industries were produced during the next four years. These studies required much new conceptual and statistical work. The informal exchange of information in GATT allowed a dialogue among state representatives to begin. The opposition to trade in services in developed market-economy countries declined during this time, while opposition from developing countries to discussion of trade in services continued (Shelp, 1986–1987; Winham, 1989; Aronson, 1988; Vernon, 1988).

Perhaps the event of most significance for the shape of subsequent policy research (which itself was an outcome of policy debate and political and diplomatic initiatives) was the placing of services even informally on the GATT agenda. The "choice of forum" was an issue of much debate among members of the nascent service policy community in the late 1970s. Developing countries argued that GATT was an inappropriate forum for services, as it was designed only to handle trade in goods. Analysis from the United

Nations Centre on Transnational Corporations pointed out that services were delivered internationally through foreign direct investment rather than through arms-length trade. The agreement to study the issue in GATT after 1982 (before its formal acceptance in negotiations) followed from the commitment of the U.S. government to the liberalization of services trade (the one sector in which the United States was still perceived to have an international comparative advantage) and because this informal exchange of information would allow other states and policy researchers time to become more acquainted with the services issue.

Being addressed in GATT—with its organizational principles, procedures, and mandate—rather than in other international organizations signified a major shift for the services issue. In particular, national regulatory practices would be subject to examination as trade barriers according to principles such as non-discrimination and most-favored nation status, with the overall goal of progressive liberalization of trade in services. Principles that guided other international organizations concerned with services—such as cooperation, harmonization, and coordination—would be downplayed, and approaches such as reciprocity and the exchange of concessions in bargaining among contracting parties would be accentuated. Even within GATT, the United States signaled a shift by suggesting that the principle of special and differential treatment for developing countries would not apply in the upcoming trade round.

With the growing number of state and international organization research programs on services, this period saw increasing *connections* among policy analysts dealing with services in different countries and the *creation* of an expert or professional specialty dealing with the service sector and trade in services. Once the issue was championed by the U.S. government, and once it became highly likely that services would be taken up by GATT (informally at first, then formally after 1986), many national and international research programs sprang up, each with its own particular purposes and orientations. These programs needed analysts, and the analysts needed to know something about services and the work of other groups. Initially research was undertaken by trade experts who applied their conceptual training to the new issue, or by analysts from international organizations who shifted to services (the United Nations Centre on Transnational Corporations, or UNCTC, and the United Nations Conference on Trade and Development, or UNCTAD, also began significant research programs on services in 1984–1985 to serve developing countries and to provide alternative sources of conceptualization and information to the work of the United States and the OECD). But as time went on, groups of academically trained analysts emerged who did research specifically on services in graduate programs. The discussions and research activities of the early 1980s not only brought together analysts whose work touched on services issues but also contributed to the creation of a new analytic specialty, once the issue was on the agenda and the need for analysts was institutionalized.

The interconnected roles of academic training and policy institutes in supporting the creation of a new expert area can be seen in the staffing of the GATT secretariat to serve the Group of Negotiations on Services. This secretariat is unique in terms of general patterns in existing international organizations: because it was a new area and could not draw solely from the existing staff of officials within GATT, an entirely new secretariat was brought in after 1986 when the decision was taken to begin negotiations on services among contracting parties. The shift to services programs in other international organizations (UNCTAD, OECD, UNCTC) did not involve such a wholesale importation of personnel, although different consultants were hired. For GATT, the academic programs and research centers (where the analysts were trained) had a direct and quick influence on the shape of policy research programs, not just in terms of policy ideas but in the embodiment of ideas in newly hired policy analysts and international organization officials. Also, the early work of the Trade Policy Research Centre and the OECD was influential in contributing to the paradigms and major questions with which these analysts worked.

Although differing perspectives followed from different sectoral, national, or international organization concerns, a common set of questions and issues was emerging by the mid-1980s. The shift in the overall set of policy ideas appears especially stark when we compare it with the policy framework guiding services in the late 1970s and early 1980s. Newly shared presuppositions included the following: that services could be viewed as commodities; that services produced rather than used value; that it was permissible to discuss services in an international trade organization; that the trade framework was generally applicable to services (although each sector would encounter specific difficulties and would need to be addressed on an individual basis); and that services trade should be liberalized for greater value creation and mutual prosperity. There were still significant disagreements over what a fair agreement for trade in services would look like, or what derogations to protect national economies and sovereignty would be acceptable.

To restate, by 1986, as the issue was finally placed on the agenda of GATT, a transnational network of policy analysts and academic research programs was already growing. It was on this network that the international negotiations initially drew for ideas and questions (when international organizations themselves organized publication projects, sponsored conferences, and promoted certain perspectives and concerns regarding services). It was also from this network that GATT and other international organization secretariats drew in staffing.

1987 to 1990: Forming a Negotiating Group
and Building a Services Agreement

In September 1986 a compromise agreement was reached among GATT
contracting parties to undertake negotiations on liberalizing trade in services
among contracting parties, but on a separate track outside of the GATT
agreement. Exploratory discussions in these parallel negotiations took place
over the next two years.

After two years of work in the Group of Negotiations on Services, efforts
were made in 1989 to negotiate specific texts for a general services agreement and to explore agreements for six test sectors. At this point the conceptual framework for a services trade agreement was in place, but the particular issues to be addressed in each sector posed new problems for research.
The test sectors included telecommunications, construction, professional services, financial services, tourism, and transportation (see GATT/GNS,
1989).

Once the issue was formally on the international agenda, it created even
broader interest in research about international services policies. There also
arose, in market terms, a large demand or need for concepts and statistical
information about services in general and in service sectors (from government departments, trade delegations, and international organization secretariats). Although the country studies prior to 1986 had caused some
resources to be dedicated to services research by trade organizations, governments, and international organizations, the amount of research activity
exploded after September 1986. These activities had various objectives: to
provide input to governments in order to formulate negotiating positions; to
provide conceptual approaches and information for negotiators; to facilitate
negotiations by educating negotiators; or to build connections among members of the services community.

Along with GATT activities, policy research programs on services in
other international organizations and within nation-states assumed greater
importance. Much of this activity was intended to provide concepts, expert
knowledge, and reflection to contribute to the GATT Group of Negotiations
on Services. UNCTAD and UNCTC continued to assign priority to services
research. UNCTAD research was consistent with its objective of providing
technical assistance to the developing countries engaged in the GATT negotiations. Just as the northern market-economy states had discussions in the
OECD and drew upon the expertise of the OECD secretariat and consultants,
it was argued, so too should developing countries have access to intellectual
resources to fully participate in formulating a balanced international service
agreement and national policies. Because the GATT secretariat was small
and was primarily intended to serve the negotiating group, it could not provide much in-house production of information. The lack of institutional

resources in GATT to undertake policy reflection and research in the new and uncharted area of trade in services created an opportunity for other research organizations.

Two research programs were mentioned by participants as especially useful once negotiations began to examine specific sectoral agreements in 1989. Throughout the negotiations, negotiators and secretariat officials sensed that they were running ahead of the academic literature on trade in services, that they had to develop their own concepts and questions, and that very little statistical information was available. The OECD work, both conceptually (in terms of a framework agreement) and sectorally (in terms of studies on specific service sectors), was most directly relevant to negotiating a GATT services agreement (Faudemay, 1989; OECD, 1987, 1989a, 1989b). For example, a paper on telecommunications was circulated informally as a discussion paper before 1990 and was drawn upon extensively in the GATT secretariat paper on telecommunications services (OECD, 1990).

The American Enterprise Institute's (AEI) series of books on international trade in services (including an overview and conceptual framework by Geza Feketekuty and seven sectoral studies) was designed and timed to be released just as the Uruguay Round of services negotiations moved into examination of concepts relevant to specific service sectors. The project included eight book-length studies covering air transport, finance, business services, construction, design and engineering services, films and television programs, ocean shipping services, and telecommunications, as well as an overview and blueprint for negotiations. The results of the AEI studies were publicized at three conferences in 1987–1988, and a full set of the books was given to each of the national delegations to GATT.

There were also studies, research, and conference programs designed to reflect the experiences and concerns of developing countries. The series of studies on services produced by UNCTAD in 1989–1990 was meant to provide resources for developing countries, in juxtaposition to the OECD—and especially to the AEI—work. A project coordinated by John Whalley of the University of Western Ontario, entitled "The Developing Countries and the Uruguay Round," was funded by the Ford Foundation. The purpose of the project was to provide basic research to enable developing countries to participate more effectively in the Uruguay Round. The Ford Foundation project included a paper by Gary P. Sampson entitled "Developing Countries and the Liberalization of Trade in Services."

In Europe and the United States, a number of non-governmental organizations actively undertook policy research and discussion on services with a distinctly transnational perspective. The U.S. Coalition of Service Industries, along with other national service industry associations, organized national service producer groups (mainly financial and accounting corporations) to provide consistent and coordinated inputs into the negotiations on a national basis. The European Service Industries Forum was composed mainly of companies in the non-traditional or "new services" sector (i.e., information, data services). Rather than focusing on only one government, as had been the case earlier, private sector advocates took on a transnational and multi-site approach to intervening in the shaping of policy discussions and negotiations (by coordinating with other national bodies). They did face one difficulty: unlike the OECD or United Nations organizations, private sector representation was not institutionalized in the GATT (persons could attend only if they were part of national delegations). The transnational strategy and the overlapping participation of certain analysts dealt fairly effectively with this potential difficulty.[8]

Another organization, Services World Forum (SWF), first based in Geneva and then in Paris, organized several conferences and published their proceedings in an attempt to "allow a community of service policy researchers to exist." From the late 1980s until 1991, the SWF's secretariat was located at PROMETHEE, a Paris-based think tank that is exploring international economic issues by using the paradigm of networks (Giarini, 1987; Bressand and Nicolaides, 1989). From the perspective of policy officials, its work had a longer-term horizon and "more conceptual tendency" than was useful for addressing the immediate issues facing negotiators.

The Centre for Applied Studies in International Negotiations in Geneva, a private organization, served on a consulting basis (to facilitate the GATT negotiations) by organizing a series of educational conferences for negotiators (which called upon the same participants who were involved in other organizations to serve as resource people), and by organizing small, informal, and personal meetings among GATT trade negotiators. Once again, the GATT secretariat's mandate of serving the negotiating group limited its formal ability to initiate informal contacts or background meetings between negotiators.

There were new efforts to encourage the exchange of ideas among all members of the policy research community during the late 1980s. The Applied Services Economic Centre, directed by Orio Giarini, Russell Pipe, and Brian Woodrow, organized conferences in 1990 and 1991 (Woodrow, 1990). Other industry and professional associations (apart from the financial sectors that led policy research in the early 1980s) also began to be interested (Federation of European Accountants, 1990). Despite the widespread interest and increasing participation of new groups and professions, the general frame of reference under which services were considered was set—although, as we shall see, the political aspects of services trade liberalization changed in 1990.

Although it is possible to compare and categorize the perspectives of the different organizations, the activities of individual participants are not so easily labeled. Although there are strong divergences of opinion on services issues among national representatives, service policy analysts participate in a number of overlapping and seemingly oppositional organizations.[9] This suggests that the international organizations and policy research institutes are less important as organizational sites but are important as funders and entry points into the services policy community.

Ironically, just as the service trade policy field was maturing and flourishing as a discipline, and just as a draft agreement was being sent to the (unsuccessful) GATT ministerial meeting in Brussels in the fall of 1990, support for liberalized services trade in the United States declined. The mobilization of non-liberal groups in the United States and elsewhere occurred when traditional and non-competitive service industries (maritime transport, air transport, and even a newly defensive financial sector) examined their costs and benefits and found that their interests would not be served by the liberalization of services trade. Also, research by the Office of Technology Assessment and the Congressional Research Service, as well as an important book by Stephen Cohen and John Zysman entitled *Manufacturing Matters*, were added to the resistance to services liberalization formerly expressed only by developing countries. These studies argued that service exports would produce few jobs in the United States, that service exports were restricted to a small number of large companies, and that service exports would take place mainly through foreign direct investment. There were questions about the usefulness of the post-industrial hypothesis, and the claim that trade in services was in the national interest came under question. The declining position of the United States in the world economy was becoming more apparent to interest groups in the United States, even to those in the supposedly strong financial services, professional services, and telecommunications services industries. The crisis and regulatory chaos in domestic financial institutions also undermined the confident external orientation.[10]

This aspect of the history leads us to proceed cautiously in equating intentions and motivations of groups undertaking and supporting certain lines of policy research with eventual outcomes (a problem that a simple instrumental view of policy research might entail). Given that the building of a hegemonic consensus required compromises with other groups, the formation of a transnational policy research community on services did not arise simply because corporations and policy researchers encouraged the U.S. government to take action on services or because they funded studies on services. Nor was the policy community immediately undermined when some of these same groups subsequently discouraged services liberalization. The arguments in favor of liberalization, the growth of research activities and institutions, and the professional investment and interest in services liberalization mean that the general frame of reference or conventional wisdom for services is no longer so dependent on policy debates centered in the United States.

DISCUSSION AND CONCLUSIONS: RESEARCH INSTITUTES, TRANSNATIONAL POLICY COMMUNITIES, STATES, AND INTERNATIONAL ORGANIZATIONS

Four arguments from a transnational application of the Gramscian perspective have been used to guide this investigation of the relationship of policy research institutes and policy communities to research programs undertaken by states and international organizations and to structural change. What contributions have these arguments brought to our understanding of services policy research?

First, did research institutes (1) assist in the creation and maintenance of a transnational group of policy analysts, professionals linked to an emerging practical activity of the services economy, a broadly defined group of intellectuals with shared purposes, questions, issues, and methodologies for solving problems, or (2) facilitate the development of common interests and shared identities? This account argues that an identifiable group of trade in services policy analysts and experts was formed. The core members included (1) state and international organization officials with responsibility for services negotiations, and (2) policy researchers and advocates. These participants can be traced physically by multiple and overlapping memberships in academic, private sector, state, and international organization research programs. The policy community can be traced theoretically by noting the unique combination of trade concepts with reflection on services in general, or by mixing trade concepts with thinking about international transactions in specific service sectors, all with a general proclivity toward liberalization. For instance, although it is acceptable for policy community members to note the difficulties of applying trade concepts to services and the regulatory adjustments that must be made, it is not acceptable to dismiss the entire project as inappropriate. Those who continue to resist the application of trade concepts to services (e.g., former experts in a policy specialization relating to a service sector) are likely to be seen as irrelevant to the flow of policy debate and find themselves increasingly peripheral to policy formation.

The group was composed of officials with on-going organizational responsibilities who encountered services in the course of their tasks. Some took up services as a transitory project; others stayed with services and became converts to the services cause. The present policy network also includes those whose education and career development was specifically focused on international economic analysis of the service economy, and those sectoral specialists who learned the language of trade disciplines as a second area of expertise after their sectoral training.

Policy research institutes contributed to both the relational and intellectual aspects of building a services policy community. For example, Services World Forum brought negotiators, policymakers, and business officials together to talk with each other. The Centre for Applied Studies in International Negotiations facilitated negotiations by organizing informal meetings as well as by mounting educational and training seminars. The U.S. Coalition of Service Industries and the British Invisible Exports Council cooperated in organizing Ditchley Park conferences on services. As these "relational" activities contributed to the shaping of ideas, other research institutes made research and publication projects their priorities. The Trade Policy Research Centre published articles that brought service issues to the fore, and the American Enterprise Institute organized and published original research on trade in specific service sectors (no other private research institute had a project this large). Although the OECD and UNCTAD were able to contribute concepts and information to the negotiating process, and although relationships and discussions grew up around these projects and working groups, they were less able to build a services policy network because of formalized representation rules.

Second, did research institutes provide links among states and international institutions, on one hand, and national and transnational civil societies, on the other? Even officials from large states do not have the resources to develop policies independently, and they need to know how the private sector, other states, and international organizations are proceeding on issues. It has been argued that states need information and consultation, and that private research bodies and "volunteers" can provide this. The services problem and policy prescriptions were not organized by bodies or consultation processes initiated and managed by the state; rather, private research institutes initially identified problems and organized the process to coordinate "civil society" interests. This was often done in consultation with academics and key state officials. These groups recognized that their strength was not in demanding policy changes and then leaving state officials to sort out and reconcile competing demands, but as much as possible in building coalitions among service producers in single nations and with service producers in other parts of the world in order to provide a coherent and consistent set of problems, questions, and policy directions. Hence, the networks and communities of individuals may be more useful for understanding these dynamics than a focus on the organizational sites of policy research. Individual analysts often work with a number of research institutes, states, and international organizations, even though these seem to have divergent objectives and mandates.

Third, group efforts to reshape national and international institutions were portrayed not as narrow-interest representation but as forward-looking intellectual leadership on behalf of—and in the interest of building consensus in—the larger national and transnational communities. It is notable that trade in services advocates were more successful in asserting these claims early in the 1980s, when (1) little empirical evidence was available on services (since there were no adequate statistical programs in existence); and (2) the institutional site for and the shape of a services trade agreement were not known. Services liberalization encountered growing challenges as more information from differing perspectives became available (e.g., concerns about the services trade deficit in the United States in the late 1980s) and as business groups learned which sectors would be included and excluded from the agreement, and what the sectoral annexes would contain.

A second objective of this chapter was to understand and evaluate the significance of agency by individuals and groups involved in service policy research for broader institutional and structural change. In the Gramscian approach, social classes arising from production relations are viewed as the main agents of change, rather than intellectuals or policy institutes. Did research institutes provide opportunities for dialogues to link the activities of policy communities to the larger context of the formation and maintenance of social groups, and the practical and economic activities to which these social groups are linked?

Nationally, the service economy arguments were not easily accepted at first by governments, which saw agriculture, manufacturing, resources, petroleum, and chemicals as the leading and most politically powerful sectors and viewed services only as utilities facilitating "real" production. Whatever structural changes had already occurred in the advanced industrial economies were not recognized in the early 1980s. It took leadership in the mobilization of people and ideas to prompt the recognition of these shifts.

The argument presented early on by those advocating change in states' regulation of the services sector and in international institutions guiding trade and investment in service industries was that changes were already taking place in the world economy, changes to which policymakers needed to respond. Otherwise, old-fashioned institutions designed for a different era of commodity and goods production would hamper the growth and full wealth-creating potential of the service economy. The service economy argument was compatible with the information age argument in that it saw information activities as one subsector of the service economy (the one in which interests in the United States were most highly mobilized) and argued that technological change was the driving force necessitating shifts to liberalized service economy institutions. The new aspect of trade in services was to append service economy arguments (which were post-industrial in their origins and in the general sense of the world that they provided) to neoclassical microeconomics and international trade theory (which political neo-conservatives in national polities noticed and which tied in with one strong set of ideas shared among officials of international organizations).

The changing structure of the world economy or changes in technologies were not just givens to which policymakers responded, nor were they factors exogenous to the policy process. Rather, the statistical programs and policy priorities of states and international organizations were (and are) contested sites of policy debates. The creation of policy knowledge on the service economy is part of these processes. Specific groups may argue, for instance, that the environment, development, gender issues, debt and deficits, peace and security, or trade barriers are issues requiring the attention of the international community, or at least of an expert subsection of the international community.

There was a crisis in the arrangement of production, and in the role of states and international institutions, throughout the 1970s. This crisis presented a political and ideological challenge: to find a new framework to orient policy. The challenge was transformed into an opportunity by members of the trade in services community. They provided governing and business groups that wanted to be liberal with a sector to be liberal about, without sacrificing larger national interests. The socially and politically constructed nature of the service economy arguments and of the liberal policy prescriptions presented alongside it in the United States can be seen in the recent action by the U.S. delegation to GATT trade negotiations to derogate from the telecommunications annex in the services trade agreement, and in the opposition by many services producer groups to the inclusion of other services in international trade agreements (finances, maritime shipping, air transport) for both protectionist and free trade reasons.

ACKNOWLEDGMENTS

Research for this chapter was funded by a research grant from the Social Sciences and Humanities Research Council of Canada. During 1990–1991 I had research affiliation with the Centre for International Trade and Investment Policy Studies at the Norman Paterson School of International Affairs at Carleton University, Ottawa, Canada. I would like to thank Norma Reesor for her helpful comments and suggestions.

NOTES

1. The Organization for Economic Cooperation and Development (OECD), the United Nations Centre on Transnational Corporations (UNCTC), the United Nations Conference on Trade and Development (UNCTAD), and the General Agreement on Tariffs and Trade (GATT) have all undertaken extensive research or negotiation programs on international

trade in services. Also, the Canada–United States Free Trade Agreement includes a chapter on services.

2. It should be noted that this chapter is more concerned with a re-formulation of the managerial and public policy groupings around the notion of the service economy than with a working-class movement expressing support for or opposition to greater global integration of production, exchange, and investment in service industries. Although Gramsci's main questions were about the urban proletariat, nevertheless the Gramscian approach highlights important aspects of the role of states and policy research communities, even for groups re-formulating state and international policy approaches and institutions.

3. Such an approach goes beyond a historical-comparative "sociology of knowledge" approach. It is not enough, the critical theorist would argue, to trace the history of policy networks and communities. Rather, reflection on the political and theoretic concerns that lead us to undertake such investigations should also lead us to evaluate those processes and their outcomes. Principles of evaluation relevant to histories of policies and policy communities might include (and are as contested as) concepts such as fairness, freedom, democracy, or equality. The discourse on shared or desirable political values, therefore, insinuates itself in the critical examination of policy networks and communities. Hence, although this chapter examines the role of the policy research network in the liberalization of services policy, the critical element of the Gramscian approach also suggests that we need to ask political, practical, and normative questions about the processes described (Neufeld, 1991).

4. I propose neither a radical "war of ideas" view of agency in shaping policy ideas and institutions, nor a view of ideas as derivative (of objective power relations), nor the instrumental development of ideas to serve and justify a priori "interests." There is a constitutive aspect to policy ideas; they go some way in making and defining problems and groups. Therefore, policy research programs should be related to the intended actions of the authorial groups, as well as to the importance and uses given to the documents and processes by those involved in the negotiations aimed at liberalizing international service institutions. Hence, the research strategy for this chapter involved the following: conducting bibliographic research to determine the research programs on trade in services; meeting with the researchers and authors of as many documents and programs as possible to ask about the problems they were trying to address, and with the participants and intended audiences to ask about activities related to research programs; meeting with officials in states and international organizations to ask about the research programs of most use to them, about the origins of important ideas and concepts used in re-organizing international service institutions, as well as asking interpretive questions on the importance of policy research for international negotiations and the importance of policy research for structural change. These interviews provide a guide to trace the ways in which ideas and approaches from the work of policy research institutes interacted with international organizations' policy discussions.

5. There is a line of thinking in political economy that labels any attempt to describe patterns of communication and planning among individuals and groups either as too "voluntarist" or as "conspiracy" theories. This proclivity seems to stem from an extreme structural view (Marxist or liberal) that interactions among individuals are either overridden by class relations or are akin to markets and games, and that no diplomat, academic, policy researcher, politician, or lowly international organization official (or groups of these persons) would have the power or prescience to organize a meeting or a conference, or even "have lunch" to discuss issues and conflicts with others, or that such communication would have any significance.

6. Robert Cox continues regarding policy networks:

These networks are not mere constructs of my imagination, classifications of authors whose ideas seem to have a community of spirit. Intellectual production is now organized like the production of goods or of other services. The material basis of networks is provided by formal (usually non-governmental) organizations as mobilizing and coordinating agencies with research directors and funds (from sources sometimes more, sometimes less visible) for commissioning studies, financing conferences, and symposia or informal luncheon discussions. . . . The material basis of networks allows for a selection of participants which guarantees a certain homogeneity around a basic core of orthodoxy. However, since the object of the exercise is consensus-building, narrow orthodoxy or exclusiveness would be a self-defeating criterion, and the activators of each network extend their search to those whose ideas reach the outer boundaries of what might ultimately be acceptable. (Cox, 1979)

7. These included John Jackson, Robert Stern, and Bernard Hoekman (from the University of Michigan); Knut Hammarskjold of the International Civil Aviation Organization; Jeffrey Schott of the Institute for International Economics; Jagdish Bhagwati of Columbia University; Geza Feketekuty, Jonathan Aronson, and Brian Hindley of the London School of Economics; Alasdair Smith, Harald Malmgren, Andre Sapir, Gary Sampson (first at UNCTAD, then as director of the GNS Secretariat at GATT), Richard H. Snape, Ingo Walter, and Harry Freeman.

8. For instance, Julian Arkell of the British Invisible Exports Council is widely respected by many analysts for the quality of his ideas and work, even though it is clear that he is operating as an advocate. In addition to his work with the LOTIS Committee of BIEC, he is a member of the European Community Services Group and has been a participant in the Ditchley Park meetings, as well as numerous other services conferences. One result of this broad participation is that wherever policy analysts turn, they will hear similar messages.

9. The work of Mr. Rodney de C. Grey, who headed the Canadian delegation to the GATT Tokyo Round talks, illustrates the wide participation of some service policy researchers. Grey wrote a discussion paper for an Atwater Institute conference in 1986; Karl Sauvant credits him with doing work for his 1986 book on traded data services; and Grey produced a conceptual study on services for the British Department of Trade and Industry. He has also written studies for the Canadian series organized by the Institute for Research on Public Policy and for the UNCTAD series.

10. Of specific relevance to the negotiations, a shift from a "negative list" to a "positive list" approach meant that only services specifically mentioned would be included, rather than an inclusive agreement that excluded only those sectors specifically mentioned (negative list). This inhibited efforts to build cross-sectoral coalitions, and some persons and corporations in the United States who had argued that a services agreement would be good for the United States reversed their positions in 1990. Internationally, certain shipping and accountancy groups worry that even liberal intervention by multilateral organizations will place restrictions on their activities, and they have also become less supportive of a services agreement.

6

Balancing Relevance and Integrity: Social Scientists and Canada's Asia-Pacific Policy Community

Evert A. Lindquist

INTRODUCTION

For social scientists, whose professional preoccupation is the study of human affairs, there is considerable temptation to go beyond disciplinary research agendas in order to "make a difference." To do so, they must become engaged with the phenomena they study and enter the world of action. Short of entering partisan politics, social scientists attempt to fulfill this ambition of relevance by participating in a variety of information generation, publication, and convocation activities, which I have elsewhere (Lindquist, 1990) referred to as *policy inquiry*. Although social scientists can take many different paths in order to conduct policy inquiry, it is useful to make a broad distinction between private inquiry and public inquiry.

Social scientists engage in *private inquiry* when they undertake policy-relevant activities as professionals directly for the benefit of state actors. This includes advising policymakers or undertaking specific projects on a contractual basis, inquiry that rarely enters the public domain. Social scientists who take this path are often called "hired guns," and the associated analytic output is not held in the same esteem as serious academic research. Although such views often emanate from jealous colleagues, it nevertheless indicates that for social scientists engaging in policy inquiry, maintaining academic integrity is an important issue.

The other major path is to conduct policy inquiry for relatively independent government advisory councils, royal commissions, non-profit policy institutes, and academic research centers. Because such work is destined for public consumption, it can be referred to as *public inquiry*. For social scientists who worry about preserving their academic integrity, it is arguably the organizations operating outside the ambit of government (i.e., non-profit institutes and academic research centers, commonly known as think tanks) that loom large as the most attractive sites for conducting policy inquiry. Not only do think tanks promise independence from the state, but most strive to maintain their credibility as institutions through academic ties.

This chapter emerged out of research that sought to document the activities of four Canadian think tanks on Asia-Pacific matters and to evaluate their output (Lindquist, 1991). One finding was that a considerable portion of their activities was underwritten by government agencies and private foundations. Another finding was that the output of the think tanks seemed inordinately skewed toward delivering services for their sponsors; relatively little policy inquiry involved careful examination of the efficacy of current government policy and programs. These findings indicate that in order to fully understand the activities and impacts of social scientists on public policy, we must look beyond their immediate organizational experiences and comprehend the broader workings of the larger policy community.

This chapter takes up the challenge. We explore how government agencies and foundations may encourage and stimulate development of a policy community but, in doing so, may constrain and divert the agendas of research organizations like non-profit institutes and academic research centers where social scientists should thrive. However, we will argue that the case of Canada's Asia-Pacific policy community, although not necessarily representative, suggests that social scientists can demonstrate considerable resilience in the face of such pressures. Even though ensuring their own survival dictates that institutes and centers accept many of the contracts and grants that governments and foundations throw their way, they nevertheless have found means to protect their core academic activities and integrity. What is not clear, however, is whether or not this elaborate form of accommodation, whereby funding organizations and scholars manage to have their way through institutional buffers, produces an optimal outcome for universities and society.

We begin by discussing how the literature on policy communities can enhance our understanding of the institutional choices and paths of influence of social scientists. Next, we provide a thumbnail sketch of the Asia-Pacific policy community, demonstrating its recent emergence and the influence of key government and private sector actors. We then review the activities and output of several think tanks inside and outside universities that have had interests in the Asia-Pacific region. Finally, we reflect on the implications of the findings for social scientists and academic centers in universities and broader policy communities.

SOCIAL SCIENTISTS AND POLICY COMMUNITIES

Most observers would agree that policymakers now find themselves in an increasingly complex and fluid environment. Some key factors leading to this higher degree of complexity and fluidity include technological advances permitting more powerful forms of communication, demographic trends that have brought new expectations about and patterns in career development, and the proliferation of single-interest groups and research organizations. State actors and institutionalized interest groups, although still undeniably important, are no longer the only sources of information and influence in the policy process. A new literature has emerged to account for and model this changing reality (Heclo, 1978; Pross, 1986; Atkinson and Coleman, 1989b, 1992; Coleman and Skogstad, 1990; Lindquist, 1992). Contributors to the literature argue that to understand policy processes and outcomes we should focus less on individual policy actors and more on their broader institutional networks; that we explore a new level of analysis, that of the policy community.

For those who are interested in the behavior of social scientists and the impact of social science research, the trends and realities delineated by this literature are at once troubling and exciting. On the one hand, by admitting a pantheon of new actors into the analysis, we could logically conclude that the influence of social scientists can only have diminished through dilution; they have a greater variety of competitors, many of whom specialize in policy inquiry. On the other hand, the very conditions that have made it more difficult for politicians, public managers, and more traditional interests to control the policy process have expanded the opportunities for social scientists to exert influence on policy-making. There are now considerably more opportunities for social scientists who want to go beyond traditional disciplinary work to conduct policy inquiry in other institutional contexts: research centers, think tanks, consultants, and various state advisory mechanisms. In any event, it seems clear that the literatures on knowledge utilization and the political sociology of social scientists must embrace the rapidly growing literature on policy communities.

One problem with fully embracing this literature is, ironically, its level of analysis: the policy community. Writers in this tradition would argue that it is misleading to examine the activities of any one actor or class of actors, such as the state or social scientists, when considering their impact on the policy process; rather, they would urge analysts to account for the shape and balance of power within a policy community in order to fully appreciate the dynamics of policy-making. Thus, from an analytic perspective, to focus on the activities of any particular class or actor is, by definition, narrow and parochial, inevitably missing critical parts of the full story within any sector.

But the challenge to expand our horizons should not stop us from study-ing the activities of particular actors within policy communities. Indeed, the literature may serve as a useful point of departure, helping to put their activi-ties in context so that a more informed and realistic assessment of their roles and influence may follow. For example, Sabatier (1987) has considered the role of professionals and experts, particularly their potential to moderate debate and encourage learning between different members of the policy community; and Lindquist (1992) has drawn on the literature to examine how the role of public managers varies in different policy communities. Although there is little doubt that students of knowledge utilization and the role of intellectuals should seriously embrace the policy community litera-ture, the literature should be used as a starting point and as a research instru-ment; there is no reason to give up on the core research project.

There are two ways in which the policy community approach can be applied to the study of social scientists. The first draws on the mainstream conceptualizations that have evolved in the literature to date. This approach is structuralist in that it seeks to delineate different kinds of policy communi-ties. Indeed, the argument is that within any given policy community there may exist different types of policy networks, actors who coalesce around different issues. With a focus on the relative autonomy of state agencies and key societal interests, as well as on their capacities to develop policy and exert pressure on policymakers, several configurations of policy networks have been mapped out. Although Atkinson and Coleman (1989b) have iden-tified at least seven configurations by using two basic dimensions (autonomy and concentration of power), Lindquist (1992) offers a simplified approach that collapses these dimensions in an effort to determine the essential contri-bution of the literature. Figure 6.1 shows that policy networks may vary con-siderably depending on the relative capacity of state actors and societal interests.

Figure 6.1
Different Configurations of Policy Networks

	Government Organization	
	Low	*High*
Organization of Interests *Low*	Pressure Pluralism	State Direction
		Corporatism
High	Clientele Pluralism	Concertation

For the purposes of studying the activities and influence of social scientists, the main insight is that depending on the policy sector, social scientists may be working in considerably different institutional environments. The implication is that different kinds of institutions may wield more political and financial power, and thus may be in a position to influence the research agendas and opportunities for social scientists. For example, in state-directed policy networks government agencies are primarily responsible for policy development and implementation, holding sway over business associations and unions. It stands to reason that on balance, social scientists will be forced to seek funding for projects from government agencies, putting the latter in a strong position to influence the research agenda of the former. Conversely, in a clientele pluralist network, where the relative power of state and societal actors is reversed, it is more likely that social scientists will find more opportunities to undertake inquiry for business, union, and other interests as well as for more neutral forums such as tripartite organizations. Perhaps the most important lesson from the policy community literature is cautionary: when undertaking case studies designed to throw light on how social scientists interact with and influence other policy actors, it is critical to control for the policy community in which they work. Some findings, which masquerade as generalizations about the behavior of social scientists, may simply reflect broader power relationships within a given policy community.

One difficulty with the structuralist approach is that it is limited to providing the backdrop against which social scientists engage in their activities. The literature does not aspire to show how social scientists, or other experts, work in or with different institutions throughout policy communities. Lindquist (1990) sketched out a micro-level approach that sees the organizations within policy communities as providing different sites for the activities of social scientists. Each site should be evaluated in terms of the extent to which it solicits private or public inquiry, insists on projecting a particular ideology, attempts to develop a consensus, and works in a hierarchical mode. Each site, as a result, provides a considerably different environment or client for the work of social scientists. This approach is best referred to here as an *organizational* approach to policy communities, one that emphasizes the institutional choice that social scientists must make when undertaking public inquiry.

We can use this approach to speculate about the comparative advantage that think tanks might hold for social scientists in policy communities. Many think tanks tap into academics as disciplinary experts because of their specialist knowledge and their legitimacy. However, no matter how attractive such opportunities are for social scientists, they must also be defensible in terms of academic professional development. It is a myth that academics, having secured tenure within the university system, ignore the views of colleagues; promotion and prestige are contingent on the views of colleagues within the university as well as those who work in similar traditions at other universities. The same criteria could be used to support serving as consultants and as bureaucratic or political advisors to policymakers, but the essential difference is that such activity crosses into the realm of private inquiry. Although some think tanks may well have a clear ideological disposition, their activities are more public in nature and arguably share the same quality with disciplinary academic research. Indeed, it is the perceived quality of *independence* that suggests that think tanks (whether in the university or the non-profit sectors) would be attractive environments for academics who wish to conduct public inquiry, because even though such organizations have a problem orientation rather than a disciplinary orientation, their members are not beholden to the interests and policymakers who attempt to solve the problems.

An interesting question concerns how think tanks in a university setting differ from those in the non-profit sector. Although they may look similar, it is best to view university think tanks as organizational solutions to the problems of particular universities or as institutional ratification of cross-disciplinary interests among professors.[1] Despite being vast storehouses of talent and expertise, universities may constrain developing new research directions because they are organized around disciplines and professions, and new research initiatives may not fit into the pigeonholes provided by extant disciplinary and professional groupings. It is almost inconceivable to do away with disciplines and professions; it is much easier, when funding is available, to create new institutional focal points. Research centers not only offer a meeting place or home for students and scholars from different parts of the university but also provide a nameplate and springboard for tapping into outside funding to support research on contemporary problems. This rationale for creating a research organization differs somewhat from the typical non-profit think tank, which tends to meet a relatively specific mandate or cater to a particular audience and members. Most academics (with the possible exception of the most policy-oriented researchers) find the research agendas and regime of related activities such as the conferences of non-profit think tanks to be too constraining.

In studying social scientists, neither the structuralist approach nor the organizational approach should take precedence. Just as it is important to locate the kinds of policy networks and communities in which social scientists work, it is also important to understand the particular organizational contexts in which they work. The approaches are highly complementary. Moving between the two levels of community analysis promises to produce more defensible findings. Accordingly, the next part of this chapter sketches out the structure and evolution of Canada's Asia-Pacific policy community and then gives a more detailed analysis of four non-profit institutes and academic centers.

THE EVOLUTION OF CANADA'S
ASIA-PACIFIC POLICY COMMUNITY

Fifteen years ago, if one had been asked to define Canada's Asia-Pacific community, the entire exercise might have taken a few short paragraphs. A satisfactory survey might have included pertinent branches of the Department of External Affairs, the diplomatic corps representing Asia-Pacific nations in Ottawa and other major Canadian cities, the handful of companies conducting business in the region, and one academic think tank—what was then known as the Joint Centre for Modern East Asia of the University of Toronto and York University. But circumstances have changed dramatically. A database recently developed by the Asia Pacific Foundation lists over 400 organizations and thousands of experts with interests in the Asia-Pacific region.

This chapter cannot provide a full account of the remarkable expansion of this policy community. Of particular interest is the subtle hand of the Canadian government as well as those of key foundations behind the growth of business and research organizations with interests in the Asia-Pacific region during the 1980s. Government influence on think tanks is more obvious because of the relatively high visibility of grants. Moreover, the government has encouraged the creation of business councils and nurtured their development by granting them access to elected and appointed officials. At the very least, it is fair to say that the evolution of the Asia-Pacific policy community in Canada has not been entirely spontaneous and displays the characteristics of a state-directed policy network.

Growing Interest of the Canadian Government in the Asia-Pacific

The Canadian government is a huge organization with diverse interests; it is impossible to review all the departments and agencies that have been involved in Asia-Pacific matters. The best strategy is to focus on those parts of the government that have had the most prominent role in supporting the activities of think tanks—the Department of External Affairs (DEA) and the Canadian International Development Agency—and simply acknowledge that a good number of other agencies at the federal and provincial level support many other members of the Asia-Pacific policy community.

Given its mandate, it is not surprising that the Department of External Affairs has an extensive bureaucracy centered in Ottawa with specific expertise in the Asia-Pacific region. For our purposes, it is sufficient to note that there is an Asia and Pacific Branch consisting of the Asia and Pacific Programs Division, the Asia and Pacific North Bureau (with divisions specializing in North Asian Relations, East Asian Relations, and Japan Trade Development), and an Asia Pacific South Bureau (with divisions in Asia Pacific Relations and Asia Pacific Trade Development). These go beyond coordinating, monitoring, and supporting the many consular offices in the region to (1) stimulate research and education on relevant topics, and (2) solicit advice from experts in Canada. Until the early 1980s, the Canadian government contributed little more than moral support to Canadian business participation in the Pacific Basin Economic Council (PBEC) and academic participation in the Pacific Trade and Development Conference (PAFTAD), both of which were established in 1968.[2] This was also the case when the Pacific Economic Cooperation Conference (PECC) was formed in 1980. PECC is an organization that brings together representatives of business, government, and academe from fourteen member nations to discuss and encourage cooperation on a variety of regional issues such as trade, investment, and natural resources.

However, the posture of the government began to change. DEA officials granted PBEC quasi-official status as the sole business representative to the Canadian government on Asia-Pacific matters and later took a behind-the-scenes role in encouraging the development of bilateral business or trade councils. During the early 1980s, the government supported a series of Pacific Rim Opportunities conferences that were organized through PBEC. The most concrete expression of interest in the region occurred in June 1984 when the outgoing Liberal government passed legislation authorizing the creation of the Asia Pacific Foundation, a non-profit organization intended to improve cultural and trade linkages throughout the region.[3]

Following the arrival of the Progressive Conservative party to power in late 1984, the government started to adopt a more pro-active stance toward the Asia-Pacific region. There were several reasons for this shift. First, the government was generally interested in improving Canada's trade performance. Second, although the strategic lynchpin was to be a Canada-U.S. Free Trade Agreement, there was a political need and economic rationale to increase trade linkages with other nations; thus, a focus on the Asia-Pacific region loomed as one possible counterweight. Third, Canadian trade linkages with the region were expanding rapidly, and it made sense to find ways to improve the capacity of Canadian business to penetrate the potentially lucrative export markets. Finally, the Pacific Economic Cooperation Conference (PECC) was slated to have its fifth meeting in Vancouver in November 1986, providing an opportunity for the government to show its interest in the region, at least symbolically. In 1985, the Department of External Affairs provided funding ($560,000 over five years) to establish the Canadian

National Committee (CNC) to coordinate Canada's participation in PECC. The Canadian National Committee now consists of twenty-five representatives from the business and academic communities as well as from the federal government and several provincial governments.[4]

The most recent and far-reaching initiative of the Mulroney government and Department of External Affairs during the 1980s was Pacific 2000, part of the broader $95 million "Going Global Strategy" announced in 1989 to increase Canada's competitiveness in the region. Part of the initiative repackaged programs such as the 1985 National Trade Strategy, existing trade offices, related programs, and funding for the Asia Pacific Foundation and its support of PECC and the Canadian National Committee. However, three new funds were created: the Japan Science and Technology Fund, the Pacific 2000 Language and Awareness Fund, and the Pacific 2000 Projects Fund. The funds were designed to support a host of projects administered by groups outside the federal government and, in some instances, Canadian think tanks such as the Joint Centre for Asia Pacific Studies, the Asia Pacific Foundation, and Simon Fraser University.

The other major player in the Asia-Pacific region is the Canadian International Development Agency (CIDA), which was established in 1968 to coordinate (1) Canada's emergency assistance to nations ravaged by natural disasters and political turmoil, and (2) technical and economic assistance to developing nations. The latter activities are typically undertaken in cooperation with business and non-profit organizations. CIDA has developed many programs to achieve these objectives: a Business Cooperation Program, which provides seed money for joint ventures; the Management for Change Program, which funds projects that show promise of facilitating the exchange of ideas between nations to solve problems; and the Nongovernmental Organization Program, which monitors the activities of churches in developing countries. Each of these programs reaches the Asia-Pacific region. The Institute for Research on Public Policy, for example, received funding from the Management for Change Program to support a series of Asia-Pacific workshops. CIDA's Asia Branch monitors developments in particular nations and negotiates "Country Focus Agreements" to coordinate Canadian assistance. One such agreement underwrote Dalhousie University's Environmental Management Development in Indonesia project. It was likely under such an agreement that the Institute for Research on Public Policy received funding to assist in establishing the Thailand Development Research Institute during the 1980s.

The Department of External Affairs and CIDA wield the most influence when it comes to providing funding for think tanks and assisting business in the development of export markets. However, several other government agencies have a piece of the action as well. They include the following: the International Development Research Corporation, which sponsors research that adapts science and technology to meet the needs of developing nations; Investment Canada, which encourages more foreign investment; and International Trade Canada and the Department of Industry, Trade, Technology, which have an interest in developing export markets. Joining these federal agencies are a panoply of provincial government trade offices as well as trade and tourism ministries. The provinces most heavily involved in these activities are British Columbia, Alberta, Ontario, and Quebec.

The Proliferation of Asia-Pacific Business Organizations

A host of Canadian business organizations are important members of the Asia-Pacific policy community. Some emerged out of bilateral interests, others have multilateral roots, and others represent specific sectoral interests of Canadian business. It is best to begin with the Canadian involvement in the Pacific Basin Economic Council (PBEC). This organization was formally established in 1968 by representatives of the business communities of Australia, Canada, Japan, New Zealand, and the United States to promote cooperation in the region. Canada was originally represented by the Canadian Chamber of Commerce (CCC) and the Canadian Manufacturers Association. The PBEC Canadian Committee organizes Canadian involvement in PBEC meetings and associated committee work and now has approximately 80 Canadian business corporations as members. Membership fees offset the administrative costs, a service provided by the International Division of the Canadian Chamber of Commerce. The Canadian Committee not only sponsors research but also provides opportunities for business leaders to meet with senior elected and appointed officials to discuss Asia-Pacific issues.[5] The Committee also works with the various arms of the British Columbia, Alberta, Ontario, and Quebec governments involved in promoting increased Asia-Pacific trade and investment.

In its early days, the PBEC Canadian Committee was designated the sole private sector advisor on Pacific affairs by the federal government.[6] However, during the late 1970s and early 1980s, there developed a view within the Department of External Affairs that PBEC was losing its relevance,[7] perhaps because Canada was interested in developing more meaningful ties with ASEAN (Association of Southeast Asian Nations) countries. During this time DEA started to quietly encourage the creation of bilateral business councils, which were to also work with PBEC. A host of councils were established during the 1980s, many of which relied on the International Division of the Canadian Chamber of Commerce to provide administrative support. They include the Canada-Korea Business Council (est. 1980), the Canada-Pakistan Business Council (est. 1981), the Canada-India Business Council (est. 1982), the Canada-Taiwan Business Council (est. 1985), the

Canadian Trade Office in Taipei, and the ASEAN-Canada Business Council
(est. 1986), which includes in its membership Brunei, Indonesia, Malaysia,
Singapore, Thailand, and the Philippines. Outside the Canadian Chamber of
Commerce administrative orbit stands the Canada-China Business Council,
the Canada–Hong Kong Business Council, and the Canada-Japan Business
Council. Members of these councils have chosen to fund and operate their
own secretariats on an independent basis, but this has not precluded cooperation with the CCC-related councils. Generally, the bilateral business councils
are not involved in developing policy positions, although they do seek to
represent the views of business and have strong associations with key government departments on trade and related matters. They provide their members with relevant data and research, opportunities to become acquainted
with other cultures, and forums for the exchange of views. It also seems
clear that the proliferation of bilateral councils has eroded the monopoly that
PBEC once held on providing advice to the government.

Until recently, Asia-Pacific business relations have been largely the
domain of the bilateral and multilateral business councils and the Canadian
Export Association. This area had not piqued the interest of the Business
Council on National Issues (BCNI), one of the nation's most influential business organizations, but now BCNI may be changing its stance. Robinson
notes that both the Business Council on National Issues and the Canadian
Chamber of Commerce now participate in organizations whose goals are to
lobby and partake in research with the OECD and the United Nations.[8] It
may only be a matter of time before their sights are turned toward the Asia-
Pacific region.

Think Tanks with Asia-Pacific Concerns

The following review of think tanks with interests in the region begins
with academic research centers and then moves to non-profit institutes,
because it was the think tanks in the former sector that first expressed an
interest in the region. This is attributable to the fact that before the 1980s,
aside from the federal government it was universities that provided a home
for most of the expertise in Canada on the Asia-Pacific region.

The first think tank with an exclusive focus in the Asia-Pacific region,
the Joint Centre on Modern East Asia, was established in 1974 as a joint
venture of the University of Toronto and York University. Its name was later
changed to the Joint Centre for Asia Pacific Studies. If a characterization of
its research can be made, it seems to emphasize (though not exclusively) the
politics and culture of Asia-Pacific nations. It stood alone until the Institute
of Asian Research was founded in 1981 at the University of British
Columbia. Its publications list reveals much greater emphasis on the

economies, trade, and investment dimensions of the Pacific Basin. Some of its funding has come from the Japan Foundation and the Canadian International Development Agency. In 1983, full regional balance was achieved in university-based Asia-Pacific think tanks when the Environmental Management Development in Indonesia (EMDI) project was initiated at the School for Resource and Environmental Studies at Dalhousie University in Nova Scotia. This project, still in progress and undertaken in cooperation with Indonesia's Ministry of State for Population and Environment, has been funded by the Canadian International Development Agency as one of its Country Focus Agreements. In 1990, Carleton University in Ottawa established its own Asian Pacific Research Centre. Although this list is not exhaustive, it identifies the university-based think tanks that have the highest profile in Canada.

Before we identify key think tanks in the non-profit sector, it is worth noting that most of these organizations typically have interests that go beyond a narrow focus on the Asia-Pacific region and have only recently developed these focused interests. For example, even though the Institute for Research on Public Policy (founded in 1972) was the first major Canadian think tank to sponsor a significant amount of Asia-Pacific research, its research program did not get under way until the late 1970s and early 1980s. Likewise, the Conference Board of Canada, a major economic and management think tank that was overhauled in 1971 after its move to Ottawa from Montreal, did not establish its International Business Research Centre until 1983. This was later joined by its International Studies and Services Development Group in 1988. Neither of these research centers within the Conference Board focus exclusively on the Asia-Pacific. The exception is the Asia Pacific Foundation, a think tank established by the Canadian government in 1984. Other think tanks, like the C.D. Howe Institute, the North-South Institute, the Canada West Foundation, and the Canadian Institute for Peace and Security, have evinced only passing interests in the region.

The emergence of interest in Asia-Pacific affairs by Canadian think tanks in the non-profit and academic sectors during the early 1980s, whether in the form of entire organizations or as branches of existing organizations, is striking and difficult to overlook. It parallels the proliferation of bilateral business councils and increasing government interest in the Asia-Pacific region during the 1980s. Indeed, much of the increased numbers and expanded activities of academic research centers and non-profit institutes resulted from increased funding from government, business, and foundations. Later in this chapter we will focus more closely on the specific activities and funding of a select group of think tanks in terms of their linkages with the broader Asia-Pacific policy community.

The Role of Private Foundations

Several foundations, inside and outside Canada, have taken a keen interest in developing the capacity of Canadian institutions to educate students, train professionals, and conduct research on Asia-Pacific issues. Many of the programs offered by the think tanks discussed later in this chapter were developed with foundation support. Their contributions have not been few: most think tanks have received substantial support from foundations. The most prominent are the Canadian Donner Foundation, the Japan (Tanaka and Naskone) Foundation, and the Max Bell Foundation.

The foundation with the greatest influence has been the Donner Foundation. It has provided support for a surprisingly diverse set of Asia-Pacific related projects at six Canadian universities. The foundation provides either start-up funds for new research centers or support for multi-year research projects. The following have received start-up funds: the Centre for Foreign Policy at Dalhousie University (1970), and the York University–University of Toronto Joint Centre for Southeast Asia Studies (1974). Substantial project grants have gone to the Institute of Asian and Slavonic Research at the University of British Columbia to establish a China Resources Centre (1974), to Dalhousie's Centre to study changes in the international system (1976), to the Institute for Research on Public Policy to study changes in the international economic order (1980) and to bolster its International Economic Program (1984), to assist McGill University's MBA (Master in Business Administration) program in developing a Chinese concentration (1988), and to University of Toronto researchers to develop the Kanji card and computer software for a variety of Asian languages. The York University–University of Toronto Joint Centre received substantial project support to develop more focus on Northeast Asia (1980), to analyze the work of Canadian missionaries in China, Japan, and Korea (1984), and to initiate an exchange program with Hong Kong (1988). During the last two decades, the Canadian Donner Foundation has contributed roughly $2.5 million toward these activities.

The other foundations have not been as dominant as the Donner Foundation but have nevertheless played a significant role in helping to expand Canada's capacity to understand and interact with the region. The Japan Foundation was established in 1972 to assist in the promotion of Japanese studies in the humanities and social sciences, and to encourage greater appreciation of Japanese culture. It has close ties to the Japanese government; its funds are administered by the Ministry of Foreign Affairs. The foundation has two programs. The Naskone program provides seed money to encourage Canadian universities to hire Japanese specialists[9] and to support visiting scholars, and the Tanaka program is directed toward language promotion. For example, seed money was provided for several Japanese specialists at York University and the University of Toronto. However, the Japan Foundation rarely sponsors specific research projects. In contrast, the Max Bell Foundation supports research projects and conferences. For example, it has sponsored the working groups of the CNC-PECC in 1985 as well as research on Southeast Asian nations and a seminar series by the Joint Centre at the University of Toronto.

Concluding Remarks

Like any policy community, the Asia-Pacific policy community in Canada will always be evolving, although by the early 1990s it seemed easier to characterize it as congealing or maturing rather than fledgling. It is a complex community comprising many organizations with different niches and competencies—this chapter has only hinted at the overwhelming abundance of interrelationships and interdependencies. The larger Asia-Pacific community constitutes an institutional environment that frames the activities of think tanks and social scientists alike, consisting of benefactors and competitors who provide a set of constraints and opportunities for think tanks. Nevertheless, with this brief profile of the Asia-Pacific community in Canada as a backdrop, we should be able to develop a qualitatively better understanding of the environment in which Canadian social scientists conducting public inquiry must work.

CANADIAN THINK TANKS AND THE ASIA-PACIFIC

To develop a better understanding of the pressures that are exerted on social scientists who conduct public inquiry in think tanks in the non-profit and academic centers, it is necessary to describe in some detail the activities and sponsorship of the organizations. The pages that follow[10] review the Asia-Pacific activities of the Joint Centre for Asia-Pacific Studies, the Institute for Research on Public Policy, the Conference Board of Canada, and the Asia Pacific Foundation. The other think tanks mentioned previously have made interesting contributions to Asia-Pacific studies, but there is neither time nor space to describe them in detail here. However, being selective does not mean that the four think tanks under consideration do not provide us with an interesting range of approaches to policy inquiry on the Asia-Pacific region. Each think tank caters to somewhat different audiences; one conducts research and data collection "in-house" whereas the other three rely heavily on outsiders to conduct inquiry; and two specialize in Asia-Pacific matters whereas the other two are "generalists" that have managed to launch programs in this area. Such organizational diversity allows us to deduce whether pressures experienced by academic research centers are unique or part of a more general phenomenon.

Joint Centre for Asia-Pacific Studies

One way to conceive of university-based think tanks is to view them as organizational solutions to structural rigidities spawned by disciplinary departments and professional programs. A perfect example is the Joint Centre for Asia-Pacific Studies at the University of Toronto and York University. By the early 1970s the University of Toronto had considerable depth in East Asian studies, having a complement of scholars with research interests in the literature, economics, history, and politics of China, Japan, and Korea. Though already housed in their own Department of East Asian Studies, both the faculty and courses were essentially locked into historical and cultural views of these nations. With burgeoning interest in a region in the midst of economic and political transformation, with profound implications for Canada and its other major trading partners, the need for more contemporary research on politics, economics, and business was recognized both inside and outside the university.

The opportunity for taking a positive step forward emerged when the Canadian Donner Foundation indicated its interest in supporting projects that examined Canada's role in the world. When East Asian specialists at the University of Toronto began to explore the possibility of support, they were soon joined by entrepreneurial academics at York University who sought to expand their capacity in this area as well. Because the Canadian Donner Foundation was not interested in funding arrangements that would result in the duplication of resources, it was agreed to put forward a joint proposal and the Joint Centre for Modern East Asian Studies was established in 1974. Its objectives were to pool and expand the resources and instruction of both universities, to conduct and disseminate research, and to cultivate better linkages with many other institutions with similar interests. Although the Joint Centre would tap into the faculty resources of both universities and had the clear intent of expanding those resources on both campuses, it would not mount its own teaching program.

Like many fledgling think tanks, the Joint Centre began with only one full-time staff person. During its early years, the center relied exclusively on a series of major grants. The first was the original five-year grant from the Canadian Donner Foundation. A second grant was obtained from the Japan Foundation in 1980 to expand the amount of Japanese scholarship, particularly at York University. This was followed in 1983 by a major grant from the Max Bell Foundation that expanded research on Southeast Asian nations and sponsored the Pacific Trade Seminar. However, the funding strategy was not without problems. Reliance on single sources of funding made it difficult for the Joint Centre to grow in different directions if new programs did not fit under the terms of an existing grant. Moreover, a secure source of funding—however temporary—made it easy for the Centre to let down its guard when it came to planning and searching for replacement funding. During the final year of a multi-year grant there would be a frenzied search for new support, which, if not immediately successful, would lead to lean times until the necessary funds were secured.

To respond to these problems, the Joint Centre engaged in several activities during the mid-1980s as part of a strategy of diversification. In 1984 it took responsibility for administering the Ontario-Jiangsu Education Exchange (OJEE), a cooperative program sponsored by the Ontario government and the Jiangsu government in China to assist scholars and students undertaking research. In 1986 the Joint Centre was awarded the contract for managing the Ontario Regional China-CIDA Orientation Centre (OROC) for the Canadian International Development Agency. The Centre also received a grant to help the Asia Pacific Foundation establish a database on organizations and specialists with expertise and interests in the Asia-Pacific region. Another project, one that was also funded by the Donner Foundation, involved research and conferences on aspects of missionary activities in China, Japan, and Korea. By 1990, the full-time staff at the Centre had expanded to six. To reflect the greater breadth of interest that had developed, the center's title was adjusted to the Joint Centre for Asia-Pacific Studies (JCAPS).

These more recent developments could be interpreted as a wholesale shift by the Joint Centre from a relatively pure research orientation to a project-based operation. However, associated faculty are still involved in their traditional research and teaching roles. As such, faculty are still directly involved in training the many individuals who will soon assume positions of responsibility in the worlds of government, business, and academe. One has only to review the publications list of the Joint Centre to get a sense of the work that has been conducted under its auspices, and this does not even reflect the many books and articles published by faculty during the same period.

Institute for Research on Public Policy

Founded in 1972, the Institute for Research on Public Policy (IRPP) stands out not only as Canada's best-endowed think tank but also as the one with the broadest research agenda, spanning economic, international, and social policy. At any one time IRPP has always had five or six research programs in progress, which have been modified or dropped as circumstances warranted. These programs, driven in large measure by grants from the federal government or private foundations, are often administered out of offices in different cities by a program director and perhaps one or two full-time research staff who obtain and administer the research grants. Most of the research is undertaken by professors at universities, and sometimes by staff on leave from government agencies or business corporations. Research projects and conferences are organized in collaboration with other research institutions such as university research centers.

Despite its constantly evolving program of research, IRPP has had a sustained interest in Asia-Pacific issues. Asia-Pacific activities have been handled under three programs: the Technology and Future Studies Program, the International Economics Program, and most recently, the Governability Research Program. If one country has been emphasized, it has been Japan. Because IRPP's activities in this area have varied considerably across the three programs, it is useful to organize this discussion into three different clusters: conferences and proceedings; a series of short monographs; and the Asia-Pacific workshop series.

IRPP sponsored two major conferences related to Asia-Pacific issues. The first was held in 1979 to celebrate 50 years of diplomatic relations with Japan. This was IRPP's first substantial effort on the Asia-Pacific.[11] The event was co-sponsored with the University of Toronto–York University Joint Centre on Modern East Asia with funding from the Canada-Japan Trade Council. Eleven papers, produced mainly by Canadian academics (the rest were from the United States), reviewed a variety of topics concerning diplomatic relations, trade, and corporate and business structures in Japan. The second conference on Canada and International Trade was held in 1984, reflecting the gathering momentum of the International Economics Program and an expanding interest in the Asia-Pacific region. The conference consisted of two concurrent mini-conferences: one focused on Canada, one on the Pacific Rim. Twelve papers were presented on Japan, Southeast Asia, China, and joint ventures undertaken by Canada in the region. The bulk of the proceedings, accompanied by a review of all the papers that were presented, was published in 1985. Even though IRPP provided synopses for both the 1978 and 1984 conferences, no attempt was made to draw on the insights for either a policy statement or commentary—the papers were left to stand on their own.

The second cluster of activity involved several short monographs, generally undertaken by university professors. Yohshi Tsurmi, a marketing and international business professor from the City University of New York, wrote *Sogoshosha* (1980), which examined the organization and activities of the large Japanese trading firms. A revised version of the monograph was printed in 1984. Roy Matthews, an economist from the Economic Council of Canada, produced *Canada and the Little Dragons* (1983), a profile of the economies of Hong Kong, Taiwan, and South Korea and an assessment of the trade opportunities for Canadian business in each nation. Richard Wright, who taught in McGill University's Faculty of Management, explored the nature of Japanese investment in Canada and the bases for improving the trading relationship in the future in *Japanese Business in Canada* (1984). W. Roy Hines, a federal official on leave from the Department of Regional Industrial Expansion, wrote *Trade Policy Making in Canada: Are We Doing It Right?* (1985), offering a critique of the newly reorganized trade policy machinery of the federal government. IRPP turned to Richard Wright once more, who, with co-author Susan Hugget, examined the ability of Canadian banks and securities firms to penetrate the Japanese market in *A Yen for Profit* (1987). Each monograph averages 125 pages in length.

The third cluster of work is the result of IRPP's creative initiative to establish bilateral and multilateral linkages with other think tanks throughout the Asia-Pacific region. Each project has resulted in the publication of a collection of essays under a common theme. The bilateral projects involved China and Japan. IRPP cooperated with the staff of the International Trade Research Institute (ITRI) of China's Ministry of Foreign Economic Relations and Trade to produce a collection of articles on China's trade policy posture during the last decade as well as a profile of its bilateral trading relationships with several nations.[12] In April 1988, representatives from IRPP and Japan's National Institute for Research Advancement (NIRA) presented papers on domestic trends and challenges and the state of the bilateral relationship.[13] The multilateral efforts were centered in the Asia-Pacific workshop series, which brought together representatives from several countries to discuss topics of mutual concern. Three symposia led to three volumes of papers: *The Changing Shape of Government in the Asia-Pacific Region*, *Economic Policy-Making in the Asia-Pacific Region*, and *Think Tanks and Governance in the Asia-Pacific Region*.[14]

IRPP also discovered novel ways to expand its presence in Asia-Pacific policy networks. First, the Institute agreed to publish the proceedings of the Pacific Trade Policy Forum of the Pacific Economic Cooperation Conference (PECC), which met in Vancouver during late June 1989.[15] Second, the Institute arranged to have its own conference, "Canada, the Pacific, and the Uruguay Round," take place immediately after the PECC meetings. Thus, many of the business leaders, government representatives, and academics could explore the implications and challenges of regional initiatives for Canada. The proceedings were published in a companion volume.[16]

Conference Board of Canada

For a variety of reasons, the Conference Board of Canada provides an alternative model for the organization of think tank activities in Canada. First, the Conference Board has always conducted all its research, analysis, and data-collection in-house. Given the breadth of its programs, ranging from economic forecasting to management research and extensive conference activities, it is not surprising that it has approximately 130 staff members. Second, the Conference Board generates much of its own data by conducting surveys of members and other organizations and by gaining access to other data sets and mining them for alternative purposes. Third, although the Conference Board aims to produce timely and relevant research, it has avoided taking policy positions or making policy prescriptions on the issues it examines. However, although the Board offered a considerable range of research programs and services to members, it was not until the early 1980s that it decided to explore international issues directly.

In 1983 the Conference Board established the International Business Research Centre (IBRC). According to its annual reports, IBRC was to be "an information centre for the fields of international trade, finance, and management," and its research activities would focus on "the ability of Canadian firms to compete effectively in the international economy." One-third of its seed funding came from agencies connected with the federal government, one-third from private sector organizations and some provincial governments, and one-third from the Conference Board itself. The fact that IBRC was even established was an accomplishment, because it occurred as Canada was emerging from a serious recession. An important new niche had been identified, and this organizational experiment would lead to a broader research orientation of the entire organization.

It is best to think of IBRC as a separately funded think tank within the larger organization. Members of the Conference Board pay an extra fee to become IBRC members. IBRC has close to 50 members from both the private sector and the public sector, including the federal departments of External Affairs, Finance, Investment Canada, and Consumer and Corporate Affairs, as well as the Canadian International Development Agency. IBRC holds meetings for members three times a year. These consist of updates on issues and trends affecting international business, presentations by guest speakers, and opportunities to exchange views. Staff members produce quarterly reports on trade and other international developments, conduct surveys of members on specific issues, and respond to requests by individual members for information.

The IBRC staff also undertake longer-term research contracts with outside organizations of interest to members. Although funding for such projects is secured following negotiations over the methodology and object of the project with the sponsors, the Conference Board retains total control of the research-in-progress and the right to make the findings available to its members and the public. The first major project, which received partial funding from the Canadian government, involved three studies on patterns in foreign investment; particular attention was given to current and potential foreign investors' perceptions of how the Foreign Investment Review Agency influenced the investment climate.[17] A second major project, funded by the Department of Finance, was to develop an econometric model and assess government policy toward export financing. Another project reviewed Canada–U.S. trade relations, and a fourth examined the competitiveness of Canada's corporate tax structure in five different industries: telecommunications, machinery, steel, newsprint, and polyethylene. These studies expanded the domestic focus of the Conference Board to embrace a more internationalist stance, but generally the work addressed trading relationships between Canada and the United States. The first study that moved the Conference Board a step closer to examining the Asia-Pacific region was a series of case studies of business linkages between Canada and six developing nations— India, Thailand, Brazil, Peru, Zaire, and Ghana—a project jointly sponsored by the Conference Board and the Canadian International Development Agency.[18]

These longer-term research studies raised a thorny question for the Conference Board. On the one hand, such studies diverted valuable resources from servicing the day-to-day and month-to-month needs of IBRC members. On the other hand, the fact that a market for similar studies clearly existed, as well as the success of the Conference Board in completing the studies to the satisfaction of clients, suggested that there was room for further growth in this direction. The organizational solution to these competing demands was to establish a separate research capacity within the Conference Board called the International Studies and Service Development Group (ISSD). This happened in June 1988. Its research agenda is based on requests from members inside and outside the IBRC orbit; and although ISSD is not obligated to directly service members, one hoped-for benefit is that new information products might be developed to enhance the offerings of IBRC to its current and prospective members. In short, ISSD is a special studies group that obtains funding by undertaking longer-term research projects rather than charging membership fees. It now has one director, five full-time research staff members, and one secretary.

Like IBRC, the ISSD group has only partial interests in the Asia-Pacific region; but it has conducted at least two major projects in this area. The first explored the nature of Canadian investment in ASEAN member countries.[19] The project identified which Canadian corporations had invested in the region on the basis of data from the Canadian and ASEAN governments, and then it surveyed Canadian corporations about their experiences in the region. The end result was a good profile of the nature of the Canadian presence and a realistic assessment of its business experiences to date. The project was sponsored by the ASEAN-Canada Business Council of the Canadian Chamber of Commerce. In 1991, ISSD was involved in another major project; sponsored by the Canadian International Development Agency, the project explored joint ventures and technology transfer between Canada and India, Japan, and Pakistan.

The Conference Board has clearly begun to address some of the issues presented by the globalization of trade and has developed a partial interest in the Asia-Pacific region. An entire division within the Conference Board is now called Management and Global Research. The management side includes the Compensation Research Centre and Human Resource Centre; the international side embraces the International Business Research Centre, the International Studies and Service Research Group, and the Financial Services Research Program (the latter group, which may have grown out of IBRC in 1988, also endeavors to monitor and assess global trends and their implications for industry in areas such as tax reform, free trade, and financial services). Although both IBRC and ISSD represent a departure for the Conference Board in terms of substantive focus, its organizational approach to serving members has been consistent.

Asia Pacific Foundation

The Asia Pacific Foundation is the only non-profit think tank that devotes its full attention to the Asia-Pacific region. Established in 1984 by an Act of Parliament, the Asia Pacific Foundation (APF) is supported not only by the federal government but also by several provincial governments and private corporations. It currently has a staff of 12 and a budget of over $2 million. Its main objective is to make Canadian business more competitive in Asia-Pacific markets. It seeks to increase the awareness of Canadians of the many different cultures, governments, and business practices in Asia-Pacific nations. The focus of APF is not only on business per se but on all institutions (universities, schools, ministries of education, the media, and cultural organizations) that might have a role in educating Canadians in these matters.

Programs and outreach activities are tailored to the needs of each of the audiences just mentioned. Exchange programs as well as cultural and language training are arranged for promising business leaders. These services are supplemented by a set of publications (*Backgrounder*, *Newsletter*, and *Issues*) that summarize and update pertinent details about the nations of the region. APF also seeks to expand the resources available to teachers in schools and universities for instruction, curriculum development, and special events. Recognizing that both teachers and education institutions are constrained by broader institutional environments—namely, provincial ministries of education—APF attempts to work with ministries to shape curriculum standards and develop instructional materials that can be widely distributed. APF staff also keep in touch with editorial staff and journalists who monitor developments in the region, providing them with a list of commentators to contact when important Asia-Pacific stories break. APF also offers fellowships to journalists that will enable them to conduct more in-depth research into the region.

Perhaps the most innovative activities that APF has undertaken to date involve the creation and cataloguing of databases pertinent to Asia-Pacific trade. These efforts have involved letting contracts to several other institutions with Asia-Pacific interests. The first project involved creating a database of all individuals and organizations in Canada with expertise or interests in the region. In 1987, APF contracted to the following institutions the responsibility for developing the databases: the Institute for Asian Research at the University of British Columbia, the International Centre at the University of Calgary, the Joint Centre for Asia-Pacific Studies of York University and the University of Toronto, the Conference Board of Canada, the Centre d'Etudes of the University of Montreal, and the Atlantic Provinces Economic Council. Over 1,400 experts and 400 other organizations were identified. More recently, another database with over 500 corporations has been developed. The databases are on-line, and data can be obtained on a user-pay basis. The Pacific Information Exchange (PIE) project is even more ambitious. It has pulled together, with the assistance of the Conference Board of Canada, all the domestic and international databases that could be of use to Canadian business in exploring opportunities in the region. APF first developed this database for use on local area computer networks but has recently made it available for on-line use.

Aside from achieving the goal of making databases available, these efforts brought about collaboration among a number of different institutions that may have not previously crossed organizational paths. Fostering networks is an important goal of APF, and this has been done in other ways as well. In 1988 the APF organized the Pacific Cooperation and Information Technology conference, a meeting of decisionmakers from 16 Asia-Pacific nations to discuss their respective and common economic futures. The conference was organized in cooperation with the Atwater Institute and with funding from the governments of Japan and Canada. The Foundation also provided funding for the 1988 NIRA/IRPP Symposium discussed earlier in this chapter and has cultivated links with other research and granting concerns that share similar interests. In 1989, APF initiated the Business Association Network, an effort to introduce promising Asian business leaders to their counterparts in Canada. These activities, along with those that target educational institutions and the media, indicate that APF has a serious commitment to networking.

Asia-Pacific Think Tanks as Environments for Social Scientists

The foregoing profiles provide considerable detail on the ethos and activities of several think tanks. For academic social scientists who are interested in conducting public inquiry, each provides a different working environment. The Joint Centre, of course, was designed for and by social scientists. Not surprisingly, it offers a location where professors and graduate students can undertake research and exchange ideas among colleagues and outsiders alike. For academics, the Conference Board would not provide many opportunities because it conducts most of its research in-house; but, like the Asia Pacific Foundation, it can call upon professors to speak at its conferences and symposia. Finally, the IRPP provides an interesting contrast because it has published the work of many academics and has provided networking opportunities for participants in its Asia-Pacific workshop series.

Perhaps the most striking and disturbing similarity among the four think tanks has been their increased reliance on project-based funding. Project funding can be of two varieties: contracts to carry out specific activities for sponsoring organizations, or grants for limited research projects that do not cater to particular clients. Donors seem to have become less willing to make large sustaining grants to think tanks that leave themselves substantial maneuvering room to determine their activities. Although the Joint Centre, IRPP's International Economics Program, and the Asia Pacific Foundation each received significant start-up grants to launch their programs, their leaders eventually all shifted to project-based funding to maintain support of activities pertaining to the Asia-Pacific region. Such a shift in funding pattern should not, by itself, be problematic; but when it is combined with a surprising lack of strategic and institutional analysis, there is cause for concern.

One would think that an important component of the output of these think tanks would be analysis of trade and governance problems posed by the Asia-Pacific region, particularly in terms of strategic and institutional considerations. Although many of the studies identify and document challenges emanating from the Asia-Pacific region, they have offered relatively little in the way of solutions or action programs. To the extent that governance issues have been discussed at all, focus has been on the governance problems of *other* nations, not those of Canada. Only the C.D. Howe Research Institute published such a study (English, 1991). Otherwise, not much more has been done beyond monitoring regional developments and sponsoring language and exchange programs. The tasks of designing new policy and implementation strategies have been left entirely to policymakers and those who seek to influence them.

There is nothing wrong or improper with project-based funding—indeed, I have recommended this avenue as a good way for think tank leaders to expand their funding bases, to develop contextual understanding of policy problems, and to establish better contacts with those who wield power in policy communities.[20] In this view, think tanks would eventually produce more perceptive, engaging, and effective policy inquiry consisting of critiques of government policy as well as credible alternatives. The findings of my own study suggest that in the case of Asia-Pacific studies, this had not happened by the early 1990s. I believe it is fair to say that hegemons within the policy community use think tanks as convenient focal points for the distribution of funds and as contractors for selective pieces of research. In the final part of this chapter I consider how such financial pressure impacts on social scientists.

SOCIAL SCIENTISTS, THINK TANKS, AND POLICY COMMUNITIES

That an academic think tank like the Joint Centre for Asia Pacific Studies has lurched from grant to grant and seems dependent on the whims of other organizations gives cause for concern; this certainly has been discussed in internal university reviews of the Centre. Of even greater concern is that an organization like the Joint Centre does not appear to be very different from other organizations like the Institute for Research on Public Policy, the Asia Pacific Foundation, and the Conference Board of Canada. Whether they are located inside or outside universities, these think tanks seem to be increasingly project-driven. This raises important questions for social scientists who are evaluating career opportunities. Has academic integrity been compromised? Should academic centers in particular resist the support of government and foundations for specific projects?

Disciplinary academic purists would certainly argue that such activity ought to be curtailed. However, if one agrees that some of the problems taken up by academic centers do need to be addressed, from what other sources are professors to obtain financial as well as interdisciplinary support? Bourne (1988) has noted that unless these centers obtain financial support to sustain themselves over the medium term, they are likely to stagnate (or, I might add, disappear). Infrastructure support for research centers is not likely to be forthcoming from other sources: the Canadian university system has been starved by provincial governments for years, and Trent (1988) points out that it has been a policy of the Social Sciences and Humanities Research Council of Canada not to provide infrastructure support and instead to fund individual scholars and projects. Confirming my own observations, Trent also notes that foundations are reluctant to provide long-term infrastructure support to academic centers. Thus, in the current situation it is difficult for academic centers and individual social scientists not to seek outside support for projects that may have policy relevance.

Does this mean that academic integrity has been compromised? My view is that it has not. Our review of the many contributions of social scientists to organizations inside and outside the academic sphere does not account for the considerable quantity of academic research that is still conducted by these individuals. Indeed, one has only to look at the list of working papers produced under the auspices of the Joint Centre to see that many professors and graduate students continue to pursue their own academic interests. Moreover, when an academic center obtains a large project grant, it is usually not professors who carry out most of the administrative activities. Rather, these responsibilities provide employment for graduate students and university staff; professors typically limit their involvement to securing the grants and then performing an oversight role. To the extent that academics are compromised, it is because some of their valuable research time is diverted to these limited administrative duties.

If academics are not being unduly compromised by a project-driven world, then what is happening? There can be little doubt that in a tight fiscal climate academics are under enormous pressure and considerable temptation to undertake research and other activities that are relevant in the eyes of government and foundation supporters. However, academics are not without their defenses. I believe that a parallel exists between the emergence of academic centers in Canadian universities and the view of Myer and Rowan (1977) that education organizations have developed elaborate institutional structures in response to assorted environmental pressures, such as affirmative action and teaching excellence, but have left untouched the core activities of classroom teaching. Following this logic, academic centers constitute a form of organizational defense whereby social scientists, for a minimal amount of time spent performing administrative chores, are able to convince outside funders that they are engaged in policy-relevant activities. Academic integrity is protected because most administrative work is conducted by staff and graduate students and does not directly divert professors from pursuing disciplinary research agendas, for which they are promoted within the university.

However, to evaluate the merits of university think tanks in terms of their implications for maintaining academic integrity is to invoke overly narrow criteria and to invite cynicism about their public purpose. They provide other significant benefits. First, an important function of university-based think tanks is to attract students with interests in particular areas, to increase their awareness of the range of academic and professional opportunities in

those domains, and to educate and train the future generations of individuals
who will populate business and government organizations. Indeed, one professor with whom I spoke ran his finger down the page of a federal government telephone directory and pointed to the names of student after student
he had taught who now worked for the Canadian International Development
Agency.[21] Second, we should not downplay the potential intellectual benefits of the dialogue between practitioners and academics through seminar
series, exchange programs, and training sessions. The knowledge utilization
literature has concluded that social scientists have an impact on decision-
making in indirect and diffuse ways.[22] For academics, any interaction with
practitioners and students (many of whom will be practitioners of the future)
provides opportunities for the diffusion of new concepts and theories.
Knowledge, of course, also flows in the reverse direction. Practitioners will
inform academics about emerging problems and provide feedback on the
salience of previous theoretical approaches for addressing these new realities.

If anything, the greatest concern about the proliferation of academic centers has less to do with their potential for undermining academic integrity
and more to do with how they corrode the traditional bases for engendering
community and coherence at universities, that is, the disciplinary and professional structures around which universities are organized. The worry is that
if too many professors become members of such centers or think tanks, they
are less likely to contribute to their departments and professional schools.
Moreover, there is a sense that organizing to attract funds, albeit necessary,
undermines the traditional emphasis on pure academic research. These concerns are important, but they fail to acknowledge how much universities
have evolved over time. There has been a proliferation of disciplines and
professions over the last hundred years or more; academic centers are only
the most recent organizational response to changing demands. Moreover,
rather than viewing the emergence of academic centers simply as shrewd
ways to acquire more financial resources, we should see them as genuine
intellectual efforts to grow toward emerging problems that pose the greatest
uncertainties, as a means for tapping into the best information and expertise
available for grappling with those problems (Stinchcombe, 1990). In this
view, academic centers create community in a manner consistent with the
larger intellectual tradition of universities; the resulting panoply of communities within universities simply mirrors the complexity of society.

A troubling problem remains. This chapter has identified a lack of a critical policy inquiry from non-profit and university think tanks that receive
considerable government and foundation support. Perhaps this is a natural
response of supplicants in a state-directed policy community, reflecting a
fear of offending key sponsors and losing precious financial support. No
doubt some criticism is articulated through other channels, such as expert

advisory groups to ministers and government departments, and to other academics in scholarly journals and books. However, academics should not use university think tanks simply as sites for undertaking discrete projects and educating students. They must also be seen as platforms for articulating informed views about the assumptions, direction, and trajectory of government policy and its management of the policy community. After all, academics have a degree of professional independence enjoyed by few others in society. But the responsibility must be shared. For academics to use centers in this manner they must have confidence that government and foundation sponsors also recognize the importance of encouraging critical views; and, moreover, that articulating such views in no way undermines their ability to undertake policy-relevant projects and educate students who will later assume important positions in organizations throughout a given policy community.

ACKNOWLEDGMENTS

This chapter was presented as a paper to the Annual Meeting of the International Political Science Association in Buenos Aires in July 1991. I would like to thank the individuals who consented to be interviewed for this study, many of whom also supplied documents. I would also like to acknowledge the superb research assistance provided by Maire O'Brien.

NOTES

1. Indeed, Bourne (1988) points out that there is no single model for academic research centers. Each is unique in mandate and organization because they are addressing a particular set of research problems within and across disciplines as well as attempting to overcome particular organizational problems at the university.
2. The origins of PBEC will be discussed in greater detail in the next section.
3. On these points, see Woods (1987), pp. 11–13.
4. See Woods (1987).
5. This information was obtained through research interviews and from Woods (1987).
6. Woods (1987), p. 11.
7. See Woods (1988), p. 176.
8. See A. Robinson, "New Lobby Groups Set Up for Business," *Globe and Mail* (Toronto), January 15, 1990.
9. The program covers the salary costs of new professorial positions for a period of three years. The university is then expected to take up the responsibility at the beginning of the fourth year. Trent (1988: 226) points out that this is a common practice of foundations. However, the problem is that in the long term, universities are left holding the bag for increased infrastructure costs.
10. This section draws heavily on Lindquist (1991), pp. 199–208.
11. It should be noted, however, that Professor Tsurmi had already been approached by Zavis Zeman to begin work on what would become an IRPP monograph entitled *Sogoshosha.*

162 THE ROLE OF INSTITUTES

12. Z. Peiji and R.W. Huenemann (eds.), *China's Foreign Trade* (Halifax: Institute for Research on Public Policy, 1987).

13. K.L. Brownsey (ed.), *Canada-Japan: Policy Issues for the Future* (Halifax: Institute for Research on Public Policy, 1989).

14. See J.W. Langford and K.L. Brownsey (eds.), *The Changing Shape of Government in the Asia-Pacific Region* (Halifax: Institute for Research on Public Policy, 1988); J.W. Langford and K.L. Brownsey (eds.), *Economic Policy-Making in the Asia-Pacific Region* (Halifax: Institute for Research on Public Policy, 1990); and J.W. Langford and K.L. Brownsey (eds.), *Think Tanks and Governance in the Asia-Pacific Region* (Halifax: Institute for Research on Public Policy, 1991). The three volumes contained papers from Australia, Bangladesh, Canada, China, Hong Kong, Indonesia, Japan, Malaysia, New Zealand, Papua New Guinea, the Philippines, Singapore, South Korea, Thailand, and the United States, though not every country was represented in each volume.

15. See H.E. English (ed.), *Pacific Initiatives in Global Trade* (Halifax: Institute for Research on Public Policy, 1990).

16. See M.G. Smith (ed.), *Canada, the Pacific, and Global Trade* (Halifax: Institute for Research on Public Policy, 1990).

17. See Conference Board of Canada, *A Fit Place for Investment? Foreign Investors' Perceptions of Canada in a Changing World*, Study No. 81 (Ottawa: 1984); *The Foreign Investment Review Agency: Images and Realities*, Study No. 84 (Ottawa: 1984); and *The Future of Foreign Investment in Canada*, Study No. 85 (Ottawa: 1985).

18. See *Building Partnerships for Tomorrow: Canadian Business Linkages with the Developing Countries, Volume 1: The Asian Experience* (Ottawa: Conference Board of Canada, 1987); *Building Partnerships for Tomorrow: Canadian Business Linkages with the Developing Countries, Volume 2: The Latin American Experience* (Ottawa: Conference Board of Canada, 1987); *Compendium Report: Building Partnerships for Tomorrow* (Ottawa: Conference Board of Canada, 1987); and *Building Partnerships for Tomorrow: Canadian Business Linkages with the Developing Countries, Volume 3: The African Experience* (Ottawa: Conference Board of Canada, 1988).

19. See J. Higgins, D. Balcome, and M. Grant, *Canadian Investment in the Association of South-East Asian Nations*, Report 33-88-DF (Ottawa: Conference Board of Canada, November 1988).

20. See E.A. Lindquist, "Making Canadian Policy Institutes More Relevant to the Policy Process," Ch. 9 in "Behind the Myth of Think Tanks: The Organization and Relevance of Canadian Think Tanks," doctoral dissertation, University of California at Berkeley, 1989.

21. Due to their size and relatively smaller turnover in staff, non-profit think tanks have less of a role to play in training; but this role should not be downplayed—they expose generalists and experts in other areas to Asia-Pacific issues as a matter of course and may convert them, at some point, into bona fide experts.

22. For citations and a review of this literature, see E.A. Lindquist, "The Third Community, Policy Inquiry, and Social Scientists" and C.H. Weiss, "The Uneasy Partnership Endures: Social Science and Government," Chs. 2 and 5 in Brooks and Gagnon (1990b).

7

Foundations, Social Scientists, and Eastern Europe

Joan Roelofs and Erkki Berndtson

INTRODUCTION

Dramatic changes in countries that at the end of the 1980s still constituted an area labeled as Eastern Europe (i.e., Albania, Bulgaria, Czechoslovakia, the German Democratic Republic, Hungary, Poland, Romania, and Yugoslavia) pose problems for those who study the role of social science policy communities.[1]

This chapter explores the question from one specific perspective: the interaction of Eastern European social science with western foundations. The funding aspect is too often forgotten in addressing the development of social science and its impact on public policy. However, it must be remembered that especially in the United States the major part of funding for the social sciences has always come from private foundations; and although public funding has been readily available in Western European states, especially following World War II, foundation money has often been crucial in these countries. In addition, U.S. foundations have had an indirect impact on social science communities in other countries as foundations have influenced American social science, which then has influenced social science worldwide.

We are mainly interested in two questions. First, we consider how different kinds of scholarly exchanges, particularly in the social sciences, may have played a role in shaping policy communities that accelerated recent ideological shifts in Eastern Europe. Second, we speculate about the role of newly emerging social sciences in these countries. Although it is too soon to say anything certain about the future, there are signs that the development will be more one-sided than it should be. American and other western foundations, western scholars and scholarly networks, Eastern European universities and institutes with political actors East and West, form a policy community of asymmetrical relations of influence and dependency. How this policy community functions in different countries will surely make a difference in the future of Eastern European societies.

Social Sciences and Eastern European Revolutions

Eastern European revolutions have been largely attributed to (1) dissatisfactions among citizens paralleled by decline of ideology among the ruling elite, which led to both corruption and poor maintenance of the ruling myths; and (2) changes in the former Soviet Union, and the perception of Soviet tolerance (even encouragement) of radical change in Eastern Europe. In addition to the "push," we may posit a "pull," which included both material goods and public diplomacy of the United States and other western nations. Cultural factors also played a role. Gradually, English became the dominant foreign language in Eastern Europe, and "just as American culture and scholarship began to dominate the attention of East European intellectuals, so American subcultures and countercultures began to prove irresistible to millions of East European young people" (Brown, 1987: 41). Also contributing to the "pull" were the Helsinki accords. Not only did these promote intellectual cooperation, but their emphasis on civil liberties substantively reinforced western standards for political evaluation.

Of course it would be preposterous to claim that western social science has been the major factor in East European revolutions, but many close observers have indicated that scholarly exchanges have had considerable impact. Even before the East European transformations, the United States International Research and Exchanges Board (IREX), which manages the exchange programs with the former Soviet Union and Eastern Europe, assumed that they had:

Recent articles in the press have shown that many alumni of these [Eastern European] programs now occupy important positions in the institutions responsible for the economic and political reform that could take place in Eastern Europe should current leadership in the Soviet Union remain in power. Past IREX participants can now be found in the Central Committees of several countries in Eastern Europe, in ministerial posts, and also in the policy-making hierarchies of educational institutions and Academies of Sciences. The placement of former grantees in decision-making bodies is certain to have a positive impact on the exchange process. (Social Science Research Council, 1987–1988: 84)

After 1989 many Eastern European social scientists acknowledged this influence. A leading Hungarian political scientist, for instance, has seen political science as one aspect in the democratization of state and society, and he claims that political science accelerated change in Hungary (Agh, 1990a: 10). The scientific base for reform was developed with the "'import' of Western, mostly American, social sciences, with their terminologies, ideas and international contacts for the establishment of oppositional 'reform sciences'" (Agh, 1990a: 5).

Mechanisms of Cultural Imperialism

The doctrine of cultural imperialism has not, to our knowledge, been applied to relations between the West and Eastern Europe, but it may be relevant in the current situation. This theory posits among other things that:

Dependency relations derive from the dominant theories and methodologies in developed countries that are world-wide reference points for research and teaching; from resources available in developed countries for advancing knowledge, including the availability of means for publishing and distributing research findings; and from the existence of major university centers in Europe and the United States that continue to attract, and often retain, first-rate social scientists from all parts of the world. . . . There is a tendency for those who participate in transnational activities to be an elite that can tap resources and opportunities not available to most social scientists in their country. (Alger and Lyons, 1974: 2–3)

There is some evidence that cultural imperialism was a strategic tool. In the mid-1960s, the premise that the West would "roll back" the communist systems of Eastern Europe through invasion was losing favor in U.S. foreign policy circles. This was the theme of Brzezinski's book *Alternative to Partition* (1965), which suggested instead a multi-pronged approach that included trade and cultural interaction. In *Between Two Ages* (1970), Brzezinski welcomed the emergence of "transnational elites":

The creation of the global information grid, facilitating almost continuous intellectual interaction and the pooling of knowledge, will further enhance the present trend toward international professional elites and toward the emergence of a common scientific language. (Brzezinski, 1970: 59)

He believed that the "technetronic revolution" would permit global responses to human problems that were pragmatic and scientific rather than ideological. In fact, attempts to create such an intellectual community had already been under way for quite some time:

[Cultural and scholarly] exchange programs with the countries of Eastern Europe began in the late 1950's. The Helsinki Final Act, signed in 1975, provided new impetus for expansion of these activities, particularly with Bulgaria, Czechoslovakia, East Germany and Hungary, whose relations with the United States in this field had been severely limited. The Final Act encouraged the East European governments to engage in exchanges and provided political sanction to private groups to expand their activities. (United States Congress, 1986: 3)

The private groups involved in these exchanges have overwhelmingly been foundations and foundation subsidiaries such as the IREX and the Institute of International Education, which has administered the Fulbright program for the U.S. government. In addition, churches and other nongovernmental organizations (NGOs) have sponsored programs. Private organizations created to serve as "pass-throughs" for government funds (e.g., Congress for Cultural Freedom) have also played a role.

Today, in addition to the Ford, Rockefeller, and Carnegie foundations, the Olin, MacArthur, Bradley, Mcknight, and Mellon foundations and Merck and Rockefeller Brothers funds support East European scholars, universities, and institutes as well as "East-West" integrative organizations such as the Fondation pour une entraide intellectuelle européenne (Paris), Center for East-West Security Studies (New York), and Salzburg Seminar in American Studies in Austria.

The energy and initiative seem to have come primarily from the private sector. This is not surprising, as foundations and offshoots such as the Council on Foreign Relations have had a long history of international interaction, whereas the U.S. government has been officially isolationist for much of the time. Since 1956, at the request of the U.S. State Department, the Ford and Rockefeller foundations had been conducting exchange programs with Poland. By 1964, it was the view of the Ford Foundation and the U.S. State Department that "its chances of breaking down the Iron Curtain would be better served by inviting scholars in the social sciences and writers [rather than technicians] who would presumably be more influenced by Western ideas" (Ashley, 1970: 135). Similar programs were undertaken with Yugoslavia and Hungary, which were later administered by the foundation-supported American Council of Learned Societies.

The U.S. Mutual Educational and Cultural Exchange Act of 1961 (known as Fulbright-Hays) was intended to "focus primarily on individuals of exceptional talent, promise, or influence in selected fields of importance to our long-term foreign relations" (United States Department of State, 1974: 3). This enterprise, known as "Public Diplomacy," was intended to encourage change through peaceful means. Along with scholarly exchanges, it included "high and pop culture, broadcasting, trade and travel" (Gordon, 1987: 90). More prominent aspects were Voice of America, Radio Free

Europe, and Radio Liberty, along with trade union interactions: "The AFL-CIO [was] almost a foreign service of its own" (Gordon, 1987: 97).

These programs, of both public and private organizations, were to serve a "civilizing mission":

[T]he United States should expand relations with senior officials in all these countries and enlarge contacts with the technocracies and the scientific-intellectual communities, in order to learn more about them and even to help shape on the margin the decisions of these oligarchies which will inherit power over the next decade. IREX . . . should be supported and expanded. (Luers, 1987: 980)

Private organizations were the channel for public diplomacy not only because of their expertise but also because many believed that narrow-minded congressional interference would restrict the range of programs and create a U.S. foreign policy aura that would deter the participation of foreign scholars.

It would be an oversimplification, however, to claim that the flow of information moved only in one direction. Beginning in the 1970s there even seemed to be an opening, cross-fertilization, and dialectic resulting from the exchanges between the West and Eastern Europe. There also seemed to be some "blowback"; that is, western social scientists found Marxist concepts to be of some use (Gruchin and Zamochkin, 1972). Besides, the IREX programs enabled less ideological westerners to study Eastern Europe in the manner of "history from the bottom up" (Lapidus, 1980). Not that this was a golden age of social science research, but looking back on it, we can see how far the ideological pendulum has swung to the right in both East and West.

Cultural Imperialism and Scientific Communities

Cultural imperialism does not imply absolute domination by one actor, but the existence of a hegemonic climate that slowly molds the intellectual discourse. It is quite often the case, as Evert A. Lindquist suggests in this volume, that while they are acquiring funds for research, social scientists can demonstrate considerable resilience in the face of external pressures and are often able to protect their own interests. On the other hand, it is also probable that the interests of financiers and researchers must meet somewhere, and in the long run it is difficult to obtain money for research that is totally against the interests of those holding the purse.

We have to focus also on the power struggle between scholars themselves and on the strategies they use to market their skills to decisionmakers and financiers of research. As Pierre Bourdieu (1984) has shown, scientists use different power resources in the scientific arena to advance their own positions in the struggle for money, fame, and career mobility. According to Bourdieu there are three kinds of scholars: those who base their power on institutional positions within academia, those who have close relations with mass media and use them to advance their fame, and those who concentrate purely on research. We can add to these strategies an ability to forge alliances with different political interests and movements (Gagnon, 1989). A scholar can base his/her position on political power structures or political movements that give him/her the needed publicity. An additional power base is an ability to attract outside financiers.

It is interesting to apply this mode of thinking to the changing situation in Eastern Europe. Under socialist governments the most important power base for social scientists was their relationship with the party, which then gave access to institutional positions. Often the quality of research was not very important. In the new situation the rules of the game have changed considerably, because in most cases Marxism is regarded with suspicion. However, in many cases former party loyalists are still heads of research institutes or university departments, which means there will be a growing conflict of interest between social scientists who achieved their positions before 1989 and those who try to rise into power now. To be able to demonstrate a relationship with the former opposition forces will be an asset. The ability to do research that has international acceptance is also a resource in itself. These channels will open doors for money, contacts, and positions in the future.

Foundations have a significant role in this respect. As has been the case in the West, foundation grants bestow not only resources but also legitimacy, and they aid with future publication possibilities. Having succeeded by following the correct approach, social scientists will likely continue to accept the "gatekeeper" function of the foundations along the path to success (i.e., publications, appointments, promotions, professional recognition). Besides, one of the most potent devices of foundations is their ability to create, endow, and monitor other organizations. These may be peak organizations that bestow grants and technical assistance. They may be research institutes, advocacy groups, or "grassroots" organizations. By these means the foundations keep their hands in both the production of knowledge and all major "credible" social reform efforts. As social science and reform have been historically inseparable, it is nearly impossible to function as a social scientist today without being enveloped in this network of foundation-created and -funded institutions.

In the writings of Eastern European social scientists there is an increasing tendency to identify foundations and their subsidiaries with the essence of democracy. This is because of the emphasis on "civil society," "social movements," and "parallel polis" in the opposition to communist government sponsorship of all social, political, and cultural life. Pluralism is held to be the true way to represent the interests of citizens. The western critique of pluralism, as fostering both inequality and fragmentation, seems to have been unnoticed by the aspiring democrats. In a similar way, the "non-profit" or "third sector" is not examined closely in regard to the source of the funds, domestic or foreign; the self-perpetuating, non-accountable boards of directors; and the objects of such organizations. Thus, at a 1990 conference of Independent Sector, the research arm of U.S. foundations and charitable organizations, the keynote speaker, a Hungarian scholar, extolled the revival of Freemasonry as a contribution to pluralism and democracy.

EASTERN EUROPEAN SOCIAL SCIENCE BEFORE 1989

The Nature of Eastern European Social Science

The nature of Eastern European social science before 1989 is more difficult to assess than is usually thought to be the case.[2] In principle, an intellectual center for these countries was the former Soviet Union (except for Albania, Yugoslavia, and to some extent Romania). Some comprehensive studies of social sciences in the Soviet Union (e.g., Fischer, 1964; Brown, 1984) suggest that one important external influence on Eastern European scholars was the work of counterparts in the Soviet Union. However, we do not assume that all changes in Eastern Europe were mere reflections of twists and turns in Soviet scholarship (including moves toward westernization). The parallels are clearly present, but causation, whether western or Soviet, is difficult to attribute. In that sense it is important to focus on differences between the countries.

An important factor in explaining the dissimilarities is the character of the different communist party-states (Wiatr, 1990: 2). This includes structures and processes governing social science research and teaching within academia, scientific traditions, the ways in which social scientists participate in the policy process, communication to policymakers, the uses made of ideas and information generated by social scientific research, the political influence of social scientists, and the nature of policy process itself (cf. Gagnon, 1989). How much critical scholarship was permitted and what kinds of practical needs there were behind social science research are also crucial questions in evaluating the situation country by country.

A major problem in determining the political role of the social sciences is the great difficulty in segregating social scientists from the vast mix of philosophers, party ideologues, dissidents, journalists, historians, and others in the intellectual milieux of these countries (Hollander, 1989). Social scientists were much more likely to be members of the ruling elite than those of the West.

Disciplinary boundaries were also vague. Because of the Marxist tradition the western social sciences were regarded with suspicion. Economics had its own place under Marxist political economy, but sociology and political science were more problematical. The nature of these two sciences was not at all clear, and it was often difficult to legitimate them or even separate them. On the whole, however, sociology was more accepted, because it could be linked to information needs of the party bureaucracy. Political science, on the other hand, was often considered to be too "political"; as Buchstein and Göhler (1990: 668) note, for instance, about the German Democratic Republic (GDR), "unlike history and sociology, political science had no traditional academic niche where it could withdraw from time to time. Its primary subject, politics, was in the center of the ideological interest of the regimen." That is why political science was often ignored and the questions of politics were treated within the discipline of historical materialism (Tarkowski, 1987: 3).

Differences in Eastern European Sociology: Bulgaria and Czechoslovakia

We can highlight differences between Eastern European countries in regard to social science by comparing the position of sociology in Bulgaria and Czechoslovakia. Bulgaria (with Poland) seems to have been an Eastern European country in which sociology had an accepted position. Sociology experienced rapid development there after the communists came to power in 1944. It was considered to be an heir to a long tradition of Marxist sociology and a tool in the "reconstruction of the whole system of social relations. . . . socialism and sociology prove to be inseparable" (Vasilev et al., 1983: 36).

Bulgarian sociology was from the beginning empirically oriented. In 1962, a massive survey on religious beliefs was conducted and was soon followed by other studies of village life, time-budgets, youth socialization, crime, and the like, which all reveal a practical orientation. An intense interest in industrial sociology, the sociology of science, and issues connected with the computerization of education and society began in the 1970s. Until recent years the mood was extremely optimistic, with no suggestion of intractable social problems that could not be solved by the application of social science to society.

The critique of "bourgeois sociology" was at the same time a lively field (see Grigorov, 1968; Iribadjakov, 1960). One of the functions of the Institute of Contemporary Social Theories of the Bulgarian Academy of Sciences was to analyze "various bourgeois ideological conceptions as soon as these are made public and even before they are churned out by the imperialist propaganda mill" ("The Power of Advanced Theory," 1982: 32). However, this critique was also used as a means to introduce western concepts and theories to Bulgarian audiences. At the same time Bulgarians were eager to have a dialogue with western scholars. They were very active in the International Sociological Association, hosting, for instance, the World Congress in 1970. In spite of that, Bulgarian sociology continued throughout the 1970s and early 1980s to be almost totally committed to Marxist approaches (see Genov, 1984; Goranov, 1986).

One can compare this favorable position of sociology in Bulgaria with the situation in Czechoslovakia, where during the 1950s only orthodox Marxism was permitted. Although sociology experienced a period of liberalization during the 1960s (Bina, 1983), after 1968 orthodoxy was again imposed, and the social sciences in general appear to have missed the cross-fertilization of the "convergence" period that occurred in some other Eastern European countries.

Political Science as a Case Study

Dissimilarities among Eastern European countries are very clear in the case of political science. The International Political Science Association was founded in 1949, but only two Eastern European countries participated in its activities at the beginning: Poland became a member in 1950 and Yugoslavia in 1952 (Wiatr, 1990: 2). After the Soviet Union was recognized as a member in 1955, other Eastern European countries followed: Czechoslovakia was recognized in 1964; Bulgaria, Hungary, and Romania in 1968; and the GDR in 1975 (International Political Science Association, n.d.; Buchstein and Göhler, 1990: 668).

However, in most cases political science was only a label for creating international contacts (cf. Buchstein and Göhler, 1990: 668), and the discipline did not really exist as an independent academic discipline. Yugoslavia and Poland were the first Eastern European countries to establish chairs for the study of politics in universities at the beginning of the 1960s (Bibic, 1982; Tarkowski, 1987), but at least in the case of Poland political science was established as a state-controlled discipline in order to supply young citizens with the basic values of a socialist society. Courses in "introduction to political sciences" were made compulsory for all students in higher education, and "in order to secure a proper number of instructors there was a recruitment drive among first of all jurists and 'professional Marxists'" (Tarkowski, 1987: 6).

In practice this meant that there were "scientific associations" for political science, but no academic disciplines. However, there were times when an independent study of politics had its moment even in these circumstances:

Poland since 1956, Czechoslovakia before and during the "Prague Spring" of 1968, Yugoslavia during most of the period since the break with the USSR in 1948, and to some degree Hungary and the USSR during the late seventies and the eighties provide examples of political science developing as an intellectual blueprint for democratic reforms. Poland and Yugoslavia have also had—for most of this time—a political climate of relative academic liberty which made possible there a kind of Western-type empirical political study, for a long time unacceptable in the other East European states. (Wiatr, 1990: 5)

In the "other" East European states political science seems to have begun to develop only following its introduction in the Soviet Union. For instance, Powell and Shoup (1970: 582) state that "In addition to the influence of Western political science, the new Soviet interest in the field stimulated Czech developments in this area." Agh (1990a: 8) confirms this by writing that in the 1970s "the Soviet leadership felt that an official acknowledgment of political science was a necessity for the foreign policy and more intensive contacts with the West, and a regional conference of IPSA was organized in Moscow."

With regard to Bulgaria, there is no evidence of political science during the early period (in contrast to sociology); political sociology was the concern of a staff agency of the Central Committee of the Bulgarian Communist Party (BCP). Only the 1979 Congress of the International Political Science Association (IPSA), held in Moscow, seems to have stimulated the development of a separate political science identity in Bulgaria.

The picture one draws from Eastern European papers in political science conferences reveals basic differences between these countries. We can take as examples general trends displayed by Eastern European political scientists at the International Political Science Association World Congresses during the period 1979–1988.[3] Counting of papergivers from these countries indicates something about the political science community of each. See Table 7.1.

Table 7.1
Papergivers/Congress

Country	1979	1982	1985	1988	Total
Bulgaria	-	4	8	2	14
Czechoslovakia	4	4	4	2	14
GDR	7	5	2	3	17
Hungary	4	2	7	10	23
Poland	7	9	5	17	38
Romania	8	12	2	2	24
Yugoslavia	9	21	14	13	57
Total	39	57	42	49	187

Yugoslavia and Poland seem to have been the leading Eastern European countries in political science according to this data. Hungarians, on the other hand, took steps to develop the discipline before 1989, whereas the "enthusiasm" of Romanians in the late 1970s and early 1980s seems to have disappeared. The other countries did not show much development.

The image is reinforced by reading papers and abstracts. In general the Polish papers were more "western" and empirical than those of other Eastern European social scientists. Even in 1979 it was possible to argue in Poland that "the characteristic feature of the politico-economic systems of Eastern European countries is a high degree of centralization. The system is organized along hierarchical lines of vertical subordination" (Tarkowski and Siemienska, 1979: 119). The 1985 Polish papers addressed, among other things, problems such as "conflict of public allocation of goods," "political clientelism," and "the Polish crisis of 1980–1981." However, in regard to Poland, a special note is needed. Because of the ideological role of Polish political science proper, it has been mainly Polish political sociologists who have been active in research. Different roles of Polish sociologists and political scientists may be seen in the attitudes toward "Solidarity":

a number of sociologists spontaneously went to Gdansk and Szczecin to act as advisers to the strike committees. Alongside the process of building "Solidarity," more and more sociologists were involved in the activities of the Union as experts, advisors, instructors and elected officials. These activities were formalised by the signing of an official agreement about co-operation between "Solidarity" and the Polish Sociological Association. (Tarkowski, 1987: 16)

but:

Only very few [political scientists]—as different from the sociologists—took active role in the Solidarity movement. Many, however, have been active in the reformist wing of the ruling Polish United Workers Party or, after 1982, in the Patriotic Movement for National Revival. Their most important theoretical contribution to the reformist politics was the concept of power-sharing ["Contractual democracy"] based on negotiated agreements. . . . the Polish Association of Political Sciences expressed its pro-reform position in collectively elaborated memoranda in 1980 and 1987. . . . the second—presented by the Executive Committee of the Association personally to General Mojciech Jaruzelski—has been considered one of the elements in elaborating the strategy of gradual democratization of Polish politics. (Wiatr, 1990: 13)

Polish social science is an excellent example of how it is necessary to understand relations between different academic disciplines and their intellectual traditions in a given country. It is also an example of how different social sciences may play different roles in politics.

The Yugoslavian case is quite different. Its relatively free intellectual climate was the same as that of Poland, but if we look at the IPSA papers during the last ten years, it is striking how the majority of Yugoslavian papers addressed one topic: self-management. Titles such as "Pluralism of self-managing interests and the political system" (1979), "Problems and experiences of big cities in Yugoslavia—actual problems of self-management organization and social behaviour" (1982), "Contradictions of institutionalisation within the system of socialist self-management" (1985), and "Political culture, self-management and social crisis" (1988) are a random selection of examples. Self-management is taken for granted, but not without critical observations: "The new society, which I envisage as socialism, must be based on economic self-management and political self-government. Self-government is not a panacea. It creates its own problems and dangers. These risks are real but possibly avoidable. Yet, it is certain, that without participatory democracy enormous developmental potentials simply cannot be exploited" (Horvat, 1979: 195–96).

The other topic frequently addressed is non-alignment. In that sense Yugoslavian political science in the IPSA congresses took up problems following the official national framework, although sometimes critically. Published descriptions of Yugoslavian political science in general confirm the interpretation evolving from the IPSA papers (Bibic, 1979, 1982), and in that sense Yugoslavian political science may be interpreted as having been both radical and conservative at the same time.

Most papers from other Eastern European countries followed the official party line more rigidly. Czechoslovakian papers reveal the strict adherence to communist orthodoxy that we have already noted in regard to sociology: "Czechoslovakia's post-war history has shown that the possibility of socialism, thanks to its historically progressive socioeconomic nature for the settlement of the nationality issue, has become a reality" (Plevza, 1979: 60). Also, East German papers displayed a firm conviction of the inevitable triumph of socialism, and even Bulgarian political scientists seem to have been more conservative than their colleagues in sociology. They were often eager to advance the official policy of the government—as, for instance, in papers advancing the idea of a Balkan nuclear-free zone, which Bulgaria had proposed.

It is interesting that the development of Romanian and Hungarian political science communities seems to have taken opposite directions. Romanians were very active in 1979 and in 1982. Some papers followed the same arguments as were made in Czechoslovakian and East German papers; but there were others that aimed at empirical research, and still others addressed political norms and values in a creative way. Then in 1985 and in 1988 Romanians seem to have dropped out of the international political science community for some reason. On the other hand, Hungarians began to participate in earnest only in 1985, but they already showed an inclination to critical thinking. Problems of democracy started to be taken up and there emerged a new fashion, comparisons between the Hungarian political transition and those in Southern Europe, first and foremost in Spain (Agh, 1990a: 19). The approach was reformist, but socialism was still considered to be a social goal.

Beginnings and Conditions of the Change

Because political conditions in Eastern European countries differed and because social sciences had different roles in them, it is no wonder that the reception of new ideas did not follow the same path in these countries. The first real change came about before and during the "Prague Spring" in Czechoslovakia when even within the party faithful, critical theory could develop. Zdenek Mlynar, a party bureaucrat, questioned repression and corruption but:

was exiled to the Czechoslovak Academy of Sciences where he studied political theory and worked until 1968. . . . Mlynar was one of the architects of the Action Program which outlined a plan for broad democratization of Czechoslovak society, and became the official line of the CPC during the "Prague Spring." . . . The Action Program was designed to encourage mass political participation through the formation of a "National front" consisting of political parties, social organizations and interest groups. This would constitute a broad and pluralistic base for democratic planning and administration. (Antonio, 1980: 234)

Because of the new orthodoxy after 1968, the Czechoslovakian policy community was very resistant to foreign ideas. We can again compare Czechoslovakia with Bulgaria, where the ideological change began before 1989. The material available shows instances of deep pessimism and a turning away from Marxism. K. Petkov (the author of *Chrestomathy on History of the BCP*, published by the party press in 1985) found in 1989 that "the major causes of the alienation of citizens in our society are built into the existing system of ownership" (Petkov, 1989: 51). He claimed that:

[A]lienation became massive in the 1970s, when embezzlement, mismanagement, "escaping" labour and plain passivity among workers on the shop floor became widespread. . . . Alienation from political institutions and their representatives is now most glaring and concentrated, the catalyst here being social deviations and distortions, such as privileges, nepotism, corruption and the like. (Petkov, 1989: 52).

He looked forward to a "de-ideologisation of social science" that would lead to the development of a "modern theory of alienation." The rational society making progress under Marxist social science had simply disappeared.

Parallel with these changes was increasing support of western foundations for Eastern European social science, although we cannot know exactly
how much influence was wielded in this way. The influence seems to have
been more complicated than simple theories of cultural imperialism suggest.
Bulgarian political scientists and political sociologists were supported in the
United States by IREX, Fulbright, and ACLS funds. The titles of their projects indicate that their work had an interest in the U.S. political system:

- Julia Vladikova-Bokova: "The Political Culture of the U.S." 85-86 IREX
- Nora Ananieva: "Contemporary Political Science in the U.S." 86-87 IREX
- Julia Dilova: "American Theories of Leadership and New Managerial
    Paradigms." 1989 ACLS
- Stephan E. Nikolov: "The Role and Activity of Interest Groups in the
    Decision-Making Process in the U.S." 1989 ACLS

However, party-approved Czechoslovakian scholars participating in
IREX exchange programs in the United States were more likely to be studying "Application of Steel-Bearing Systems in Dwellings and Urban Construction for Minimization of Corrosive Loss."

After 1989 the ideological change seems to have been more dramatic in
Czechoslovakia than in Bulgaria. It may be that those social science communities that in the past were more susceptible to western influence will in the
future be more resistant to it than others. Although Bulgarian scholars studied the U.S. politics with foundation money, they often had a critical attitude
toward foundations. For instance, Nikolov presented a paper at the 1990
Research Forum of Independent Sector entitled: "Is Nonprofit Activity Possible under Socialism?" In it he mentions that non-profit organizations in
socialist countries have been used by the powerful to hide and launder
embezzled public funds. Many of these scholars also still adhere to socialist
ideas. Ananieva and another IPSA participant, Alexander Lilov, assumed
national leadership in the reformist Bulgarian Socialist Party (the former
BCP) in 1990, Lilov as head of the party and Ananieva as deputy prime minister.

These examples do not yet refute our hypothesis of cultural imperialism.
As will be seen in the next section, foundations have had a role in
Czechoslovakia. These examples also indicate that the mechanisms of cultural imperialism cannot be analyzed without taking note of general differences between countries and many intervening variables.

One of the intervening variables is the class position of intellectuals. We
can take Hungary as an example, as a tradition hopeful of reforming socialism remained strong (until very recently) in Hungarian social science (Hegedus, 1980, 1982; Gyorgy, 1988). Of particular interest is the 1974 work of
the exiles G. Konrad and I. Szelenyi, *The Intellectuals on the Road to Class*

Power (1979). Their assumption that intellectuals were gaining ascendency, in Hungary and in similar societies, would endow social science with a significant role in legitimating the power of this new class. Yet they were thinking primarily of intellectuals inspired by the new humanistic version of Marxism. Later Szelenyi stated:

I am convinced that the image of socialism as superrational, as the system with a scientific and research edge over anarchistic and only formally rational capitalism, played a crucial role in persuading intellectuals throughout the Eastern bloc. . . . These Hungarian intellectuals, who graduated during the 1960s, were ethically motivated in their careerism. They had a sense of mission, or calling. They wanted to lead society towards an enlightened, rationalistic, humanistic, and definitely socialist future. (Szelenyi, 1986–1987: 108–9)

At the same time Szelenyi doubts that this model has much validity anymore. He sees in Hungary the ascendency of the petty bourgeoisie, with not much prospect for democratization: "I see more signs of capitalist greed than of civic responsibility among them" (Szelenyi, 1986–1987: 137). If Szelenyi's analysis is correct, the rise of the petty bourgeois attitude among intellectuals will make them more eager to grasp the monetary and other rewards from anywhere available, not much questioning the conditions attached to them—and not only in Hungary.

FOUNDATIONS AND THE DEVELOPMENT OF SOCIAL SCIENCE

Foundations and Western Social Science

To understand the possible impact of foundations on social science in Eastern Europe, it is useful to look at the history of western social science, which has in many respects been the product of the funding decisions of big, mainly American, foundations (the Carnegie Corporation, the Rockefeller Foundation, and the Ford Foundation). This is largely due to their impact on American social sciences, which in turn had a major influence on social science enterprise around the globe following World War II. Even before the war the Rockefeller Foundation supported social science in Europe in many ways. Between 1919 and 1940, Rockefeller funding (close to $5 million) provided "the mainstay of the support social science received" in Britain (Fisher, 1980: 240). In a similar way, the development of American-style social science was stimulated by grants to the Royal Institute of International Affairs (London), the Graduate Institute of International Studies (Geneva), the Centre d'études politiques étrangères (Paris), the Notgemeinschaft der Deutschen Wissenschaft (Berlin), the Institute of Economics and History at

Copenhagen, Stockholm University, University of Oslo, the Dutch Economic Institute, and others (Fosdick, 1952).

In the United States the foundations played a key role in directing the development of American social science from the beginning of the twentieth century (Roelofs, 1990). The Carnegie Corporation and the Rockefeller Foundation with its affiliates (the Laura Spelman Rockefeller Memorial, 1918–1928, and the Spelman Fund, 1928–1949) were particularly active in financing the research agenda of scholars who had close relations with the Progressive movement. The study of public administration and the activity of municipal reform movements received foundation support that was decisive for the development of both. Without foundation support the Social Science Research Council (founded in 1924) could not have functioned, and university research was almost totally dependent on outside financing (social sciences in Chicago were one of the foundation pets).

After the war there was still not much provision for federally supported social science. Instead, private foundations continued their support for social science. Because the United States was now the foremost power in the world, many foundation trustees felt the need for more scientific and reliable knowledge about society and politics. One of the results was the establishment of "area studies" centers in major universities. For instance, the Carnegie Corporation funded the Russian Research Center at Harvard, and the establishment of the Russian Institute at Columbia occurred with money from the Rockefeller Foundation (Geiger, 1988).

Foundations paid much attention to other aspects of society also. The Social Science Division of the Rockefeller Foundation distributed $21 million in 1939–1949. This money went into programs such as the following: functioning of political democracy ($1.5 million), functioning of the economy and economic history ($6.3 million), international relations ($3.7 million), and interpersonal and intergroup relations ($1.3 million). During these years $1.7 million were also given to development of social sciences in Europe (Geiger, 1988: 323–24).

In 1949 the Ford Foundation became a new national giant foundation, and it remains the largest in the United States. The foundation designated five objectives at the beginning: establishing world peace, strengthening the economy, strengthening democracy, addressing problems of education, and promoting the scientific study of man. In that sense the foundation continued the programs that Rockefeller and Carnegie had previously funded. Most of the money was given to major U.S. universities and the Social Science Research Council. During 1946–1958, the Ford Foundation supported social sciences with over $60 million, of which Harvard, Columbia, and the University of Chicago received almost half (Geiger, 1988: 333–35).

Without making a thorough analysis of the impact of the Ford Foundation on social science development, one example is revealing. The foundation's Behavioral Sciences Division spent $23 million between 1951 and 1957 to advance the building of a more rigorous social science. From its beginning it focused on problems of low voter turnout and the questioning of the classical democratic image (Seybold, 1982: 29). It was no wonder that Robert A. Dahl wrote in 1961 an "Epitaph for a Monument to a Successful Protest" (the behavioral approach in political science), arguing that an important factor in the emergence of the behavioral study of politics was "the influence of those uniquely American institutions, the great philanthropic foundations, especially Carnegie, Rockefeller, and more recently Ford—which because of their enormous financial contributions to scholarly research, and the inevitable selection among competing proposals that these entail, exert a considerable effect on the scholarly community" (Dahl, 1961: 765). Although behavioralists may not agree, it is apparent "that the currency of the term was attributable to the desire of the officers of the Ford Foundation rather than to the intellectual merit of the idea" (Geiger, 1988: 329).

Currently the Ford Foundation works through a program division encompassing six broad categories: Urban Poverty, Rural Poverty and Resources, Human Rights and Social Justice, Governance and Public Policy, Education and Culture, and International Affairs. The program budget for 1990–1991 was $599,700,000, out of which approximately 35 percent was allocated for work in selected developing countries (Ford Foundation, 1990).

Foundations and Eastern Europe

Although Eastern Europe has not been the main target of the Ford Foundation, some reimbursements have been directed to it. In 1990 the foundation's International Affairs division announced:

As part of its new initiative in the Soviet Union and Eastern Europe, the Foundation is supporting research on the mechanisms and consequences of economic reform in the region. Among the organizations receiving such grants are the University of Pittsburgh on behalf of the International Management Center in Budapest, the Center for Foreign Policy at Brown University, and the Foundation for the Development of Polish Agriculture in Warsaw.

and

Along with the Foundation's Education and Culture Program, . . . International Affairs grants will continue to focus on the Soviet Union and Eastern Europe. Among the institutions that have received support are the American Council of Learned Societies and the American Institute for Contemporary German Studies in

Washington, D.C. New grants will support academic programs in East European studies in the United States and abroad. Support is also planned for collaborative research and policy analyses on Eastern Europe and the Soviet Union by scholars from the region as well as from Western and developing countries. (Ford Foundation, 1990: 30, 34)

The foundation (among other financiers) has also supported the East European Cultural Foundation (EECF) in London, which, according to an undated publication of the EECF, was

created in response to requests from Central and Eastern Europe for effective assistance in maintaining cultural, intellectual and civic life in these countries and to prevent their isolation from each other and from the West. The EECF encourages and helps to facilitate various forms of creative work by Czechs, Slovaks, Hungarians and Poles, and dialogue between Polish Solidarity, Czechoslovakia's Charter 77, the Hungarian democratic opposition and unofficial peace and human rights activists in East Germany, and between these groups and the West.

The East European Cultural Foundation belongs to a group of new foundations established during the 1980s to promote western-style pluralism in Eastern Europe, and they have now taken an active role in renewing social sciences in these countries. In this sense they may be more important than the old American foundations for the future of Eastern European social science.

In more recent years the EECF has published a journal, *East European Reporter* (founded in 1985), which has focused exclusively on dissenting theories and leading dissenters, many of whom were social scientists. It is dominated by anti-communists and tends to exclude reformist thought or those critical of western democracy.

Emigré and dissident views have also been featured in the *Journal of Democracy*, a publication of the U.S. government foundation, the National Endowment for Democracy. The possibility of democratic socialism or social democracy is usually dismissed in the articles; the democratic revolution has to be based on the emancipation of civil society and modeled on "the successful transitions to democracy in Spain, Portugal and elsewhere," according to the Czech historian Vilem Precan (1990: 81).

The Jan Hus Educational Foundation, a British foundation, indicated in its 1988–1989 report that it had supported the underground in Czechoslovakia but now could name names. Among those financed was Tomas Jezek, chief adviser to the minister of finance, who "for many years, worked secretly with Pavel Bratinka on translations of the works of Friedrich von Hayek" (Jan Hus Educational Foundation, 1990: 3). Other social scientists whose work was translated into samizdat editions included Alexis de Tocqueville and Karl Popper.

Two western-style foundations in Bulgaria have among their objectives support for the social sciences. One is the Lyudmila Zhivkova Foundation (its name has recently been changed to International Foundation St. Cyril and Methodius), which began in 1982 with a stellar cast of founders including Armand Hammer (United States), Pierre Cardin (France), Dr. Rifaat Assad (Syria), and Robert Maxwell (Great Britain). Many Bulgarian scholars were connected to the foundation, and overseas branches were established, such as one in Germany initiated by the head of the Krupp Foundation.

In 1990 an "Open Society Fund" was created by George Soros (a Hungarian-born American): "The Foundation finances numerous educational and cultural initiatives of Bulgarians in this country and abroad. By its various programs, it establishes new contacts and channels of information in the social sciences, economics, state and economic management, and education" (Soros Foundation, 1990: 3). The objectives are similar to those of the other Soros foundations in the former Soviet Union, China, Poland, and Hungary (the first Soros Foundation was established in Hungary in 1984). The Open Society Fund grants financial assistance to study in foreign universities, to participate in international conferences, to conduct research projects, and so on. The American University in Bulgaria was also founded with the Fund's assistance. From October 1990 to October 1991 the foundation granted 872,000 U.S. dollars and 2,682,000 levs in total and claimed that "the additional financial assistance solicited from other organizations abroad with the aim of implementing the Fund's programs exceeds 15 million U.S. dollars" (Soros Foundation, 1990: 10). The foundation has a promise of matching funds from the Bulgarian government and tax-exempt status for all its activities, even those that may be profit-making enterprises. The chairman of the board is Professor Bogdan Bogdanov of Sofia University, who has elsewhere argued that the University should be converted to a private, joint stock company (Engelbrekt, 1990: 7).

The Soros Foundation has been the most active in Hungary. According to George Soros:

The objective of the Soros Foundation is to support the evolution and development of Hungarian society. As a foreigner I am not qualified to determine what shape that society should take, but I have a strong conviction that it ought to be many-faceted and rich in opportunity. This is precisely what the Foundation seeks to accomplish: to expand the possibilities for creative activity and to support new initiatives in culture and education. (Soros Foundation, 1987: v)

In addition to exchange programs, the foundation has undertaken a comprehensive curriculum reform and textbook revision for the Budapest University of Economics (former Karl Marx University) "to create the appropri-

ate environment and conditions for management training." The Sociology
Department also received a three-year grant for modernization (Soros Foundation, 1988: 29). The foundation has undertaken a joint venture with two
Italian organizations and three Hungarian agencies to create the Budapest
Institute of Management (Soros Foundation, 1987: 7). Notable among the
grants in other fields is a heavy emphasis on folk arts and religious history,
and provision for Hungarian high school students to attend Choate/Rose-
mary Hall in Connecticut.

A Hungarian economist, Miklos Marschall (1989), who spent a year as a
Fulbright scholar in the United States, claimed that Soros funds were an
essential support for independent research in Hungary and that even socialist
scholars received grants (to study at the New School in New York City).
Marschall is himself a specialist on foundations and non-profit activity in
Hungary, and he has estimated that by 1989 there were at least 1,000 foundations in Hungary (with foreign, domestic, or joint funds and management).

THE FUTURE OF EASTERN EUROPE
AND EUROPEAN SOCIAL SCIENCE

Neither the future of Eastern Europe nor its social science development
can be seen clearly today. As this chapter's section on "Eastern European
Social Science before 1989" suggests, the nature of social sciences has varied from country to country (as has the role of social scientists). The variation has been due to different intellectual traditions and the nature of political systems. However, because of new interaction with developed capitalist
countries, there is a possibility that social science communities in these
countries will become more similar in the future.

As capitalism becomes the dominant ideology, social scientists seem to
be silent or applauding. IREX notes that their exchange scholars are now in
important positions in Eastern Europe, but the implications for social science
are not yet clear. The ideologists may again become dominant, and critical
social scientists ignored. As domestic funds are currently scarce for any cultural or intellectual work, it is unlikely that much will be produced in social
science apart from that which receives foreign sponsorship.

We may take Hungarian political science as an example, as Hungarian
social scientists have participated actively in the major foundation-supported
exchange programs and conferences (IREX, SSRC, American Center for
International Leadership, American Council of Learned Societies, etc.). The
Budapest School of Economics and Social Sciences plans to establish: "a
'joint venture' with Western, mostly American, political scientists, that is, to
establish some kind of an 'Institute for Democracy' for political education."
The Institute for Political Studies would be founded with "the active and

direct assistance of American and West European foundations and universities, first of all that of the SUNY at Albany" (Agh, 1990a: 25). The Hungarian Political Science Association has also established official contacts with the American Political Science Association, and these two organizations have agreed upon a system of annual conferences. In addition, political scientists of Hungarian origin living abroad, mostly in the United States, have taken an active part in establishing a new Hungarian political science.

The crucial question is the future of the systems of higher education in these countries. Will universities be state-owned or private? How much resources will be allocated to the social sciences (from public or private funds)? What kind of policy communities arise in different countries that want to develop social sciences? Much depends on the strength and position of the existing social science communities. Scholars who sided with communist parties may lose their jobs, as, for instance, has already happened in the former GDR, where hundreds of professors and other researchers are now out of work. On the other hand, those who were integral parts of the political change may benefit. Whatever the case will be, it is probable that there will be a general conflict between established scholars who have an institutional position in academia, and new scholars who are only now trying to get into the profession. Other conflicts will arise from the splintering of the political spectrum. Nationalist-populist movements will clash with more urban and cosmopolitan intellectuals; adherents of new parties will clash with each other. How to succeed (or survive) in this game will depend as much on political and social relations as on one's ability to do research.

There are critical scholars in Eastern Europe who are interested in creating a new kind of democracy. They are not satisfied with the narrow definition of democracy as a certain kind of electoral system; they are trying to find answers to questions raised by "new" social movements in the West (Agh, 1990b: 27–28). Many of these scholars held prominent positions in the opposition movements (e.g., in Ecoglasnost in Bulgaria), and in that sense they have no political stigma.

However, these scholars may turn out to be too radical for foundation funding. When the political system is created anew with political parties and electoral politics, many scholars may not be interested in thinking about the problems of democracy, but rather in the mechanisms and operation of a new system. These scholars, who easily find their counterparts in the West, may readily find support for their research. In this way the foundation equation of democracy and pluralism may be uncritically accepted by Eastern European social science. For instance, in political science the main focus of research now seems to be on electoral research and the pluralist theory of democracy. Research projects led by known western empiricists (e.g., Ronald Inglehart, Richard Rose, Samuel Barnes), such as "The European Value Systems Survey and World Value Survey," "Free Elections and the

Development of New Party Systems in Central and Eastern Europe," and "Attitudes towards Authorities and Regimes," do seem to receive funding and be able to coopt scholars from all Eastern European countries (see Klingemann, 1991). The same trend could also be seen in the 1991 IPSA World Congress in Buenos Aires, where there were only 24 papergivers (according to the program) from Eastern Europe, but 15 of the papers dealt with parties, elections, or the democratization process in Eastern Europe.

This clearly points to a need, East and West, for social scientists to resume work on a critical theory of democracy. If one-party rule is rejected, it does not mean that rule by entities however financed, and of unknown representativeness, can be equated with democracy. The problem is not simple, as political parties may appear to represent numbers primarily; but today, techniques of manipulative technology (available for a price) have a great deal to do with producing those numbers.

The general political climate in Eastern European countries seems to be moving to the right. There is a real possibility of the emergence of right-wing authoritarianism in these countries (Agh, 1990b: 23). The political right has never been interested in widening democracy, although it has approved the empiricist conservatism of non-radical social scientists. To combat this trend, critical social scientists should get on with developing theories to support democracies that are humanistic as well as egalitarian, and seek to resolve the greatest problems East and West, which are not the lack of consumer goods and profits but the destruction of the biosphere and deterioration of the quality of life for rich and poor alike.

NOTES

1. It is important, however, to remember that none of these countries were and are similar. Because of cultural reasons it is necessary to make a distinction at least between countries belonging to Central Europe (Czechoslovakia, the former GDR, Hungary, and Poland) and Eastern Europe proper (Albania, Bulgaria, Romania, and Yugoslavia). Also, from the disintegrating Yugoslavia at least Slovenia and Croatia should be understood to belong to Central rather than Eastern Europe (Agh, 1990b; Wiatr, 1990: 1). For simplicity, however, we use the term "Eastern Europe" throughout the chapter.

2. One might reasonably inquire how the authors (not versed in Eastern European languages) know what social scientists in Eastern Europe have produced. The answer provides a clue to the process itself. There are abstracts and papers that have been presented in English at international conferences. Such conferences and international organizations are generally subsidized by foundations, so this scholarship is where one would expect the most western influence. Articles and books have been translated into English. One important source is the U.S. journal *Telos*, which for many years was a bridge among dissidents in Eastern European countries (e.g., for Poles and Hungarians who did not know each others' language but could read English). Furthermore, print databases such as International Political Science Abstracts, International Bibliography of the Social Sciences, and Public Affairs

Information Service (international) Index contain brief summaries of works indexed; and CD-ROM databases, especially Sociofile, provide longer abstracts that illustrate the changing concerns of Eastern European social scientists. These sources give access to works that were not written in English and may never have been translated. It might be expected that these articles would differ from those intended primarily for an international audience, perhaps being more representative of traditional or orthodox approaches; this hypothesis deserves further analysis. Of course, it may be that significant work is being carried out that has neither been translated nor abstracted. It is certainly possible that important pieces of the picture are missing. We hope, however, that even these sketches will raise some crucial questions about the future of Eastern European social science.

3. During this period four Congresses were held within different social climates. The 1979 World Congress was held in Moscow, 1982 in Rio de Janeiro, 1985 in Paris, and 1988 in Washington, DC. Because of the locations, scholars from different countries have had different chances to participate. That is why the counted figures are merely suggestive. Moreover, the papergivers have been counted on the basis of information contained in the programs. In reality, some of the papers were never given, and there were many unlisted papergivers. This is a general problem of scientific conferences that is hard to avoid, but we believe that "no-shows" and their replacements roughly balance each other.

8

From Radio Research to Communications Intelligence: Rockefeller Philanthropy, Communications Specialists, and the American Policy Community

William Buxton

LASSWELL'S FORMULA AND MARSHALL'S CHART

Who
Says What
In Which Channel
To Whom
With What Effect?

These words of Harold Lasswell, introducing an article that he wrote in 1948 (Lasswell, 1948: 37), have come to enjoy a mantra-like status within the field of communication studies. For mainstream thinkers, Lasswell's formula has been recurrently used as a framework for discussing research findings in the discipline (DeFleur and Ball-Rokeach, 1975: 208). Even scholars of a more critical disposition have found Lasswell's prophetic statement to be of value in orienting research in the field. William Leiss devoted the 1990 Southam lecture (given each year at the annual meetings of the Canadian Communication Association) to an exploration of how the "message transmission" theory, as developed by Lasswell and elaborated a year later by Shannon and Weaver (1949), could serve as the basis for integrating research results in the area of public policy communications (Leiss, 1991: 2).

In deploying the message transmission theory to codify research initiatives in communications, writers like DeFleur, Ball-Rokeach, and Leiss have assumed that understanding its meaning is unproblematic. As a matter of course, they have treated Lasswell's formula as nothing more than a set of abstract categories that could serve as a template for imparting coherence to research in communications. They have, in effect, largely begged the questions of where the words originated, why they were selected by Lasswell, what they had come to mean at the time they were written, through which channels they had been directed, and to whom they had been addressed. In what follows, I use an exploration of the origins of Lasswell's formula as a point of departure for critically examining how the field of communications emerged in the United States during the decade prior to the end of World War II. In doing so, I give particular attention to how the Rockefeller Foundation was able to shape and direct the course of communication studies in accordance with its views on how the production of social scientific knowledge could be brought to bear on matters of public concern. It is hoped that an analysis of this kind might help communication studies learn from the lessons of its past in order to confront the nature and meaning of current intellectual practices in the field.

As Morrison (1978) has pointed out, Lasswell's formula can be traced to a series of seminars held in 1939–1940, sponsored and organized by the Rockefeller Foundation. A number of leading figures doing research in communications took part with the intent of "conceptualizing and organizing the field." It was during these meetings, Morrison claims, "that Lasswell first developed his now celebrated model of the communication process—who says what to whom in what channel with what effect—a conceptual model which had tremendous importance for the field's future history" (Morrison, 1978: 358).

Morrison is correct in attributing the origins of Lasswell's formula to the seminars. But a closer reading of the relevant documentation reveals not only that the concept had a different authorship but that it had a much different meaning and purpose within its original context. To a large extent, the authorship and purpose were closely related. Although undoubtedly all the members of the seminar contributed to the genesis of the communications schema,[1] it was John Marshall, associate director of the Humanities Division of the Rockefeller Foundation, who appears to have provided its initial formulation. And this formulation, as we will now examine, was inherently linked to Marshall's practical vision of the role in public life to be played by the emergent field of communications.

The formula first emerged at a meeting of the seminar held on May 8, 1940 (Rockefeller Archive Center, 1940c). In order to conclude the seminar with a coherent account of the year's work, Marshall suggested the need to systematize what had been discussed:

He hoped that a "chart" of research in the communications field might be developed, clarifying the need for such research, outlining the research itself, showing the interpretations that might develop from it and their significance, and suggesting the outcomes which might be expected. Such a chart is needed to lay the basis for the co-ordination and supplementation of parallel studies in the three fields of communication. (Rockefeller Archive Center, 1940c: 1)[2]

After considerable discussion of the issues raised by his initial comments, Marshall summarized what had been said in the following manner:

General answers of a valid character are not to be expected. Valid answers can be found only when specific problems are framed. The field of communications research lacks basic data on how people's experiences are being modified by communications. A "chart" is necessary, applicable in any study, which would remind those carrying it of the context which must be taken into account; a "chart" fixing the context within which studies, to be adequate, must be undertaken. In addition to defining the context, it should list the resources for implementing that context. If studies were structured in this way, it would furnish an integrating mechanism. (Rockefeller Archive Center, 1940c: 5)

The members of the seminar agreed that the process of charting would be attempted at the next meeting, to be held in June 1940. This was to involve the listing of a series of questions, along with the sources that were available to answer them. A number of the seminar members were assigned particular parts of the chart to complete (Rockefeller Archive Center, 1940c: 5).

Although no record of the subsequent—and possibly final—session of the seminar could be found, a number of the "parts" of the chart, as prepared by seminar members, have been preserved. Taken together, they reveal that Lasswell's formula not only originated in the seminar but had begun to serve as a framework for ordering and systematizing research. Marshall (1940a) wrote the introduction to the chart, which now took the form of a draft memorandum. He drew particular attention to "mass communication" and how it might be analyzed.[3] The analysis of mass communications was of "value to those who direct their use—particularly those who are conscientious in meeting the responsibilities that entails" (Marshall, 1940a: 2). Overall, the thesis of the memorandum was "that study of what mass communications are today doing in American society can yield knowledge which will be of practical value both to those who direct the use of the media of mass communication and to those concerned with their control in the public interest—not only governmental agencies, but industrial and civic groups as well (Marshall, 1940a: 4). The memorandum could be considered a success if "it will lead others to agree that the time has come to undertake systematic observation and reporting on the current flow of mass communications, its trends through time, and its effect through time" (Marshall, 1940a: 5).

Research of this kind was of practical value to those in control of mass media because it would provide "knowledge of what effect can be expected for a given type of communication, at a given time, and under given circumstances." Knowledge of this kind would be built up from the results of specific studies. These, in turn, could be of immediate practical value "if they are made to deal with communications bearing on questions of evident social importance." As Marshall emphasized, special studies must have a "general view of mass communications" as their context, if they are to realize their full value:

Analysis of the effect of any given communication . . . involves answering the basic question, *to whom was it said*. To generalize any specific finding on effect, the investigator . . . must be able to relate *what was said* to *what was being said* through the various media at the time in question and at earlier times. Finally, he must be able to relate *what is said* to *who said it*, and if possible, to the intention that the communicator had. (Marshall, 1940a: 6; emphasis added)

The remainder of the "parts," written by other members of the seminar, fleshed out the schema. Lasswell (1940) addressed the question of who communicates. Gorer (1940) discussed how content could be classified. Waples (1940) wrote a short account of how effects might be examined. Finally, Lazarsfeld (1940a) wrote on audience research, in effect addressing the "whom" to which mass communication is directed.

Mass communications was not simply chosen for study because of its inherent fascination; it was of interest because it was so closely bound up with problems of generating public consent for the policy measures undertaken during the "emergency" period of World War II. The draft document arising from the seminar can best be viewed as a strategic vehicle for institutionalizing communications research along particular lines. It represented an effort by communications researchers to make their emergent field relevant to the problems faced by policymakers with the onset of a period of emergency. What remains to be better understood is how and why this institutionalization occurred, and the role of the Rockefeller Foundation in the process. We will now examine more in detail how a "communications group" developed to the point of being poised to make its presence felt in the wartime effort. This will involve an examination of the background to the group's formation with particular reference to how Rockefeller philanthropy became involved in communications through its sponsorship of the Princeton Radio Research Project and related initiatives. I will conclude by briefly considering how the Rockefeller Foundation was instrumental in mediating between communications researchers and governmental officials after the conclusion of the communications seminar of 1939–1940.

THE PRINCETON RADIO RESEARCH PROJECT

In May 1937, the Rockefeller trustees approved a grant to Hadley Cantril of $67,000 over two years to be administered by the School of Public and International Affairs at Princeton University (Rockefeller Archive Center, 1937a). The main concern of the study was to examine "the essential value of radio to all types of listeners." Cantril maintained that "if radio is to serve the best interests of the people, it is essential that an objective analysis be made of what these interests are, and how the unique psychological and social characteristics of radio may be devoted to them." Moreover, the study sought to develop methodological techniques appropriate to the analysis of the radio audience (Cantril, 1937).

Cantril's study was part of a broader program of research administered by the Federal Radio Educational Committee (FREC). The body had been formed by the Federal Communications Commission in 1935 to "formulate plans for furthering cooperation between broadcasters and various non-profit groups."[4] Composed of representatives from both broadcasters and educators, FREC had as one of its major goals the undertaking of "a thoroughgoing study of how educational broadcasting is to be financed, or more particularly how the expense involved is to be shared by the broadcasters, educational agencies, the foundations, and possibly the government" (Marshall, 1935: May 15–16). To this end, it formed numerous research committees whose collective goal was to produce findings that would help to reconcile differences between educators and broadcasters. As it became increasingly evident that the projects proposed by the research committees were potentially far too costly and badly in need of streamlining, a "Committee of Six" was formed, consisting of three broadcasters and three educators.[5] It was given the task of combining some of the studies in order to reduce its costs (Studebaker, 1937). Ultimately, the Committee of Six evolved into FREC's executive committee, charged with the responsibility of overseeing the projects and generating funding for them from the broadcasting industry and other private sources.

John Marshall, working on behalf of the Humanities Division of the Rockefeller Foundation, adeptly worked through FREC to advance his agenda for communications research. The Committee of Six, in this sense, served a dual purpose. On the one hand, through his contacts on the committee (particularly Willis, Tyson, and Cantril), he was able to have some influence on the committee's choice of research projects. Working closely with the committee, the Foundation was able to generate funding from a variety of sources for a focused set of research initiatives. In effect, by virtue of its own prestige and influence the Rockefeller Foundation had been able to give FREC credibility in the eyes of industry, so much so that they were willing to provide funding for some of its projected studies. Having thus established the credibility of this committee, John Marshall was able to argue to the Rockefeller Foundation trustees that any funding allocated to FREC-sponsored studies would be subject to review by a group who had "the public interest" of radio broadcasting in mind.

This argument appeared to be crucial for generating support for Cantril's research proposal. In making the case to the trustees for support of the study, Marshall stressed that the project was part of a broader program of research within FREC, which had been supported by the radio industry. As he noted, not only had the industry's representatives supported the Committee of Six as a coordinating agency, but they had agreed to underwrite some of the projects at considerable cost (Marshall, 1937). Evidently swayed by the case Marshall had made, the trustees attached a good deal of weight to the fact that Cantril's study would be vetted by the Committee of Six:

As findings are to be released only through this Executive Committee, they will automatically carry the approval of three representatives of the industry whose authority cannot be questioned. At the same time, the presence on the Executive of three prominent educators assures due protection for educational and cultural interests. (Rockefeller Archive Center, 1937a)

Hence, they viewed the proposal as potentially significant because work of this kind was "fundamental for the success of the co-operative efforts of the radio industry and non-commercial agencies that are directed towards broadening radio's range of public service" (Rockefeller Archive Center, 1937a).

The Princeton Radio Research Project was initially supported because Rockefeller officials felt that it potentially could yield important insights into how commercial broadcasting could incorporate more educational material into its programming. It was believed that if the tastes and interests of the listening audience were better understood (assumed to be the desire for a greater diversity of non-commercial fare), commercial broadcasters would begin to offer more programs of an educational, artistic, and public interest nature. This would mean, in turn, that the tastes and standards of the listening audience would be elevated. Although such a goal might now seem naive and unrealistic, it was fully consistent with the Humanities Division's notion that radio could be used as a vehicle for enhancing the cultural levels of the mass public.

Once the Princeton Radio Research got under way, however, it began to move inexorably away from its original purpose of "broadening radio's range of public service" through encouraging cooperation between educational and commercial broadcasters. Undoubtedly, the rapid decline of advocacy for educational radio after the Communications Act of 1934 made the issue of mediating between the two interest groups appear less pressing.

However, much of the change in the orientation of the Project could be attributed to the selection of Paul Lazarsfeld as its first director in the summer of 1937, after neither Cantril nor Frank Stanton was willing to assume the position. Even as Lazarsfeld worked within the guiding framework of the Princeton Project, namely that of "studying the meaning of radio to all types of listeners" (Lazarsfeld, 1938b: 1), he sought to place it on a much more rigorous methodological footing. As he noted, the study of "who listens to what, why, and with what effect" is "a rather large order and one of our primary problems is to restrict the scope of our activities." This meant that "the *theoretical* and *conceptual analysis* of the listener problems confronting radio today is, therefore, one definite part of our activities" (Lazarsfeld, 1938b: 1–2). Lazarsfeld shifted the project away from its original goal of reconciling the differences between educators and broadcasters; it became much more oriented toward methodological questions and the study of a broad range of issues related to radio broadcasting and its effects.[6]

Nevertheless, given that the Project was still part of the research program coordinated by the FREC, an effort was made to give the appearance that its results would be of direct or at least indirect benefit to educational broadcasting. This presentation of the Project was evident in a report submitted to the Committee of Six in November 1938 (Rockefeller Archive Center, 1938b). The report contained accounts of the principles by which the research was guided, the plans for publication, and the kinds of research that were slated for the next phase of the Project's activities. It also included a statement on the general purpose of the Project as it had been summarized in the 1937 Annual Report of the Rockefeller Foundation. Following from its mandate to examine "the use of radio for educational or cultural purposes," the report emphasized how the Project sought to meet the needs of educational broadcasters. This included the development of "short-cut methods" to help undertake listener research, the stimulation of interest by "universities and other research agencies" in listener research, setting an example for educational researchers of how cooperative ventures with private agencies could be developed, and collecting the results of studies done by "commercial research agencies" and making them available to educators (Rockefeller Archive Center, 1938b: 4–5). More generally, the Project was guided by the concern to develop a "theoretical framework" that would "guide us in empirical research and in our interpretation of the findings." This would involve "the systematic study of actual efforts made currently with educational programs." Along the same lines, the Project sought to survey the "main fields in which radio obviously has its greatest social effects" (such as music, news broadcasting, and politics), and to determine the "social, regional and other differences" in the radio audience.

These principles, however, were not particularly in evidence in the list of eleven publications that had been planned; most were only marginally related to the needs and concerns of educational broadcasters. Indeed, only one projected volume (on studies in educational broadcasting) had any direct bearing on their concerns. The rest were either narrowly methodological in orientation[7] or discussions of various aspects of contemporary radio.[8] The only publication resulting from the Project at that point was a "radio issue" of the *Journal of Applied Psychology*, which was due to appear in February 1939. Clearly, the Project had strayed significantly from its goal of furthering the cause of educational and cultural broadcasting through research. It had embarked on a bewildering range of studies whose state of development was unclear and ill-defined.

Nevertheless, in its report on the Project, the Committee of Six of the Federal Radio Education Commission found that it was "being conducted in full accordance with the original plans" and recommended that "funds for its completion over an additional three years . . . be provided by the Rockefeller Foundation." Overall, the Committee commended "the progress of the work thus far" (Tyson, 1938).

Despite the positive recommendation of the Committee of Six, Marshall believed that "the disinterested opinion of a group of qualified specialists" should be solicited before the Foundation Board of Directors could consider a renewal of the Project's grant (Rockefeller Archive Center, 1938b). That the Foundation found it necessary to enlist the services of an additional reviewing committee was an indication of the degree to which the Committee of Six, as the executive body of FREC, had failed to live up to its expectations as an agency to direct and validate studies in radio research. There were other signs that the Project had not been as successful as its directors and the Committee of Six had claimed. Judging by the response of publishers to the Project's proposed series, it was unlikely that the proposed volumes would ever appear in print. As D.C. Poole (the Princeton University official responsible for the Project) noted to Stevens, the three publishers that had been approached[9] unanimously agreed that "the studies are of value but that their publication in the ordinary commercial way is not feasible" (Poole, 1938).

The reviewing committee for the Princeton Radio Survey met with its three directors in January 1939.[10] It was the Committee's view that although the Project had done "an excellent and intelligent job of exploration," it should "be focused in a general way upon certain important problem areas" (Rockefeller Archive Center, 1939a: 1). Members of the Committee then went on to indicate what some of these areas might be. The issue also came up of the relationship of the Project to educational concerns. Gilbert Seldes felt that the Project had an "educational bias" and that "the commercial and entertainment aspects of broadcasting should not be neglected." Cantril responded:

the Princeton Project is one of a series set up by the Committee of Six of the Federal Education Commission; . . . the Committee of Six feels that the Project should have an educational slant and expects to review all of the material collected by the Project before publication; . . . the Project finds itself in a situation involving conflicting allegiances and responsibilities; . . . the Directors would like to see the Project divorced entirely from the Committee of Six. (Rockefeller Archive Center, 1939a: 5)

Replying to a question posed by Robert Lynd about "whether the Directors were bound to confine themselves to a study of educational broadcasting," Marshall stated "that they were not; that the word 'educational' was not mentioned in the Foundation's grant to the project; and that the field was wide open, at least as far as this Reviewing Committee is concerned" (Rockefeller Archive Center, 1939a: 5).[11] Taking its lead, the Committee agreed that "the Project should be free to study all kinds of programs, including commercial and entertainment programs" (Rockefeller Archive Center, 1939a: 5).

Although the ostensible purpose of the Committee was to evaluate the Project, its actual function appears to have been to set it on a particular course. This was evident in its suggestions for future research. Rather than continuing to concern itself with questions of relevance to educational broadcasting, the Project was to devote itself to such matters as "the effects of radio listening" and the determination of "whether radio can accomplish certain effects independently or only as part of a more general process or situation" (Rockefeller Archive Center, 1939a: 9). Under the general categories of "attitudes toward authority" and "levels of anxiety," it was suggested that the Project give attention to how well radio was able to accomplish the following social objectives:

1. to supply listeners information not otherwise available
2. to restore the spontaneity and freshness of local viewpoints
3. to assist in decreasing the social lag incident to technological change
4. to increase the selective response of groups to the radio
5. to increase tolerance toward experts and expert knowledge in social affairs (Rockefeller Archive Center, 1939a: 10).

The directors responded enthusiastically to the suggestions. Stanton indicated that "a good deal of the groundwork for carrying out the Committee's suggestions had already been done." Along the same lines, Lazarsfeld "accepted that the work already begun points in the direction suggested by the Committee and can be pointed still more; and that a real attempt had been made during the first year and a half of the Project's work to decide

problems on just such bases as those the Committee had in mind" (Rockefeller Archive Center, 1939a: 10).

That the directors of the Project took the Committee's suggestion to
heart is evident in the proposal they submitted during the next month for a
renewal of their grant. A number of the suggestions of the Committee were
reiterated almost verbatim, followed by a statement that "the present proposal seems to the officers to give adequate consideration to most if not all
these recommendations of the Reviewing Committee" (Rockefeller Archive
Center, 1939c).

Despite the Committee's conviction that the Project was promising, it
recommended that "the evidence accumulated be fully formulated before
proceeding with any additional research" (Rockefeller Archive Center,
1941). Such an assessment only served to fuel the growing impatience of
Foundation officials with the Project. As Marshall noted in an internal memorandum,

There has been a good deal of scepticism as to what the Project could accomplish.
J.M. [John Marshall] naturally believed with Lazarsfeld that the Project can and
does offer much information of significance for better broadcasting; but others do
not share his belief. The burden of proof is now Lazarsfeld's. More generally there
is a scepticism about what the methods of social psychology can accomplish. . . .
Finally J.M. said quite candidly, that in some quarters Lazarsfeld himself suffered
from the reputation of being a starter and not a finisher. (Marshall, quoted in Morrison, 1978: 356)

Marshall communicated the Foundation's concerns to Lazarsfeld in a
telegram:

Discussions in office indicate reluctance to invest in new research pending formulation of present findings stop feeling here that need is for breathing spell to save project from being victim of its own success stop no recommendation to trustees now
stop ready to review situation in June if formulation is sufficiently advanced by
then to proved basis. (Marshall, quoted in Morrison, 1978: 355)

The situation was indeed reviewed in June, but a final decision on the
renewal was not reached. Rather, following the suggestion of the review
committee, the Foundation "appropriated $17,500 in 1939 in addition to the
amount available from the 1937 grant" for the formulation of the evidence
that had been accumulated (Rockefeller Archive Center, 1941). In effect, the
Foundation made the renewal of the grant contingent on publication in an
acceptable form of the material that the Project had conducted until that
point.

This pressure by the Foundation appears to have galvanized the directors
of the Project into action. Lazarsfeld submitted a draft of *Radio and the*

Printed Word (1940b),[12] which was then sent by Marshall to a number of consultants for comments.[13] Stanton sent Marshall an outline of a book to be entitled *Listener Research Techniques*.[14] Indicating some impatience with its formulation, Marshall posed these questions to Stanton: "Is this book or the project elsewhere to suggest not only the ways of getting information but also the information it seems desirable to get? . . . Has the project formulated any notion of what an educational station needs to know about its audience?" (Marshall, 1939b). Cantril requested a subsidy for the publication of his study of the Orson Welles broadcast "The War of the Worlds," which had originally been supported by a grant-in-aid from the General Education Board (Cantril, 1940). Marshall explained to Cantril that "the interest which promoted this grant-in-aid . . . goes no further than having the study made and available for general education" (Marshall, 1939d: July 25).

By the end of August 1939, Lazarsfeld was able to provide for the first time a clear indication that the works in progress would be forthcoming as publications.

The monograph [Lazarsfeld, 1940b] will appear jointly with Dr. Stanton's text on the measurement of radio audiences and Dr. Cantril's text on the mass hysteria study [Cantril, 1940]. We feel that these three publications, together, will give a very good start, and will enable the public to get a picture of what the radio project of Princeton University is doing. (Lazarsfeld, 1939)

The flurry of activity by the directors over the summer apparently convinced Marshall that the Project was finally on track. He noted the following to Herbert Brucker, who was in the process of preparing a report on the Project:

It [the Princeton Project] has now been whipped into pretty good shape. But, as that implies, some whipping was necessary. With some reason, the Directors of the Project had let their work range pretty widely—so widely in fact that it seemed fairly clear that steps would have to be taken to pull the various leads together. As a result, the terms of the grant made last spring were such as to insist on the formulation of data already in hand. . . . that job is now progressing to a satisfactory conclusion. But "complete satisfaction" would neglect an earlier feeling that the Project had got a bit out of hand and was, as we put it last spring, in danger of becoming the victim of its own success. Certainly an enterprise of this kind needs firm administration, and I am not satisfied that this particular enterprise has always had it. (Marshall, 1939c)

Marshall's earlier lack of confidence in the administration of the Project had led him to consult with Robert Lynd, professor of sociology at Columbia University, who had been closely involved with the Project since its inception. Lynd noted to Marshall:

I think what he needs is a stronger hand (you, a committee on?) holding him to a *defined* program. I don't believe he had a clear-cut set of definitions and of criteria as to priority in undertaking the job. . . . the Foundation did not know what it wanted but wanted a field of alternative possibilities opened up. This played into Paul's over-wide field of interest and aided and abetted him in following his curiosity rather than narrowing a program.

He is so darned able that there is no point in throwing out baby and bath. Every researcher has an Achilles heel. His is his intellectual curiosity about everything interesting. He can be channelled. . . . The need, therefore, is to use his great strength but to see that his sailing orders are more explicit. (Lynd, quoted in Morrison, 1978: 356)

THE COMMUNICATIONS GROUP

The "sailing orders" materialized in the form of a series of seminars, which began in September 1939 and continued until June 1940.[15] The purpose of the seminars was to channel Lazarsfeld's research along more systematic lines. Marshall recalled:

We felt that Lazarsfeld's research for the first period was admirable, but that it was scattered and unfocused. With Lazarsfeld's agreement we therefore subjected him to a day's examination. We had a group of people and we sort of cross-examined Lazarsfeld all that day, trying to get him to define some focus for his work in the next period of his work. While we did get Lazarsfeld to agree to certain foresight to what he would go on to do, the work was still in a conceptual muddle. There was no sharpness to it whatsoever. So we came to agree in the spring of 1939 that we should hold this series of meetings at monthly intervals throughout the coming academic year. (quoted in Morrison, 1978: 357)

The first meetings of the committee took place on September 20 and 23, 1939. Dubbed the "communications group," it would subsequently meet on a regular basis throughout the academic year. These meetings led to the production of numerous memoranda, commentaries, and working papers, culminating in two summary documents, "Research in Mass Communications" (Rockefeller Archive Center, 1940d) and "Needed Research in Communications" (Rockefeller Archive Center, 1940e).

Although the initial plan for the seminar was to embark on a theoretical discussion of mass communication, the "war situation" changed its orientation. As Marshall stated, "it now seemed advisable that instead it consider what research studies might be undertaken at once . . . studies that would be of immediate significance and would furnish immediate returns through current reporting of results" (Rockefeller Archive Center, 1939b: 1). After indicating the trends that would likely occur during this period of "emergency psychology," the members of the committee "made various suggestions for research which might be undertaken at this time" (Rockefeller Archive Center, 1939b: 2). The subsequent discussion addressed the issue of how informed public opinion could be cultivated during the emergency, with particular reference to the role of communications in this process. It was felt that "the committee should attempt to make the public more keenly aware of trends resulting in America from the war situation, so that the people would know what was going on and would not be swamped by these trends but could cope with them, combat them, or adjust to them more readily and intelligently" (Rockefeller Archive Center, 1939b: 1–2). In order to address the issues raised by the committee's concerns, it was decided that documents would be prepared and would serve as the basis for seminar discussions. The preparation of the documents, at least initially, was primarily the responsibility of two subcommittees, namely research (consisting of Lasswell, Gorer, and Marshall) and government (consisting of May and Slesinger). In addition, other members of the seminar were to occasionally prepare reports on particular topics.

From the outset, it was evident that Harold Lasswell and John Marshall both played a particularly crucial role in the development of the seminar. Both worked from a broad vision of how systematic research in communications could have a practical bearing on the changing political circumstances. Marshall acted as a guiding force, ensuring that the group kept to its focus of defining the field of communications. To a large extent his views coincided with those of Lasswell, who consistently spoke in favor of "the creation of a body of social scientists and experienced public characters which would construct probable outcomes of trends and policies, then measure the flow of communications regarding them in terms of standards of communication it would develop, with particular emphasis upon clear reporting" (Rockefeller Archive Center, 1939c: 2). Lasswell and Marshall undoubtedly bore most of the responsibility for the production of the major document considered by the seminar in its early meetings, judging by its orientation and emphasis. The final section of the memorandum (pp. 53–55) discussed the "Role of the Central Coordinating Agency," maintaining that it would be necessary to have a coordinating body to "stimulate concurrent researches, to perform continuously approximate coordinations, and to provide a channel for intercommunication and interstimulation between the separate studies" (Rockefeller Archive Center, 1939c: 53).

Evidently both Marshall and Lasswell believed that the seminar itself should serve as a coordinator of research. In response to the suggestion of Bryson that it begin to map out the field of communications, Lasswell suggested that "the seminar might discuss going and proposed research." When Marshall pointed out that the seminar was to act as a coordinating agency for specific research projects, Lasswell stated that "it was this problem of coordination and integration that interested him especially. He suggested that the seminar might be able to effect such integration after it became a coordinating agency." To this end, he "felt that a secretariat for the seminar should be created, which would be useful in coordinating activities and also in connection with preparation for the meetings of the seminar." Building on Lasswell's suggestions, "Slesinger moved that the seminar become a body to discuss going and prospective research projects, with a view toward later developing a more general theory of communications" (Rockefeller Archive Center, 1939d: 6). This view gained assent from the other seminar members.

From this point on, the texture of the seminar changed. A number of sessions were given to the discussion of particular research projects and working papers.[16] The work of the communications group culminated in a draft document framed by the communications formula. It was on the basis of this schema that the field of communications was to develop. The practical impulse of the communications group's work is evident in the two memoranda they produced after the seminar's completion (Rockefeller Archive Center, 1940d, 1940e). To a large extent, they drew on the earlier discussions as articulated in the draft memorandum produced for the June 1940 meeting.

The purpose of the communications group, according to the first of these memoranda, was to "throw light upon the ways and means by which, given the necessity for change, the public mind can most effectively be helped to adapt itself in time to necessary change" (Rockefeller Archive Center, 1940d: 1). To this end, with its interest in "the relevance of research to public policy," the group was concerned with what Walter Lippmann (and Noam Chomsky) would have considered to be "the manufacture of consent":

Government which rests upon consent rests also upon knowledge of how best to secure consent. Policies which there are no real grounds to question risk defeat unless account is taken of public predisposition and of public need, unless the interpretation of purpose and probable result is actively communicated. Research in the field of mass communication is a new and sure weapon to achieve that end. (Rockefeller Archive Center, 1940d: 2)

It was in this sense that the "vast, existing resources of mass communication can influence profoundly the speed and success of adaptation in the human mind" (Rockefeller Archive Center, 1940d: 4). To illustrate how such ideals might be realized in practice, the memorandum discussed at length how communications research could intervene to deal with the hypothetical case of how an address on a radio program "dealing with the dangers of subversive activities on the part of the aliens" led to "outbreaks of feelings against alien groups" (Rockefeller Archive Center, 1940d: 8). The memorandum then went into some detail about how the resources of communications research could be effectively mobilized to address a problem of this kind (Rockefeller Archive Center, 1940d: 8–17). It was concluded that "the critical situation of our fable . . . rather than exaggerating, perhaps only puts into perspective the consequences of mistaken use of mass communications and the help which research can give in avoiding such mistaken use" (Rockefeller Archive Center, 1940d: 16). Indeed, the point of the fable was to "[make] clear what the job of research in mass communications is . . . that job is to learn what mass communications do in our society." This involved "getting evidence with which to answer four basic questions":

What they do became a question of *what effects* do mass communications as a whole, or any single communication, have. What effects they have likewise inescapably involved discovering *to whom what was said*. How these effects occurred necessitated analysis of *what was said*. And that analysis . . . required answers to a fourth and final question—*who said it and with what intention*. In brief, then, the job of research in mass communications is to determine who, and with what intention, said what, to whom, and with what effects. (Rockefeller Archive Center, 1940d: 17; emphasis added)

The second memorandum, which appeared in October 1940, was much more sharply focused on the direct practical relevance of communication research to the affairs of state (Rockefeller Archive Center, 1940e). As it had become increasingly evident that the "emergency period" was going to be of long duration and that the United States could very likely be drawn into the conflict, the communications group began to reflect more seriously on how their initiative could gain public and governmental support. It was on the basis of support of this kind that their vision of an institutionalized agency coordinating communication could become a reality. These considerations likely account for the shift away from technical and academic discourse toward a much more direct and accessible form of expression. Originally, the group had planned to assemble several documents from the seminar and circulate them to a wider audience. However, "the problems of national defense have become so urgent that it was agreed that a briefer statement would be of interest." Nevertheless, the group pointed out that the "general remarks" of the memorandum "are fortified at all points by the more technical material that was considered by the conferees" (Rockefeller Archive Center, 1940e: 1).

The opening paragraph of the document made its intent clear:

Facts, not now available, are urgently needed to provide a basis for more effective communication. Second, that the means of getting the needed facts are ready at hand. Third, that getting them must be closely geared to making communication more effective. It recommends that the work of getting them be begun at once. (Rockefeller Archive Center, 1940e: 1)

The communication in question was that which took place between the government and the people. It was through new forms of research, the group stated repeatedly, that communication between government and the people could be developed as a genuine two-way process. At face value, the memorandum appears to advocate a dialogical model of communication, as based on new research initiatives and findings. However, when it is examined more closely, a much different conception of the relation between government and the public seems to have formed the basis for the group's proposals for the development of the field of communications. The memorandum took its point of departure from the "wider and wider responsibility for the welfare of the people" that events imposed on "our central government" (Rockefeller Archive Center, 1940e: 3). This involved the making of decisions "with a maximum of speed." These decisions, in turn, were communicated to the people along with proposals and explanations. In response, "from the people comes an answering stream of counter-proposal, explanation, and consent." The government then takes these into account "in final decision and administration." However, the memorandum stresses, "if this two-way process of communication does not function, democracy *is* endangered" (Rockefeller Archive Center, 1940e: 3).

As the group appeared to suggest, the course of recent events had caused strains in this process of communication, thereby imperiling democracy. It noted that "the pace of governmental decision in this country, particularly in foreign affairs and national defense, is outstripping that of explanation." This meant not only that "adequate explanation" did not reach the people affected by the decisions," but that "the gap between the government and the people is widening." Hence, there was a need to create more effective ways of communicating. The government required better ways of explaining its decisions and proposals to the people, and the people needed "better ways of explaining to the government how they feel themselves affected by its proposals or decisions" (Rockefeller Archive Center, 1940e: 4).

It was the group's contention that research was essential if this "two-way process" of communication was to be restored:

[F]irst, to supply facts needed to make explanation both prompt and adequate; and, second, to bring back from the people an equally prompt and adequate response. With such research, the present gap between the government and the people can be closed. The government can then exercise its wider responsibility without risking loss of confidence and impaired morale. The people then can sanction changes in their lives with the assurance that their government has taken their responses into account. (Rockefeller Archive Center, 1940e: 5)

According to the group, democracy depended on a two-way process of this kind. For if explanation by the government was to be effective, it "needed to get behind the opinions of the moment, and enable the people intelligently to consent or dissent" (Rockefeller Archive Center, 1940e:8). However, the democratic process "has been endangered in times of increased tension more by ignorance than by intention. Those responsible have lacked the knowledge that they needed to make democracy strong enough to meet new stress and strain. One means to strengthen it lies in such research as it is here described which gives them a factual basis for distinguishing between consent or dissent of the moment, and genuine agreement or justified objection" (Rockefeller Archive Center, 1940e: 15–16).

In this sense, "the widening gap between the government and the people will close only when that flow removes the feeling of being governed by remote control, and substitutes a feeling of belonging to something that is worth belonging to." Research, then, "can ensure the flow of communication that is vital to the democratic process." This gives it "an urgency which seems to justify any risk or possible misuse" (Rockefeller Archive Center, 1940e: 15).

Even as the memorandum concentrated on the domestic aspects of communication, it was already looking ahead to the role that communications could play if the United States were to enter the fray.

If . . . events force this country into a belligerent part in world politics, communications will have still other tasks, particularly that of conveying to the enemy countries information calculated to be effective in the winning of the war. Again, research will be essential, both for the process of communicating effectively with the people of the enemy countries, and for gauging their response. (Rockefeller Archive Center, 1940e: 16)

The memorandum concluded by examining how an initiative of communications research of this kind could be institutionalized. It stressed that "research can make its contributions promptly enough to be of practical use, if [it] is properly organized and coordinated. The next step is to mobilize existing facilities and personnel so that they may be ready and available." This would involve the following course of action:

The need is first, to mobilize research workers already competent to apply known and tested methods of research, and to recruit and train others who are qualified for training; second, to put into usable form the facts which earlier research has already made available; and third, to agree on assignment of responsibility for further research, in ways that assure the coordination of inquiry and continual pooling of results. (Rockefeller Archive Center, 1940e: 18)

As the memorandum stressed, work in communications justified planning in terms of these three steps. As it indicated through a concise inventory, considerable work was being done in various research centers.[17] It was emphasized that those who wrote the memorandum were prepared "at once to take these first two steps, if they are able to secure the help they need—cooperation from those concerned, and funds to meet the costs" (Rockefeller Archive Center, 1940e: 20).

In the view of the group, the research in question "can probably best be undertaken within the government." Nevertheless, research would take place outside the government as well. What was needed was the "definite assignment of responsibility." This called for the formation of a central authority or agency charged with organizing and monitoring research initiatives in communications.

The ideal organization and coordination would be through some central agency, perhaps an institute of research in communication, within the government or outside it, similar to the national institutes for research in economics, which would, in assigning responsibility, ensure the comparability of findings, and their pooling in some central formulation and reporting. (Rockefeller Archive Center, 1940e: 21)

This suggested a "central institute or council for research, with local or regional offices across the country, so placed as to have ready access to representative samples of the population" (Rockefeller Archive Center, 1940e: 22). In conclusion, the signers of the memorandum appealed to its readers "to consider in severely practical terms what organization of the research it outlines will be most advantageous." They emphasized that they and other communications researchers would be "quick to do what they know they can, when others who recognize the need for their contribution are ready to help in making it of use" (Rockefeller Archive Center, 1940e: 22).

TOWARD COMMUNICATION INTELLIGENCE

Of those who signed the memorandum, it was Lasswell and Marshall who took the initiative in seeking support for the development of an agency responsible for coordinating research in communications. They met on October 2, 1940, to discuss the next steps that could be taken. It was decided that Lasswell and Cantril would organize a conference on research in communications "based probably on the memorandum in communications" that had been produced by the seminar of the previous year. The purpose of the conference followed closely from the proposals developed in the final two memoranda. A list of people qualified to direct communications research would be compiled. A plan for putting the "available knowledge of communications" in a form that would be "useable for present purposes" was to be developed. Finally, an effort would be made to reach agreement on "how responsibility for various phases of research can be assigned." Marshall told Lasswell that the Rockefeller Foundation would be able to support the meeting through its conference funds (Marshall, 1940b: October 2).

The Conference on Communication Research took place on January 18, 1941, at the Princeton Club. It brought together "specialists in communication research"[18] with "representatives of various government agencies with a present or potential interest in the results of such research."[19] After providing an overview of the various types of research in communication, Lasswell claimed that its results might be called "communication intelligence," analogous to "military intelligence." A number of the communications specialists then summed up their ongoing research and indicated the procedures that were used.

The representatives of government agencies made it clear that they were in need of the findings that communications researchers could offer. James McCamy noted that he had been "soaking up" the data reported because it was precisely what "he and his associates sorely needed." He added that there was almost a "'dangerous lack of facts' of this kind which are needed as a basis for policy formation." Saul Padower supported McCamy's remarks, stating that "with no means of predicting public response, decisions have to be made by guess and b'gorry." James Allen discussed the resistance in Washington by executive agencies to studies of public opinion. Luther Evans remarked that the Library of Congress had sought to make members of Congress aware of their inadequate information on the state of public opinion. Kenneth Kane described how the Department of Justice had begun to study current communication in order to determine when foreign government agents had not been registered with the State Department (Marshall, 1941: January 18).

Overall, it was felt that there was a need to "find some way of making available to government agencies findings arrived at by agencies outside the government." Evans reported that the Library of Congress had begun to move more in this direction with an expanded information service. It was also considering how it could help to pool research findings. Marshall raised the issue of the need to avoid duplication in research between the government and external agencies, but he was not able to get a clear answer from the government officials who were present. During informal exchanges following the conference, "more was said about the desirability for organizing and coordinating communication research and for pooling findings in a way that would make them promptly available. One possibility was that a government committee be set up which would operate much as do the other research committees of the National Defense Council" (Marshall, 1941: January 18). A few days later, Lasswell told Marshall that the government representatives at the conference all believed there was a need for "the development of research under government auspices" and that the duplication of effort would be avoided as a result of the conference (Marshall, 1941: January 20).

A valuable outcome of the conference, Marshall noted in his diary, was that it had given him access to numerous people working in government agencies who believed that research in communications was needed. In a visit to Washington to attend a conference on "Morale and Communication Research" on January 29, 1941, he met with some of these officials again. In talks with the Federal Communications Commission and the Department of Justice, particularly, he explained the kind of communications research that the Foundation would consider supporting, and he "expressed his hope that his contacts in these agencies would help him in avoiding any duplication with government activities." He also discussed the possibility that an agency coordinating research could be established. There was some agreement that this function might best be served by the Library of Congress, possibly through Lasswell's newly created office there (Marshall, 1941: January 29).

Over the next months, strategies for cooperation between government agencies began to take shape. Both the Neutrality Bureau of the Department of Justice and the Federal Communications Commission had made plans for the study of wartime communications. These provided for "advisors, drawn from private research," who would not only take part in governmental research but "relate to it the findings of non-governmental investigation." Marshall noted:

Eventually these advisors might become an advisory committee which among other things would assure the articulation and full exploitation of the findings of the two agencies—the Department of Justice dealing with print and film, and the FCC with radio. It was further agreed that the RF could serve a useful function by enabling qualified alien investigators . . . who cannot be directly employed by the government, to continue in related research. Finally, it was pointed out that the government is not yet able to undertake studies of the effects of communications analyzed, and that accordingly, the Foundation might well wish to consider support for such work to complement what the government can do. (Marshall, 1941: March 20)

This complementary function accurately describes the role that the Humanities Division of the Rockefeller Foundation had came to assume, largely through the initiatives of John Marshall, in relation to the linkage between communications research and the policy process. Initially, through its support and sponsorship of radio research, it sought to address a critical policy issue arising from the 1934 Communications Act, namely the reconciliation of educational and commercial broadcasting (see Buxton, 1993b). When this problem was no longer a matter of concern, it turned its attention more generally toward helping build the foundations for research in mass communications, largely through the vehicle of the Princeton Radio

Research Project. This initiative, in turn, provided the basis for addressing the broader question of how research could help facilitate better communications between policymakers and the public. To this end, it was instrumental in the consolidation of a "communications group" sharing a common concern to generate research of practical relevance to building public consent to new lines of policy made necessary by the "emergency period." This was carried out not only through the provision of financial support and organizational resources but also through sustained and focused intellectual guidance.

Once the network of communications specialists had been consolidated, the Rockefeller Foundation turned its attention to the problem of how the equivalent of this body—taking the form of a coordinator of communications—could be institutionalized. In the same way that it had earlier brought educators together with commercial broadcasters, it now sought to bring together communication researchers and members of the policy community. At the same time, it continued to support projects directed toward "process research," with a view to generating more effective communication intelligence. At all stages of the process, the guiding direction of John Marshall was in evidence. In this sense, Marshall's chart provides us with a much richer and more compelling understanding of the origins of communications studies than does Lasswell's better-known formula.

ACKNOWLEDGMENTS

I wish to thank the Rockefeller Archive Center for giving me permission to quote from material in its collection. This chapter has been written with the support of a research grant from the Social Science and Humanities Research Council of Canada. I am grateful to Charles Ackland for his comments on a draft of this chapter.

NOTES

1. Lazarsfeld had used the phrase "who listens to what, why, and with what effect" the previous year in describing the tasks of radio research. He claims to have come across it in an unspecified document (Lazarsfeld 1938a: 1).

2. He was referring to film, radio, and print.

3. This may have been the first time that the term "mass communication" was used in an analytical way.

4. This initiative was intended to diffuse the tension between educational broadcasters and commercial broadcasters in the aftermath of the Communications Act of 1934. Prior to the passage of the Act, educators and supporters of non-commercial broadcasting had lobbied to have a fixed portion of the airwaves reserved for educational broadcasting. However, their efforts failed; the 1934 Act supported the principle that broadcasting was to be primarily privately owned and commercial in nature.

5. The three broadcasters chosen were Frederic Willis, assistant to the president, Columbia Broadcasting System; James Baldwin, executive director of the National Association of Broadcasters; and John Royal, vice-president in charge of operations, National Broadcasting System. The three educators were W.W. Charters of Ohio State University; Levering Tyson of Columbia University; and Hadley Cantril.

6. Indeed, Lazarsfeld had little interest in mass communications per se; he apparently saw the Princeton Radio Research Project as a useful vehicle for developing new forms of methodology. As he informed David Morrison in an interview, "Look, you have to understand that I had no interest whatsoever in mass communications. I mean everything in a way is interesting to a methodologist, but I certainly didn't find that in the beginning an important topic at all. It was exclusively that it was rather a spectacular job" (Lazarsfeld, quoted in Morrison, 1978: 349).

7. This group included "The Panel as a Tool in Listener Research," "Statistical Methods as Applied to Radio Research," "Handbook of Listener Research," and "Measurement Techniques" (Rockefeller Archive Center, 1938b: 2).

8. These included "The Art of Asking Why," "Radio Commentators," "Music on the Air," and "Radio and Reading" (Rockefeller Archive Center, 1938b: 2).

9. The publishers were Henry Holt and Company, McGraw-Hill Publishing Company, and John Wiley and Sons.

10. The members of the committee were Irvin Stewart, Douglas Waples, Davidson Taylor, Harold Lasswell, R.L. La Piere, Lyman Bryson, Gilbert Seldes, James Angell, and Robert Lynd.

11. Yet in a review of Rockefeller involvement in radio written shortly after the Princeton Project was approved, Marshall included the Project as one of those that was involved in "educational and public service." He noted that the "anticipated outcomes" of projects of this kind included the "development of research procedures that will set new standards in evaluating broadcasting's educational and cultural contributions" and "the development of a more explicit appreciation of broadcasting's opportunities and responsibilities for education and public service on the part of the industry and non-profit agencies concerned with broadcasting" (Rockefeller Archive Center, 1937c: 3).

12. That the prodding of the Rockefeller Foundation precipitated the writing of the book is evident in Lazarsfeld's foreword to it:

A series of investigations covering a rather wide range of problems was undertaken [by the Office of Radio Research]. One group of studies which seemed of obvious importance related radio to other media of communication such as newspapers and books. In June, 1939, when the first general progress report was due, these studies formed a natural unit for summary. The volume on "Radio and the Printed Page" in its present form grew out of discussion of this first report. (Lazarsfeld, 1940b: vii)

13. D.S. Freeman, editor of the *Richmond News Leader,* gave the work mixed reviews. Although he was pleased with the research it showed and the inclusion of material based on George Gallup's figures, he found the text "infernally verbose" (Freeman, 1939). Marshall agreed with Freeman that the manuscript was "verbose in the extreme," and he added that this problem needed to be remedied, "if the monograph is to get any adequate publication." A.G. Crane, president of the University of Wyoming, evidently found it to be a "valuable job" (Marshall, 1939d).

14. I could find no record of this book's publication.

15. The regular seminar participants were Charles Siepmann, Lyman Bryson, Lloyd Free, Geoffrey Gorer, Harold Lasswell, Robert Lynd, Donald Slesinger, Douglas Waples, Paul Lazarsfeld, and John Marshall. In addition, R.J. Havighurst, Stacy May, I.A. Richards, and David H. Stevens took part in the discussions (Rockefeller Archive Center, 1940d).

16. These included the Cantril, Doob-Zinn-Child, Lazarsfeld, and Lasswell-Gorer research proposals for studies of public opinion (Rockefeller Archive Center, 1939e), Douglas Waples's project on reading (Waples, 1940), I.A. Richards's memorandum on content (Rockefeller Archive Center, 1940b), the studies of Slesinger and Gorer "on the movies as a medium of mass communication" (Rockefeller Archive Center, 1940c), and, finally, the "lists of social changes" that Lynd and Bryson believed to be desirable (Rockefeller Archive Center, 1940c: 6; see also Lynd, 1940).

17. Many of these were under the umbrella of Rockefeller-sponsored projects. These included the annotated bibliography written in 1935 for the Social Science Research Council (Lasswell, Smith, and Casey, 1935); the development of polling under Gallup and the Institute of Public Opinion; the *Fortune* poll under Elmo Wilson; the *Public Opinion Quarterly*; the work of the Graduate Library School at Chicago and the Columbia University Office of Radio Research; the Public Opinion Research Project at Princeton; and the Princeton Listening Center.

18. A number of the researchers (Lasswell, Cantril, Bryson, Lazarsfeld, Slesinger, Waples, and Harwood Childs of Princeton) who came to the conference had taken part in the seminar of the previous year. The others who took part were Weinberg (Professor of History at Johns Hopkins), Pendleton Herring (Department of Government, Harvard), and Ralph Casey (University of Minnesota School of Journalism).

19. The government representatives present were James McCamy (assistant to the secretary of agriculture), Saul K. Padower (assistant to the secretary of the interior), James Allen (assistant to the attorney general), Kenneth Kane (director of the Neutrality Bureau of the Department of Justice), David Lloyd (Federal Communications Commission), Lieutenant-Commander Galvin of the Navy Department, and Luther Evans (assistant general administrator of the Library of Congress).

References

Adkin, L.E. (1992). "Counter-Hegemony and Environmental Politics in Canada." In W.K. Carroll (ed.), *Organizing Dissent: Contemporary Social Movements in Theory and Practice*, pp. 135–56. Toronto: Garamond Press.

Agh, A. (1990a). "The Emergence of the Science of Democracy in Hungary and Its Impact on the Democratic Transition." Paper presented at the Conference of the International Committee for the Study of the Development of Political Science, Barcelona, May 14–20.

———. (1990b). "Transition to Democracy in Central Europe: A Comparative View." Paper presented at the first meeting of the U.S.-Hungarian Roundtable in Political Science, San Francisco, August 28–29.

Alger, C., and G. Lyons. (1974). "Social Science as a Transnational System: Report of a Seminar." *International Studies Notes* 1, no. 3: 1–13.

Almond, G.A. (1988). "The Return of the State." *American Political Science Review* 82: 853–74.

Althusser, L. (1971). *Lenin and Philosophy*. London: New Left Books.

Antonio, R. (1980). "Review of Mlynar, Nightfrost in Prague." *Telos* 44: 233–39.

Archibald, Clinton. (1984). "Corporatist Tendencies in Quebec." In Alain-G. Gagnon (ed.), *Quebec: State and Society,* 1st ed., pp. 353–64. Toronto: Methuen.

Aronowitz, S. (1992). *The Politics of Identity: Class, Culture, Social Movements*. New York: Routledge, Chapman and Hall.

Aronson, Jonathan. (1988). "Negotiating to Launch Negotiations: Getting Trade in Services onto the GATT Agenda." Pittsburgh: Pew Program in Case Teaching and Writing in International Affairs.

Ashley, W. (1970). "Philanthropy and Government: A Study of the Ford Foundation's Overseas Activities." Unpublished Ph.D. dissertation. New York: New York University.

Atkinson, M.M., and W.D. Coleman. (1989a). "Strong States and Weak States: Sectoral Policy Networks in Advanced Industrial Nations." *British Journal of Political Science* 19: 46–67.

———. (1989b). *The State, Business, and Industrial Change.* Toronto: University of Toronto Press.

———. (1992). "Policy Networks, Policy Communities and the Problems of Governance." *Governance* 5, no. 2: 154–80.

Augelli, Enrico, and Craig Murphy. (1988). *America's Quest for Supremacy and the Third World: A Gramscian Analysis.* London: Pinter.

Bashevkin, S.B. (1985). *Toeing the Lines: Women and Party Politics in English Canada.* Toronto: University of Toronto Press.

Bauer, R.A., I. DeSola Pool, and L.A. Dexter. (1972). *American Business and Public Policy*, 2d ed. Chicago: Aldine.

Beard, Charles A. (1960). *An Economic Interpretation of the Constitution of the United States.* New York: MacMillan.

Beer, S. (1974). *The British Political System.* New York: Random House.

Benda, Julien. (1969). *The Treason of the Intellectuals* (translation of La trahison des clercs). New York: W.W. Norton.

Bentley, Arthur. (1908). *The Process of Government.* Chicago: University of Chicago Press.

Berelson, Bernard. (1959). "The State of Communication Research." *Public Opinion Quarterly* 23: 1–6.

Berger, S. (ed.). (1981). *Organizing Interests in Western Europe.* New York: Cambridge University Press.

Berlin, Isaiah. (1982). "Montesquieu." In *Against the Current: Essays in the History of Ideas*, pp. 130–61. New York: Penguin Books.

Bibic, A. (1979). "Political Science in Yugoslavia." Paper presented at the Eleventh IPSA World Congress, Moscow, August 12–18.

———. (1982). "Yugoslavia." In W.A. Andrews (ed.), *International Handbook of Political Science.* Westport, CT: Greenwood.

Bina, V. (1983). "Czech Sociology and Marxism-Leninism." *Mens en Maatschappij* 58, no. 1: 53–77.

Block, F. (1987). *Revising State Theory.* Philadelphia: Temple University Press.

Bloom, Allan. (1987). *The Closing of the American Mind.* New York: Simon and Schuster.

Boardman, R. (1992). "The Multilateral Dimension: Canada in the International System." In R. Boardman (ed.), *Canadian Environmental Policy: Ecosystems, Politics, and Process*, pp. 224–45. Toronto: Oxford University Press.

Bourdieu, P. (1984). *Homo academicus.* Paris: Les éditions de Minuit.

Bourne, L.S. (1988). "On the Role of University-Based Research Institutes: Reflections on the Institutional Environment of Research." In *Culture, Development and Regional Policy*, Canadian Issues, Vol. 9, pp. 177–83. Montreal: Association for Canadian Studies.

Bradford, N. (1994). *Creation and Constraint: Economic Ideas and Politics in Canada.* Unpublished dissertation, Carleton University, Ottawa.

Brady, Alexander. (1958). *Democracy in the Dominions: A Comparative Study in Institutions*, 3d ed. Toronto: University of Toronto Press.

Brecher, I. (1957). *Monetary and Fiscal Thought and Policy in Canada, 1919–1939.* Toronto: University of Toronto Press.

Bressand, Albert, and Kalypso Nicolaides (eds.). (1989). *Strategic Trends in Services: An Inquiry into the Global Service Economy.* New York: Harper and Row.

Brock, William E. (1982). "A Simple Plan for Negotiating on Trade in Services." *World Economy* 5, no. 3 (November).

Brodie, J., and J. Jenson (1988). *Crisis, Challenge and Change.* Ottawa: Carleton University Press.

Brooks, S. (1990). "The Market for Social Scientific Knowledge: The Case of Free Trade in Canada." In S. Brooks and A. Gagnon (eds.), *Social Scientists, Policy and the State.* New York: Praeger.

Brooks, S., and A. Gagnon. (1990a). "Politics and the Social Sciences in Canada." In A. Gagnon and J. Bickerton (eds.), *Canadian Politics: An Introduction to the Discipline.* Peterborough: Broadview Press.

——— (eds.). (1990b). *Social Scientists, Policy and the State.* New York: Praeger.

Brown, A. (1984). "Political Science in the Soviet Union: A New Stage of Development?" *Soviet Studies* 36, no. 3: 317–44.

———. (1987). "Eastern Europe's Western Connection." In L. Gordon (ed.), *Eroding Empire: Western Relations with Eastern Europe.* Washington, DC: Brookings.

Brym, Robert J. (1987). "The Political Sociology of Intellectuals: A Critique and a Proposal." In Alain-G. Gagnon (ed.), *Intellectuals in Liberal Democracies: Political Influence and Social Involvement.* New York: Praeger.

Brzezinski, Z. (1965). *Alternative to Partition.* New York: McGraw-Hill.

———. (1970). *Between Two Ages.* New York: Viking.

Buchstein, H., and G. Göhler. (1990). "After the Revolution: Political Science in East Germany." *Ps: Political Science and Politics* 23, no. 4: 668–73.

Bueckert, D. (1992). "Four Women's Groups Withdraw Support." *Ottawa Citizen*, August 1, p. A5.

Buxton, William. (1993a). "The Harvard Industrial Hazards Project, 1930–1943." *Rockefeller Archive Center Newsletter*, Spring, pp. 12–15.

———. (1993b). "The Political Economy of Communications Research: The Rockefeller Foundation, the 'Radio Wars' and the Princeton Radio Research Project." In Robert Babe (ed.), *Economy and Communications.* Dordrecht: Kluwer.

Cab 124/572. (n.d.). *Cabinet–Post War Agricultural Policy.* London: Public Records Office.

Cairns, A. (1988). "The Governments and Societies of Canadian Federalism." In D. Williams (ed.), *Constitution, Government, and Society in Canada.* Toronto: McClelland and Stewart.

———. (1990). "Constitutional Minoritarianism in Canada." In R.L. Watts and D.M. Brown (eds.), *Canada: The State of the Federation 1990*, pp. 71–96. Kingston: Institute of Intergovernmental Relations.

———. (1991). *Disruptions* (ed. Douglas Williams). Toronto: McClelland and Stewart.

Cameron, D. (1989). "Political Discourse in the Eighties." In A. Gagnon and B. Tanguay (eds.), *Canadian Parties in Transition: Discourse, Organization, Representation.* Toronto: Nelson.

Cameron, D., and D. Drache (1988). "Outside the Macdonald Commission: Reply to Richard Simeon." *Studies in Political Economy* 26 (Summer).

Campbell, J.C., et al. (1989). "Afterword on Policy Communities: A Framework for Comparative Research." *Governance* 2: 86–94.

Campbell, R. (1987). *Grand Illusions.* Peterborough: Broadview Press.

Campion, F.D. (1984). *The AMA and U.S. Health Policy since 1940.* Chicago: Chicago University Press.

Canadian Advisory Council on the Status of Women. (1989). *Canadian Charter Equality Rights for Women. One Step Forward or Two Steps Back?* Ottawa: Ministry of Supply and Services.

Canadian Forum. (1936). Vol. 16, no. 184 (May).

Cantril, Hadley. (1937). "Project I." RF. RG 1.1. Series 200. Box 271. Folder 3234. Rockefeller Archive Center.

———. (1940). *The Invasion of Mars: A Study in the Psychology of Panic.* Princeton: Princeton University Press.

Carson, Rachel. (1962). *Silent Spring.* Boston: Houghton Mifflin.

Cawson, Alan. (1985). "Varieties of Corporatism: The Importance of the Meso-Level of Interest Intermediation," and "Conclusion: Some Implications for State Theory." In Alan Cawson (ed.), *Organized Interests and the State: Studies in Meso-Corporatism,* pp. 1–21, 221–26. Beverly Hills, CA: Sage.

Chomsky, Noam, and Edward Herman. (1988). *Manufacturing Consent: The Political Economy of the Mass Media.* New York: Pantheon Books.

Clarke, H., et al. (1991). *Absent Mandate.* Toronto: Gage.

Clark-Jones, M. (1987). *A Staples State.* Toronto: University of Toronto Press.

Coates, D. (1989). *The Crises of Labour: Industrial Relations and the State in Contemporary Britain.* Oxford: Phillip Allen.

Cohen, Jean L. (1982). *Class and Civil Society: The Limits of Marxian Critical Theory.* Amherst: University of Massachusetts Press.

———. (1985). "Strategy or Identity: New Theoretical Paradigms and Contemporary Social Movements." *Social Research* 52, no. 4 (Winter): 663–715.

Cohen, S.D. (1988). *The Making of United States International Economic Policy,* 3d ed. New York: Praeger.

Coleman, William D., and Grace Skogstad (eds.). (1990). *Policy Communities and Public Policy in Canada: A Structuralist Approach.* Mississauga: Copp Clark Pitman Ltd.

Commoner, B. (1966). *Science and Survival.* New York: Viking.

———. (1972). *The Closing Circle.* New York: Bantam.

Cox, Robert W. (1979). "Ideologies and the New International Economic Order: Reflections on Some Recent Literature." *International Organization* 33, no. 2 (Spring): 257–302.

———. (1983). "Gramsci, Hegemony and International Relations: An Essay in Method." *Millennium: Journal of International Studies* 12, no. 2: 162–75.

———. (1986). "Social Forces, States and World Orders: Beyond International Relations Theory." In Robert O. Keohane (ed.), *NeoRealism and Its Critics.* New York: Columbia University Press.

———. (1987). *Production, Power and World Order: Social Forces in the Making of History.* New York: Columbia University Press.

Critchlow, Donald T. (1984). "Brookings: The Man and the Institution." *Review of Politics* 46, no. 4 (October): 561–81.

Dahl, R. (1961). "The Behavioral Approach in Political Science: Epitaph for a Monument to a Successful Protest." *American Political Science Review* 55, no. 4: 763–72.

Daub, M. (1984–1985). "A History of Canadian Economic Forecasting." *Journal of Business Administration* 15.

DeFleur, Melvin L., and Sandra Ball-Rokeach. (1975). *Theories of Mass Communication,* 4th ed. New York: Longman.

Destler, I.M. (1986). *American Trade Politics: System under Stress.* Washington, DC: Institute for International Economics.

Diani, M. (1992). "The Concept of Social Movement." *Sociological Review* 40, no. 1: 1–25.

Doern, G.B. (1992a). "Johnny-Green-Latelies: The Mulroney Environmental Record." In F. Abele (ed.), *How Ottawa Spends 1992–93: The Politics of Competitiveness*, pp. 353–76. Ottawa: Carleton University Press.

———. (1992b). *The Greening of Canada: Twenty Years of Environmental Policy*. Unpublished report prepared for the Department of Environment, Ottawa.

Dyson, Kenneth. (1980). *The State Tradition in Western Europe: A Study of an Idea and Institution*. Oxford: Martin Robertson.

Easton, David. (1965). *A Systems Analysis of Political Life*. New York: Wiley.

Ehrensaft, P., and W. Armstrong. (1981). "The Formation of Dominion Capitalism." In A. Moscovitch and G. Drover (eds.), *Inequality: Essays on the Political Economy of Social Welfare*. Toronto: University of Toronto Press.

Engelbrekt, K. (1990). "The Waning of Communist Ideology." *Report on Eastern Europe*, July 27, pp. 5–8.

English, H.E. (1991). *Tomorrow the Pacific*. Toronto: C.D. Howe Research Institute.

Esping-Andersen, G. (1985). *Politics against Markets*. Princeton: Princeton University Press.

Evans, Peter B., Dietrich Rueschemeyer, and Theda Skocpol. (1985). "On the Road toward a More Adequate Understanding of the State." In Peter B. Evans, Dietrich Rueschemeyer, and Theda Skocpol (eds.), *Bringing the State Back In*, pp. 347–66. Cambridge: Cambridge University Press.

Eyerman, R., and A. Jamison. (1991). *Social Movements: A Cognitive Approach*. Cambridge: Polity Press.

Faudemay, Marie-Pierre. (1989). "The OECD Testing of the Conceptual Framework." Paper prepared for an information-sharing session organized by the Centre for Applied Studies in International Negotiation (CASIN), 20 October 1989.

Faulkner, J.H. (1982). "Pressing the Executive." *Canadian Public Administration* 25, no. 2: 240–54.

Federation of European Accountants (FEE). (1990). *The Impact of the Uruguay Round Services Negotiations on the Accountancy Profession*. Proceedings from meeting held February 1–2, Vevey, Switzerland. Brussels: FEE.

Feketekuty, Geza. (1988). *International Trade in Services: An Overview and Blueprint for Negotiations*. Washington, DC: American Enterprise Institute/Ballinger.

Feldstein, P.J. (1988). *The Politics of Health Regulation*. Ann Arbor: University of Michigan Press.

Fischer, G. (1964). *Science and Politics: The New Sociology in the Soviet Union*. Ithaca: Cornell University.

Fisher, D. (1980). "American Philanthropy and the Social Sciences: The Reproduction of a Conservative Ideology." In R. Arnove (ed.), *Philanthropy and Cultural Imperialism*. Boston: G.K. Hall.

Ford Foundation. (1990). *Current Interests of the Ford Foundation 1990 and 1991*. New York: Ford Foundation.

Fosdick, R. (1952). *The Story of the Rockefeller Foundation*. New York: Harper & Brothers.

Fowler, R. (1940). "Design for a New Dominion." *Maclean's Magazine,* January 8.

Freeman, D.C. (1939). "Letter to John Marshall. 3 July." RF. RG 1.1. Series 200. Box 272. Folder 3241. Rockefeller Archive Center.

French, R. (1984). *How Ottawa Decides*. Toronto: James Lorimer.

Friedan, B. (1963). *The Feminine Mystique*. New York: Dell.

Furet, François. (1978). *Penser la révolution française*. Paris: Editions Gallimard.

Gagnon, A. (1989). "Social Scientists and Public Policies." In *International Social Sciences Journal* 122, no. 4: 555–67.

Gagnon, Alain (ed.). (1987). *Intellectuals in Liberal Democracies*. New York: Praeger.

Gamson, W.A. (1991). "Commitment and Agency in Social Movements." *Sociological Forum* 6, no. 1: 27–50.

Geertz, Clifford. (1983). *Local Knowledge: Further Essays in Interpretive Anthropology*. New York: Basic Books.

Geiger, R. (1988). "American Foundations and Academic Social Science, 1945–1960." *Minerva* 26, no. 3: 315–41.

General Agreement on Tariffs and Trade, Group of Negotiations on Services. (1989). "Trade in Professional Services: Note by the Secretariat." MTN.GNS/W/67, 25 August 1989.

Genov, N. (1984). "Research Problems in the Area of Social Activity and Social Systems." *Sociologicky Casopis* 20, no. 2: 208–13.

Gerth, H., and C.W. Mills (eds.). (1958). *From Max Weber: Essays in Sociology*. New York: Oxford University Press.

Giarini, Orio (ed.). (1987). *The Emerging Service Economy*. New York: Pergamon.

Giddens, A. (1986). *The Constitution of Society*. Oxford: Polity Press.

Gill, Stephen. (1990). *American Hegemony and the Trilateral Commission*. Cambridge: Cambridge University Press.

Gill, Stephen, and David Law. (1988). *The Global Political Economy: Perspectives, Problems and Policies*. New York: Harvester.

Godber, G. (1988). "Forty Years of the NHS." *British Medical Journal* 297: 37–43.

Goldstein, J. (1988). "Ideas, Institutions and American Trade Policy." In G.J. Ikenberry, D.A. Lake, and M. Mastanduno (eds.), *The State and American Foreign Economic Policy*. Ithaca and London: Cornell University Press.

Goldthorpe, John H. (1984). "The End of Convergence: Corporatism and Dualist Tendencies in Modern Western Societies." In John H. Goldthorpe (ed.), *Order and Conflict in Contemporary Capitalism: Studies in the Political Economy of Western European Nations,* pp. 315–43. Oxford: Oxford University Press.

Goranov, K. (1986). "Political Relations in the Stage of Accomplishment of the Development of Socialism." Sofia: Partizdat.

Gordon, L. (ed.). (1987). *Eroding Empire: Western Relations with Eastern Europe*. Washington, DC: Brookings Institution.

Gorer, Geoffrey. (1940). "Content Classification." RF. RG 1.1. Series 200. Box 224. Folder 2678. Rockefeller Archive Center.

Gouldner, Alvin. (1970). *The Coming Crises of Western Sociology*. New York: Basic Books.

Gourevitch, P. (1986). *Politics in Hard Times*. Ithaca: Cornell University Press.

———. (1989). "Keynesian Politics: The Political Sources of Economic Policy Choices." In P. Hall (ed.), *The Political Power of Economic Ideas*. Princeton: Princeton University Press.

Gourevitch, P., et al. (1984). *Unions and Economic Crisis: Britain, West Germany and Sweden*. London: Allen & Unwin.

Gramsci, A. (1971). *Selections from the Prison Notebooks*. New York: International Publishers.

Granatstein, J.L. (1982). *The Ottawa Men*. Toronto: University of Toronto Press.

Grant, W.P., and S. Wilks. (1983). "British Industrial Policy: Structural Change, Policy Inertia." *Journal of Public Policy* 3: 13–28.

Grant, W.P., W. Paterson, and C. Whitson. (1988). *Government and the Chemical Industry.* Oxford: Clarendon.

Gray, C. (1988). "Why Can't Women Get Their Act Together?" *Chatelaine* 61, no. 11: 82–83, 232–34, 238–40.

Grigorov, K. (1968). "Modern Bourgeois Sociological Theories about the Economic Cycles." Sofia: BAN.

Gruchin, B., and V. Zamochkin. (1972). "Yesterday, Today, and Tomorrow: Remarks about the Seventh World Congress of Sociology." *American Sociologist* 17: 17–20.

Gustafsson, B. (1973). "Review Article—A Perennial of Doctrinal History and the Stockholm School." *Economy and History* 16: 114–28.

Gyorgy, S. (1988). "Theoretical Questions of the Socialist State and the Challenge of Democracy." Paper presented at the IPSA World Congress, Washington, DC, August 28–September 1.

Habermas, J. (1972). *Knowledge and Human Interests.* London: Heinemann.

Habermas, Jurgen. (1991). *The Structural Transformation of the Public Sphere* (trans. Thomas Burger). Cambridge, MA: MIT Press.

Hall, Peter A. (1986). *Governing the Economy: The Politics of State Intervention in Britain and France.* Cambridge: Polity Press.

——— (ed.). (1989). *The Political Power of Economic Ideas.* Princeton: Princeton University Press.

———. (1990). "Policy Paradigms, Experts and the State: The Case of Macroeconomic Policy Making in Britain." In Stephen Brooks and Alain-G. Gagnon (eds.), *Social Scientists, Policy and the State*, pp. 53–78. New York: Praeger.

Hamilton, M. (1989). *Democratic Socialism in Britain and Sweden.* Basingstoke: Macmillan Press.

Hansen, W.L. (1990). "The International Trade Commission and the Politics of Protectionism." *American Political Science Review* 84: 21–45.

Hardin, H. (1974). *A Nation Unaware: The Canadian Economic Culture.* Vancouver: J.J. Douglas.

Hartz, L. (1955). *The Liberal Tradition in America.* New York: Harcourt Brace Jovanovich.

Havighurst, C.C., R.B. Helms, C. Bladen, and M.V. Pauly. (1988). *American Health Care.* London: Institute of Economic Affairs.

Heclo, Hugh. (1974). *Modern Social Politics in Britain and Sweden.* New Haven: Yale University Press.

———. (1978). "Issue Networks and the Executive Establishment." In A. King (ed.), *The New American Political System*, pp. 87–124. Washington, DC: American Enterprise Institute for Public Policy Research.

Heclo, H., and H. Madsen. (1987). *Policy and Politics in Sweden.* Philadelphia: Temple University Press.

Hegedus, A. (1980). "Interview." *Telos,* no. 47: 132–37.

———. (1982). "Hungary in 1956." *Telos,* no. 53: 163–71.

Heinrich, E. (1992). "Recession Chills Out Green Groups." *Financial Post,* February 10, p. 8.

Held, D. (1991). "Between State and Civil Society: Citizenship." In G. Andrews (ed.), *Citizenship*, pp. 19–25. London: Lawrence and Wishart.

Hernes, Gudmund, and Arne Selvik. (1981). "Local Corporatism." In Suzanne Berger (ed.), *Organizing Interests in Western Europe: Pluralism, Corporatism, and the Transformation of Politics*, pp. 103–19. Cambridge: Cambridge University Press.

Higgins, W. (1985). "Ernst Wigforss: The Renewal of Social Democratic Theory and Practice." *Political Power and Social Theory* 5.

Hoberg, G. (1993). "Environmental Policy: Alternative Styles." In M. Atkinson (ed.), *Governing Canada: Institutions and Public Policy,* pp. 307–42. Toronto: Harcourt, Brace, Jovanovich.

Hodgetts, J. (1968). "Public Power and Ivory Tower." In T. Lloyd and J. Mcleod (eds.), *Agenda 1970: Proposals for a Creative Politics.* Toronto: University of Toronto Press.

Hollander, P. (1989). "Social Science and Social Problems in Hungary." *Society* 26, no. 2: 14–21.

Horowitz, G. (1968). *Canadian Labour in Politics.* Toronto: University of Toronto Press.

Horvat, B. (1979). "Some Political Preconditions for a Free Society." In R. Merritt (ed.), *International Political Science Enters the 1980s,* vol. 1. Abstracts of papers presented at the Eleventh World Congress of the International Political Science Association, Moscow, August 12–18, 1979. Oslo, Norway: International Political Science Association.

House of Commons. *Parliamentary Debates,* 5th Series, vol. 397, 25 February 1944.

Howard, R. (1991). "Reproductive Technology Commission Facing Lawsuit." *Globe and Mail,* November 30, p. A1.

Ikenberry, G.J. (1988). "Conclusion: An Institutional Approach to American Foreign Economic Policy." In G.J. Ikenberry, D.A. Lake, and M. Mastanduno (eds.), *The State and American Foreign Economic Policy.* Ithaca and London: Cornell University Press.

Ingham, G. (1974). *Strikes and Industrial Conflict.* London: MacMillan.

International Political Science Association. (n.d.). "Synthesis Report on the I.P.S.A. 20 Years Activities 1949–1969." Oslo, Norway: International Political Science Association.

Iribadjakov, N. (1960). "'Modern' Critics of Marxism." Sofia: Partizdat.

Jamison, A., R. Eyerman, J. Cramer, and J. Laessoe. (1991). *The Making of the New Environmental Consciousness: A Comparative Study of the Environmental Movement in Sweden, Denmark and the Netherlands.* Edinburgh: Edinburgh University Press.

Jan Hus Educational Foundation. (1990). *Report.* London: Jan Hus Educational Foundation.

Jenkins, J.C. (1983). "Resource Mobilization Theory and the Study of Social Movements." *Annual Review of Sociology* 9: 527–54.

Jenson, J. (1986). "Gender and Reproduction: Or, Babies and the State." *Studies in Political Economy* 20 (Summer).

———. (1989). "'Different' But Not 'Exceptional': Canada's Permeable Fordism." *Canadian Review of Sociology and Anthropology,* Winter.

———. (1990). "Representations in Crisis: The Roots of Canada's Permeable Fordism." *Canadian Journal of Political Science* 23, no. 4: 653–84.

———. (1991). "All the World's a Stage: Ideas, Spaces and Times in Canadian Political Economy." *Studies in Political Economy* 36 (Fall): 43–72.

———. (1992a). "Citizenship Claims: Routes to Representation in a Federal System." Paper presented to the Federalism and the Nation State Conference, University of Toronto.

———. (1992b). "Naming Nations: Nationalisms in Canadian Public Discourse." Paper presented to the Workshop on Culture and Social Movements, University of California, San Diego.

Jessop, B. (1990). *State Theory.* Oxford: Polity Press.

Jhappan, R. (1992). "A Global Community? Supranational Strategies of Canada's Aboriginal Peoples." Paper presented to the Canadian Political Science Association, University of Prince Edward Island.

Jordan, A.G. (1990). "Sub-Governments, Policy Communities and Networks." *Journal of Theoretical Politics* 2, no. 3: 319–38.

Jordan, A.G., and J.J. Richardson. (1982). "The British Policy Style or the Logic of Negotiation?" In J.J. Richardson (ed.), *Policy Style in Western Europe*. London: George Allen and Unwin.

———. (1987). *Government and Pressure Groups in Britain*. Oxford: Clarendon.

Jordan, A.G., and K. Schubert. (1992). "A Preliminary Ordering of Policy Network Labels." *European Journal of Political Research* 21: 7–28.

Journal of Applied Psychology. (1939). Vol. 23, no. 1 (February), "Special Issue on Radio Research."

Katzenstein, Peter J. (1978). "Conclusion: Domestic Structures and Strategies of Foreign Economic Policy." In P. Katzenstein (ed.), *Between Power and Plenty: Foreign Economic Policies of Advanced Industrial States*, pp. 295–336. Madison: University of Wisconsin Press.

———. (1985). *Small States in World Markets: Industrial Policy in Europe*. Ithaca and London: Cornell University Press.

———. (1987). *Policy and Politics in West Germany: The Growth of a Semi-Sovereign State*. Philadelphia: Temple University Press.

Kaulbars, M. (1992). "The Movement That Never Was." *CEN Bulletin* 2, no. 4. Ottawa: Canadian Environmental Network.

Keane, John. (1988). "Introduction" and "Despotism and Democracy." In John Keane (ed.), *Civil Society and the State*, pp. 1–31, 35–71. London: Verso.

Kent, T. (1958). "The Gordon Commission." *Winnipeg Free Press*, Editorial Series, April–May.

Keohane, R.A. (1984). *After Hegemony: Cooperation and Discord in the World Political Economy*. Princeton: Princeton University Press.

Kingdon, John. (1984). *Agendas, Alternatives, and Public Policies*. Boston: Little Brown.

Kitschelt, H. (1990). "The Medium Is the Message: Democracy and Oligarchy in Belgian Ecology Parties." In W. Rüdig (ed.), *Green Politics One*. Edinburgh: Edinburgh University Press.

Klandermans, B., and S. Tarrow. (1988). "Mobilization into Social Movements: Synthesizing European and American Approaches." *International Social Movement Research* 1: 1–38.

Klingemann, H.D. (1991). "Developing Research Projects in Central and Eastern Europe." *Participation* 15, no. 1: 8–9.

Konrad, G., and I. Szelenyi. (1979). *Intellectuals on the Road to Class Power*. Brighton: Harvester.

Krasner, S.D. (1978). "United States Commercial and Monetary Policy: Unravelling the Paradox of External Strength and Internal Weakness." In P.J. Katzenstein (ed.), *Between Power and Plenty*. Madison: University of Wisconsin Press.

Krauss, Melvyn B. (1984). "'Europeanizing' the U.S. Economy: The Enduring Appeal of the Corporatist State." In Chalmers Johnson (ed.), *The Industrial Policy Debate*, pp. 71–90. San Francisco: Institute for Contemporary Studies Press.

Kriesi, H. (1988). "The Interdependence of Structure and Action: Some Reflections on the State of the Art." *International Social Movement Research* 1: 349–68.

———. (1989). "New Social Movements and the New Class in the Netherlands." *American Journal of Sociology* 94, no. 5: 1078–116.

Krommenacker, Raymond J. (1984). *World-Traded Services: The Challenge for the 1980's*. Dedham, MA: Artech House.

Kuechler, M., and R.J. Dalton. (1991). "New Social Movements and the Political Order." In R.J. Dalton and M. Kuechler (eds.), *The Challenge of New Movements*, pp. 277–99. Oxford: Oxford University Press.

Laclau, E., and C. Mouffe. (1985). *Hegemony and Socialist Strategy*. London: New Left Books.

Lamontagne, M. (1954). "The Role of Government." In G.P. Gilmour (ed.), *Canada's Tomorrow*. Toronto: Macmillan.

Langille, David. (1987). "The Business Council on National Issues and the Canadian State." *Studies in Political Economy* 24 (Autumn): 41–85.

Lapidus, G. (1980). "Patterns of Daily Life." *IREX Occasional Papers* 1, no. 4.

Lash, S., and J. Urry. (1987). *The End of Organized Capitalism*. Cambridge: Polity Press.

Lasswell, Harold. (1940). "Who Communicates." RF. RG 1.1. Box 224. Folder 2678. Rockefeller Archive Center.

———. (1948). "The Structure and Function of Communication in Society." In Lymon Bryson (ed.), *The Communication of Ideas*, pp. 35–51. New York: Harper and Brothers.

Lasswell, Harold, B. Smith, and R. Casey. (1935). *Propaganda and Promotional Activities: An Annotated Bibliography*. Minneapolis: University of Minnesota Press.

Latham, Earl. (1956). "The Group Basis of Politics: Notes for a Theory." In Heinz Eulau, Samuel Eldersveld, and Morris Janowitz (eds.), *Political Behaviour: A Reader in Theory and Research*. Glencoe, IL: Free Press.

Laumann, E.O., and Knoke, D. (1987). *The Organizational State*. Madison: University of Wisconsin Press.

Laxer, G. (1989). *Open for Business*. Toronto: Oxford University Press.

Lazarsfeld, Paul F. (1938a). "Letter to the Committee of Six. 7 November." RF. RG 1.1. Series 200. Box 271. Folder 3236. Rockefeller Archive Center.

———. (1938b). "Princeton Radio Research Project." RF. RG 1.1. Series 200. Box 271. Folder 3236. Rockefeller Archive Center.

———. (1939). "Letter to John Marshall. 29 August." RF. RG 1.1. Series 200. Box 272. Folder 3241. Rockefeller Archive Center.

———. (1940a). "Notes on Audience Research." RF. RG 1.1. Series 200. Box 224. Folder 2678. Rockefeller Archive Center.

———. (1940b). *Radio and the Printed Page*. New York: Duell, Sloan and Pearce.

Lehmbruch, Gerhard. (1979). "Liberal Corporatism and Party Government." In P. Schmitter and G. Lehmbruch (eds.), *Trends toward Corporatist Intermediation*, pp. 147–83. Beverly Hills, CA: Sage.

Leiss, William. (1991). "The 1990 Southam Lecture: On the Vitality of Our Discipline— New Applications of Communications Theory." *Canadian Journal of Communication* 16: 291–305.

Lindblom, Charles. (1977). *Politics and Markets*. New York: Basic Books.

Lindquist, E.A. (1990). "The Third Community, Policy Inquiry, and Social Scientists." In S. Brooks and A.-G. Gagnon (eds.), *Social Scientists, Policy and the State*, pp. 21–51. New York: Praeger.

———. (1991). "Confronting Globalization and Governance Challenges: Canadian Think Tanks and the Asia-Pacific Region." In J.W. Langford and K.L. Brownsey (eds.), *Think Tanks and Governance in the Asia-Pacific Region, pp. 189–213*. Halifax: Institute for Research on Public Policy.

———. (1992). "Public Managers and Policy Communities: Learning to Meet New Challenges." *Canadian Public Administration* 35, no. 2: 127–59.

Lippman, Walter. (1922). *Public Opinion*. London: Allen & Unwin.

Lipset, Seymour Martin. (1968). "Moisei Ostrogorski and the Analytical Approach to the Comparative Study of Political Parties." In *Revolution and Counterrevolution: Change and Persistence in Social Structures.* New York: Basic Books.

———. (1981). *Political Man*, expanded ed. Baltimore, MD: Johns Hopkins University Press.

Lobby Digest. (1990). "Women Power: How Wiener Got Roasted." Vol. 8, p. 5.

Lowery, Shearon, and Melvin L. DeFleur. (1975). *Milestones in Mass Communication*, 4th ed. New York: Longman.

Luers, W. (1987). "The United States and Eastern Europe." *Foreign Affairs* 65, no. 5: 976–94.

Lynd, Robert. (1940). "Desirable Social Changes to Be Researched On." Memorandum to the Communications Group, May 5. RF. RG 1.1. Series 200. Box 224. Folder 2678. Rockefeller Archive Center.

Macdonald, D. (1991). *The Politics of Pollution.* Toronto: McClelland and Stewart.

Mackintosh, W.A. (1948). "Trade and Fiscal Policy." In *Canada Looks Ahead.* Ottawa: Tower Books.

———. (1953). "Federal Finance." *Canadian Tax Journal* 1.

———. (1965). "The White Paper on Employment and Income in Its 1945 Setting." In *Canadian Economic Policy since the War.* Ottawa: Carleton University.

Magnusson, W., and R. Walker. (1988). "De-centring the State: Political Theory and Canadian Political Economy." *Studies in Political Economy* 26 (Summer).

Maheu, Louis. (1983). "Les mouvements de base et la lutte contre l'appropriation étatique du tissu social." *Sociologie et Sociétés* 15, no. 1: 77–92.

Maier, Charles. (1988). *The Unmasterable Past: History, Holocaust and German National Identity.* Cambridge, MA: Harvard University Press.

Mann, M. (1984). "The Autonomous Power of the State: Its Origins, Mechanisms and Results." *Archives Européennes de Sociologie* 25: 185–213.

Marmor, T. (1970). *The Politics of Medicare.* London: Routledge and Kegan Paul.

Marmor, T., J.L. Mashaw, and P.L. Harvey. (1990). *America's Misunderstood Welfare State.* New York: Basic Books.

Marschall, M. (1989). Interview. Keene, NH. July 22–23.

Marsh, D., and Rhodes, R.A.W. (1992). *Policy Networks and British Government.* Oxford: Oxford University Press.

Marshall, John. (1935). Officer's Diary. Rockefeller Foundation Archives. 905 MAR. Rockefeller Archive Center.

———. (1936a). Officer's Diary. Rockefeller Foundation Archives. 905 MAR. Rockefeller Archive Center.

———. (1936b). "Statement on Radio. June." RF. RG 3.1. Series 911. Box 5. Folder 51. Rockefeller Archive Center.

———. (1937). "Memorandum on Cantril's Proposal." RF. RG 1.1. Series 200. Box 271. Folder 3234. Rockefeller Archive Center.

———. (1939a). "Letter to A.G. Crane. 13 July." RF. RG 1.1. Series 200. Box 272. Folder 3241. Rockefeller Archive Center.

———. (1939b). "Letter to Frank Stanton. 12 July." RF. RG 1.1. Series 200. Box 272. Folder 3241. Rockefeller Archive Center.

———. (1939c). "Letter to Herbert Brucker. 21 November." RF. RG 1.1. Series 200. Box 272. Folder 3242. Rockefeller Archive Center.

———. (1939d). Officer's Diary. Rockefeller Foundation Archives. 905 MAR. Rockefeller Archive Center.

———. (1940a). "Introduction." RF. RG 1.1. Series 200. Box 224. Folder 2678. Rockefeller Archive Center.

———. (1940b). Officer's Diary. Rockefeller Foundation Archives. 905 MAR. Rockefeller Archive Center.

———. (1941). Officer's Diary. Rockefeller Foundation Archives. 905 MAR. Rockefeller Archive Center.

Martin, A. (1984). "Trade Unions in Sweden." In P. Gourevitch et al. (eds.), *Unions and Economic Crisis*. London: Allen & Unwin.

McDowell, Stephen D. (1991). "Gender and the Liberalization of Service Institutions." Paper delivered at the meeting of the International Studies Association, Vancouver, British Columbia, March.

Meadows, Dennis L., et al. (1972). *The Limits to Growth*. New York: New American Library.

Melucci, Alberto. (1985). "The Symbolic Challenge of Contemporary Movements." *Social Research* (Winter), pp. 789–818.

———. (1988). "Social Movements and the Democratization of Everyday Life." In John Keane (ed.), *Civil Society and the State: New European Perspectives*, pp. 245–60. London: Verso.

———. (1989). *Nomads of the Present: Social Movements and Individual Needs in Contemporary Society*. London: Hutchinson Radius.

Mittelstaedt, M. (1991). "Saving the Planet Can Wait." *Globe and Mail*, November 28, p. A1.

Montaigne, Michel Eyquem, Seigneur de. (1958). *Essays* (trans. J.M. Cohen). London: Penguin Books.

Montesquieu, Charles Louis de Secondat, Baron de. (1973). *Persian Letters* (trans. C.J. Betts). Harmondsworth: Penguin Books.

———. (1989). *The Spirit of the Laws* (trans. and eds. Anne M. Cohler, Basia Carolyn Miller, and Harold Samuel Stone). Cambridge: Cambridge University Press.

Morrison, David. (1978). "The Beginning of Modern Mass Communication Research." *Archives of European Sociology* 19: 347–59.

Murray, Charles. (1984). *Losing Ground: American Society Policy, 1950–1980*. New York: Basic Books.

Myer, J.W., and B. Rowan. (1977). "Institutionalized Organizations: Formal Structure as Myth and Ceremony." *American Journal of Sociology* 83: 340–63.

Myles, J. (1989). "Introduction: Understanding Canada: Comparative Political Economy Perspectives." *Canadian Review of Sociology and Anthropology* (Winter).

Myrdal, G. (1973). *Against the Stream*. New York: Pantheon Books.

Nash, R. (ed.). (1968). *The American Environment: Readings in the History of Conservation*. Reading, MA: Addison-Wesley.

———. (1980). "The Separation of Form and Content in Liberal Democratic Politics." *Studies in Political Economy* 3 (Spring): 5–16.

Neatby, H.B. (1976). *William Lyon Mackenzie King, 1932–1939*. Toronto: University of Toronto Press.

Nettl, J.P. (1968). "The State as Conceptual Variable." *World Politics* 20: 559–92.

Neufeld, Mark. (1991). "The Reflexive Turn in International Relations Theory." Working Paper No. 4, Centre for International and Strategic Studies, York University, Toronto, January.

Nikolov, S. (1990). "Is Non-Profit Activity Possible under Socialism?" Paper presented at Research Forum of Independent Sector, Boston, MA, March 15–16.

Nordlinger, E. (1981). *On the Autonomy of the Democratic State*. Cambridge, MA: Harvard University Press.

———. (1988). "The Return to the State: Critique." *American Political Science Review* 82, no. 3: 875–85.

Odell, J. (1982). *U.S. International Monetary Policy*. Princeton: Princeton University Press.

Offe, Claus. (1980). "The Separation of Form and Content in Liberal Democratic Politics." *Studies in Political Economy* 3 (Spring): 5–16.

———. (1981). "The Attribution of Public Status to Interest Groups: Observations on the West German Case." In Suzanne Berger (ed.), *Organizing Interests in Western Europe: Pluralism, Corporatism, and the Transformation of Politics*, pp. 123–58. Cambridge: Cambridge University Press.

———. (1985). *Disorganized Capitalism* (ed. John Keane). Cambridge: Polity Press.

———. (1991). "Reflections on the Institutional Self-Transformation of Movement Politics: A Tentative Stage Model." In R.J. Dalton and M. Kuechler (eds.), *The Challenge of New Movements*, pp. 232–50. Oxford: Oxford University Press.

Olson, Mancur. (1982). *The Rise and Decline of Nations: Economic Growth, Stagflation and Social Rigidities*. New Haven, CT: Yale University Press.

Organization for Economic Cooperation and Development. (1987). "Elements of a Conceptual Framework for Trade in Services." Paris: OECD.

———. (1989a). "Testing the Conceptual Framework for Trade in Services in the Field of Tourism and International Travel." Paris: OECD.

———. (1989b). *Trade in Services and Developing Countries*. Paris: OECD.

———. (1990). *Trade in Information, Computer and Communication Services*. Paris: OECD.

Orlow, Dietrich. (1986). *Weimar Prussia 1918–1925: The Unlikely Rock of Democracy*. Pittsburgh: University of Pittsburgh Press.

Ostrogorski, Moisei. (1902). *Democracy and the Organization of Political Parties*. New York: Macmillan.

Ottawa Citizen. (1991). "Sleeping with the Enemy." *Ottawa Citizen*, October 13, p. A5.

Owram, D. (1986). *The Government Generation: Canadian Intellectuals and the State 1900–1945*. Toronto: University of Toronto Press.

Paltiel, K.Z. (1989). "Political Marketing, Party Finance and the Decline of Canadian Parties." In A.-G. Gagnon and A.B. Tanguay (eds.), *Canadian Parties in Transition*, pp. 332–53. Scarborough: Nelson.

Panitch, Leo. (1979). "Corporatism in Canada?" *Studies in Political Economy* 1: 43–92.

———. (1980). "Recent Theorizations of Corporatism: Reflections on a Growth Industry." *British Journal of Sociology* 31, no. 2 (June): 159–87.

Parsons, Talcott. (1951). *The Social System*. New York: Free Press.

Pekkarinen, J. (1989). "Keynesianism and the Scandinavian Models of Economic Policy." In P. Hall (ed.), *The Political Power of Economic Ideas*. Princeton: Princeton University Press.

Peon, M.M. (1979). *Harry S Truman versus the Medical Lobby*. Columbia: University of Missouri Press.

Peschek, Joseph G. (1987). *Policy-Planning Organizations: Elite Agendas and America's Rightward Turn*. Philadelphia: Temple University Press.

———. (1989). "'Free the Fortune 500!' The American Enterprise Institute and the Politics of the Capitalist Class in the 1970s." *Critical Sociology* 16, no. 2–3 (Summer–Fall): pp. 165–80.

Petkov, K. (1989). "The Causes of Alienation." *World Marxist Review,* October, pp. 51–52.

Phillips, S.D. (1991a). "How Ottawa Blends: Shifting Government Relationships with Interest Groups." In F. Abele (ed.), *How Ottawa Spends 1991–92: The Politics of Fragmentation*, pp. 183–228. Ottawa: Carleton University Press.

———. (1991b). "Meaning and Structure in Social Movements: Mapping the Network of National Canadian Women's Organizations." *Canadian Journal of Political Science* 24, no. 4: 755–82.

———. (1992). "Action, Meaning and Structure in Social Movements: A Project Analytic Study of Women's Organizations." Ottawa: School of Public Administration Discussion Paper Series.

Pickersgill, J. (1960). *The Mackenzie King Record*, vol. 1. Toronto: University of Toronto Press.

Pickersgill, J., and D. Forster. (1970). *The Mackenzie King Record*, vol. 3. Toronto: University of Toronto Press.

Plevza, V. (1979). "National Self-Determination and the Change of Political and Social Systems." In R. Merritt (ed.), *International Political Science Enters the 1980s*, vol. 1. Abstracts of papers presented at the Eleventh World Congress of the International Political Science Association, Moscow, August 12–18. Oslo, Norway: International Political Science Association.

Pocock, J.G.A. (1975). *The Machiavellian Moment*. Princeton: Princeton University Press.

Pontusson, J. (1987). "Sweden." In J. Krieger et al. (eds.), *European Politics in Transition*. Lexington, MA: Heath.

———. (1988). "Swedish Social Democracy and British Labour: Essays on the Nature and Condition of Social Democratic Hegemony." Western Societies Program Occasional Paper no. 19. Ithaca: Cornell University.

Poole, D.C. (1938). "Letter to David H. Stevens. 9 December." RF. RG 1.1. Series 200. Box 271. Folder 3236. Rockefeller Archive Center.

Powell, D., and P. Shoup. (1970). "The Emergence of Political Science in Communist Countries." *American Political Science Review* 64: 572–88.

"The Power of Advanced Theory." (1982). *World Marxist Review* (September): 29–33.

Precan, V. (1990). "The Crumbling of the Soviet Bloc." *Journal of Democracy* 1, no. 1: 79–85.

Pross, A.P. (1986). *Group Politics and Public Policy*. Toronto: Oxford University Press.

———. (1992). *Group Politics and Public Policy*, 2d ed. Toronto: Oxford University Press.

Razack, S. (1991). *Canadian Feminism and the Law*. Toronto: Second Story Press.

Reich, Robert B. (1983). *The Next American Frontier*. New York: Times Books.

———. (1991). *The Work of Nations*. New York: Vintage Books.

Rhodes, R.A.W. (1981). *Control and Power in Central-Local Relations*. Aldershot: Gower.

———. (1986). *Beyond Westminster and Whitehall*. London: Unwin Hyman.

———. (1990). "Policy Networks: A British Perspective." *Journal of Theoretical Politics* 2, no. 3: 292–316.

Rhodes, R.A.W., and Marsh, D. (1992). "New Directions in the Study of Policy Networks." *European Journal of Political Research* 21: 181–205.

Rice, J. (1985). "Politics of Income Security: Historical Developments and Limits to Future Change." In B. Doern (ed.), *The Politics of Economic Policy*. Toronto: University of Toronto Press.

Richardson, J.J., and A.G. Jordan. (1979). *Governing under Pressure*. Oxford: Martin Robertson.

Richter, Melvin. (1969). "Comparative Analysis in Montesquieu and Tocqueville." *Comparative Politics* 1, no. 2: 129–60.

————. (1970). "The Uses of Theory: Tocqueville's Adaptation of Montesquieu." In Melvin Richter (ed.), *Essays in Theory and History*, pp. 74–102. Cambridge, MA: Harvard University Press.

Rockefeller Archive Center. (1937a). "Hotlist." April 28. Rockefeller Foundation Archives. RF. RG 1.1. Series 200. Box 271. Folder 3234. Princeton Radio Research Project.

————. (1937b). Memorandum of May 21 Approving Grant to School of Public and International Affairs, Princeton University. RF. RG 1.1. Series 200. Box 271. Folder 3233. Princeton Radio Research Project.

————. (1937c). "Radio in RF and GEB Program: Retrospect and Prospect." RF. RG 3.1. Series 911. Box 5. Folder 51. Princeton Radio Research Project.

————. (1937d). Rockefeller Program in Broadcasting. RF. RG 1.1. Series 200. Box 271. Folder 3234. Princeton Radio Research Project.

————. (1938a). Application to Rockefeller Foundation for Renewal of Grant. RF. RG 1.1. Series 200. Box 272. Folder 3239. Princeton Radio Research Project.

————. (1938b). "Report of Activities." RF. RG 1.1. Series 200. Box 271. Folder 3236. Princeton Radio Research Project.

————. (1939a). Memorandum of 25 January, 1939 (allocating $750 for the costs of arranging for a review of the Princeton Radio Research Project by a qualified reviewing committee). RF. RG 1.1. Series 200. Box 271. Folder 3233. Princeton Radio Research Project.

————. (1939b). "Public Opinion and the Emergency." RF. RG 1.1. Series 200 Box 224. Folder 2677. Princeton Radio Research Project.

————. (1939c). Report for the Reviewing Committee, Princeton Radio Survey, 20 February. RF. RG 1.1. Series 200. Box 273. Folder 3245. Princeton Radio Research Project.

————. (1939d). Seminar Memorandum No. 1: Summary of Discussions of Communications Seminar, September 20 and 23, 1939. RF. RG 1.1. Series 200. Box 224. Folder 2678. Princeton Radio Research Project.

————. (1939e). Seminar Memorandum No. 2: Summary of Discussions of Communication Seminar, September 29, 1939. RF. RG 1.1. Series 200. Box 224. Folder 2678. Princeton Radio Research Project.

————. (1939f). Seminar Memorandum No. 4: Summary of Discussions of Communication Seminar, November 24, 1939. RF. RG 1.1. Series 200. Box 224. Folder 2678. Princeton Radio Research Project.

————. (1939g). Seminar Memorandum No. 5: Summary of Discussions of Communications Seminar, December 21, 1939. RF. RG 1.1. Series 200. Box 224. Folder 2678. Princeton Radio Research Project.

————. (1940a). "Needed Research in Communication." RF. RG 1.1. Series 200. Box 224. Folder 2677. Princeton Radio Research Project.

————. (1940b). "Research in Mass Communications." Rockefeller Foundation Archives. RF. RG 1.1. Series 200. Box 224. Folder 2677. Princeton Radio Research Project.

————. (1940c). Seminar Memorandum No. 6: Summary of Discussions of Communications Seminar, February 16, 1940. RF. RG 1.1. Series 200. Box 224. Folder 2678. Princeton Radio Research Project.

————. (1940d). Seminar Memorandum No. 7. March 15, 1940. RF. RG 1.1. Series 200. Box 224. Folder 2678. Princeton Radio Research Project.

————. (1940e). Seminar Memorandum No. 9. April 12, 1940. RF. RG 1.1. Series 200. Box 224. Folder 2678. Princeton Radio Research Project.

————. (1940f). Seminar Memorandum No. 10. May 8, 1940. RF. RG 1.1. Series 200. Box 224. Folder 2678. Princeton Radio Research Project.

————. (1941). Memorandum on the Princeton Radio Research Project. RF. RG 1.1. Series 200. Box 272. Folder 3243. Princeton Radio Research Project.

Roelofs, J. (1990). "Foundations and Political Science." Paper presented at the Workshop of the IPSA Research Committee on the Study of Political Science as a Discipline, Paris, May 21–22.

Ross, G. (1987). "Adieu Vieilles Idées." In G. Ross (ed.), *Contemporary France*. London: Routledge.

————. (1991). "French Intellectuals from Sartre to Soft Ideology." In Charles Lemert (ed.), *Intellectuals and Politics*. Newbury Park, CA: Sage.

Rothstein, B. (1985). "Managing the Welfare State: Lessons from Gustav Moller." *Scandinavian Political Studies* 13.

Rucht, D. (1988). "Themes, Logics, and Arenas of Social Movements: A Structural Approach." *International Social Movement Research* 1: 305–28.

————. (1991). "The Strategies and Action Repertoires of New Movements." In R.J. Dalton and M. Kuechler (eds.), *The Challenge of New Movements*, pp. 156–75. Oxford: Oxford University Press.

Sabatier, P.A. (1987). "Knowledge, Policy Oriented Learning, and Policy Change: An Advocacy Coalition Framework." *Knowledge* 8, no. 4: 649–92.

Salter, L. (1988). *Mandated Science: Science and Scientists in the Making of Standards*. Norwell, MA: Kluwer Academic Publishers.

Sampson, Gary P. (n.d.). "Developing Countries and the Liberalization of Trade in Services." Washington, DC: Ford Foundation Project.

Sandel, Michael. (1984). "The Procedural Republic and the Unencumbered Self." *Political Theory* 12 (February): 81–96.

Saunders, P. (1975). "They Make the Rules." *Policy and Politics* 4: 31–58.

Schattschneider, E.E. (1960). *The Semi-Sovereign People*. Hinsdale, IL: Dryden Press.

Schmitter, Philippe. (1974). "Still the Century of Corporatism." *Review of Politics* 36, no. 1 (January): 85–131.

————. (1981). "Interest Intermediation and Regime Governability in Contemporary Western Europe and North America." In Suzanne O. Berger (ed.), *Organizing Interests in Western Europe*, pp. 285–327. Cambridge: Cambridge University Press.

Schmitter, Philippe, and Gerhard Lehmbruch. (1982). *Patterns of Corporatist Policy-Making*. Beverly Hills: Sage.

Schrecker, T. (1984). *The Political Economy of Environmental Hazards*. Ottawa: Law Reform Commission.

————. (1992). "Of Invisible Beasts and the Public Interest: Environmental Cases and the Judicial System." In R. Boardman (ed.), *Canadian Environmental Policy: Ecosystems, Politics, and Process*, pp. 83–108. Toronto: Oxford University Press.

Schumpeter, Joseph. (1962). *Capitalism, Socialism and Democracy*. New York: Harper Torchbooks.

Scott, F.R. (1937–1938). "The Royal Commission on Dominion-Provincial Relations." *University of Toronto Quarterly* 7.

Seybold, P. (1982). "The Ford Foundation and Social Control." *Science for the People* 14, no. 3: 28–31.

Shannon, Claude E., and Warren Weaver. (1949). *The Mathematical Theory of Communication*. Urbana, IL: University of Illinois Press.

Shelp, Ronald K. (1981). *Beyond Industrialization: Ascendancy of the Global Service Economy*. New York: Praeger.

————. (1986–1987). "Trade in Services." *Foreign Policy* 65 (Winter): 64–84.

Simeon, R. (1987). "Inside the Macdonald Commission," *Studies in Political Economy* 22 (Spring).

Simeon, R., and Robinson, I. (1990). *State, Society and the Development of Canadian Federalism.* Toronto: University of Toronto Press.

Skocpol, Theda. (1985). "Bringing the State Back In: Strategies of Analysis in Current Research." In Peter B. Evans, Dietrich Rueschemeyer, and Theda Skocpol (eds.), *Bringing the State Back In,* pp. 3–43. Cambridge: Cambridge University Press.

Smiley, D. (1962). "The Rowell Sirois Report, Provincial Autonomy, and Post-War Canadian Federalism." *Canadian Journal of Economics and Political Science* 28, no. 1: 54–69.

Smith, Bruce Lannes, Harold D. Lasswell, and Ralph D. Casey. (1946). *Propaganda, Communication, and Public Opinion: A Comprehensive Reference Guide.* Princeton: Princeton University Press.

Smith, M.J. (1989). "The Annual Review: The Emergence of a Corporatist Institution?" *Political Studies* 37: 81–96.

———. (1990a). "Pluralism, Reformed Pluralism and Neo-Pluralism." *Political Studies* 38: 302–22.

———. (1990b). *The Politics of Agricultural Support in Britain.* Aldershot: Gower.

———. (1991). "From Policy Community to Issue Network: Salmonella in Eggs and the New Politics of Food." *Public Administration* 69: 235–55.

———. (1993). *Pressure Power and Policy: State Autonomy and Policy Networks in Britain and the United States.* Hemel Hempstead: Harvester Wheatsheaf.

Social Science Federation of Canada. (1987). *University Research Centres in the Social Sciences and Humanities.* Proceedings of a national conference held in Ottawa, March 1987. Ottawa: University of Ottawa Press.

Social Science Research Council. (1987–1988). *Annual Report.* New York: SSRC.

Soros Foundation. (1987). *Annual Report.* Sofia.

———. (1988). *Annual Report.* Sofia.

———. (1990). "Open Society Fund." Sofia.

Stinchcombe, A.L. (1990). *Information and Organizations.* Berkeley: University of California Press.

Stones, R. (1990). "Government-Finance Relations in Britain 1964–67: A Tale of Three Cities." *Economy and Society* 19: 32–55.

Struthers, J. (1983). *No Fault of Their Own.* Toronto: University of Toronto Press.

Studebaker, J.W. (1937). "Report of Progress of Federal Radio Education Committee." Address delivered at Second National Conference on Educational Broadcasting, Chicago, 30 November. General Education Board. GEB Advisory Committee. Series 1, Sub-series 2, Box 359, Folder 3706. Rockefeller Archive Center.

Swenson, P. (1989). *Fair Shares: Unions, Pay and Politics in Sweden and West Germany.* Ithaca: Cornell University Press.

Szelenyi, I. (1986–1987). "The Prospects and Limits of the East European New Class Project: An Auto-Critical Reflection of the Intellectuals on the Road to Class Power." *Politics and Society* 15, no. 2: 103–44.

Tarkowski, J. (1987). "Political Science and Sociology: Different Responses to the Polish Crisis." Paper presented at the Conference on the Comparative Study of the Development of Political Science, Cortona, September 21–26.

Tarkowski, J., and R. Siemienska. (1979). "Local Leaders in the Socialist Countries of Eastern Europe." In R. Merritt (ed.), *International Political Science Enters the 1980s,* vol. 1. Abstracts of papers presented at the Eleventh World Congress of the International Political Science Association, Moscow, August 12–18. Oslo, Norway: International Political Science Association.

Tarrow, S. (1983). *Struggling to Reform: Social Movements and Policy Change during Cycles of Protest.* Ithaca: Cornell University, Western Societies Program, Paper No. 15.

———. (1989). *Struggle, Politics, and Reform: Collective Action, Social Movements, and Cycles of Protest.* Ithaca: Center for International Studies, Cornell University.

Taylor, Charles. (1975). *Hegel.* Cambridge: Cambridge University Press.

———. (1991a). "Civil Society in the Western Tradition." In Ethel Groffier and Michel Paradis (eds.), *The Notion of Tolerance and Human Rights: Essays in Honour of Raymond Kiibansky,* pp. 117–36. Ottawa: Carleton University Press.

———. (1991b). "Comprendre la culture politique." In Raymond Hudon and Rejean Pelletier (eds.), *L'engagement intellectuel: Mélanges en l'honneur de Léon Dion,* pp. 193–207. Sainte-Foy, Quebec: Les Presses de l'Université Laval.

Therborn, G. (1989). "'Pillarization' and 'Popular Movements.'" In F. Castles (ed.), *The Comparative History of Public Policy.* Cambridge: Polity Press.

Thompson, E.P. (1981). *The Making of the English Working Class.* Harmondsworth: Penguin.

Tilton, T. (1990). *The Political Theory of Swedish Social Democracy.* Oxford: Oxford University Press.

Tocqueville, Alexis de. (1945). *Democracy in America,* vols. 1, 2 (trans. Henry Reeve, rev. Francis Bowen). New York: Vintage Books.

———. (1955). *The Old Regime and the French Revolution* (trans. Stuart Gilbert). Garden City, NY: Doubleday Anchor Books.

Toner, G. (1990). "Whence and Whither: ENGOs, Business and the Environment." Ottawa: Carleton University, Department of Political Science (unpublished paper).

———. (1991). "The Canadian Environmental Movement: A Conceptual Map." Ottawa: Carleton University, Department of Political Science (unpublished paper).

Toronto Star. (1985). "Canada Gets Blueprint for Future." September 6.

Trent, J.E. (1988). "Research Institutes in Canada: Underdeveloped, Under-appreciated and Underfunded." In *Culture, Development and Regional Policy,* Canadian Issues, vol. 9, pp. 221–29. Montreal: Association for Canadian Studies.

Truman, David B. (1951). *The Governmental Process.* New York: Alfred A. Knopf.

Tuohy, Carolyn. (1990). "Institutions and Interests in the Occupational Health Arena: The Case of Quebec." In W.D. Coleman and G. Skogstad (eds.), *Policy Communities and Public Policy in Canada: A Structuralist Approach,* pp. 238–65. Toronto: Copp Clark Pitman.

Tyson, Levering. (1938). "Letter to David H. Stephens. 19 November." RF. RG 1.1. Series 200. Box 271. Folder 3236. Rockefeller Archive Center.

Underhill, F. (1975). *In Search of Canadian Liberalism.* Toronto: Macmillan.

United States Congress. House. (1986). *List of Organizations Involved in Exchange Programs with the Soviet Union and Eastern Europe.* 99th Congress, 2d. session. Washington, DC: USGPO.

United States Department of State. (1974). *A Human Contribution to the Structure of Peace: International Educational and Cultural Exchange.* Washington, DC: USGPO.

Vacca, Giuseppe. (1982). "Intellectuals and the Marxist Theory of the State." In Anne Showstack Sassoon (ed.), *Approaches to Gramsci.* London: Writers and Readers.

Vasilev, M., et al. (1983). "Sociology in Bulgaria." *International Review of Modern Sociology* 13: 35–77.

Vernon, Raymond. (1988). "Launching the Uruguay Round: Clayton Yeutter and the Two-Track Decision." Pittsburgh: Pew Program in Case Teaching and Writing in International Affairs.

Vickers, J.M. (1988). "Politics as if Women Mattered: The Institutionalization of the Canadian Women's Movement and Its Impact on Federal Politics 1965–1988." Paper presented to the ACSANZ'88 Canadian Studies Conference, Canberra.

Vogel, David. (1989). *Fluctuating Fortunes: The Political Power of Business in America.* New York: Basic Books.

Waarden, F. van (1992). "The Historical Institutionalization of Typical National Patterns in Policy Networks between State and Industry: A Comparison of the USA and the Netherlands." *European Journal of Political Research* 21: 131–62.

Waddock, S.A. (1988). "Building Successful Social Partnerships." *Sloan Management Review* 17 (Summer): 17–23.

Waples, Douglas. (1940). "Some Considerations Involved in Studies to Describe the Effects of Communications." RF. RG 1.1. Series 200. Box 224. Folder 2678. Rockefeller Archive Center.

Weaver, R. Kent. (1989). "The Changing World of Think Tanks." *PS: Political Science and Politics* 22, no. 3 (September): 563–78.

Weber, Max. (1958). "Politics as a Vocation" and "Capitalism and Rural Society in Germany." In H.H. Gerth and C. Wright Mills (eds.), *From Max Weber: Essays in Sociology*, pp. 77–128, 363–85. New York: Oxford University Press.

Weir, M., and T. Skocpol. (1985). "State Structures and the Possibility of 'Keynesian' Responses to the Great Depression in Sweden, Britain and the United States." In P.B. Evans, D. Reuschemeyer, and T. Skocpol (eds.), *Bringing the State Back In*, pp. 107–63. Cambridge: Cambridge University Press.

Wiatr, J. (1990). "The Impact of Democratization on Political Science in Eastern Europe: The Polish Experience." Paper presented at the Conference of the International Committee for the Study of the Development of Political Science, Barcelona, May 14–20.

Wilks, S., and Wright, M. (1987). "Conclusion: Comparing Government-Industry Relations: States, Sectors, and Networks." In S. Wilks and M. Wright (eds.), *Government-Industry Relations*. Oxford: Clarendon Press.

Williams, G. (1985). "Symbols, Economic Logic and Political Conflict in the Canada-U.S.A. Free-Trade Negotiations." *Queen's Quarterly* 92, no. 4 (Winter).

———. (1986). *Not for Export*. Toronto: McClelland and Stewart.

Wilson, D. (1991). "Little Voice Becomes a Roar." *Globe and Mail*, September 16, p. A2.

Wilson, J. (1992). "Green Lobbies: Pressure Groups and Environmental Policy." In R. Boardman (ed.), *Canadian Environmental Policy: Ecosystems, Politics, and Process*, pp. 109–25. Toronto: Oxford University Press.

Wilson, V., and O.P. Dwivedi. (1982). "Introduction." In V. Wilson and O.P. Dwivedi (eds.), *The Administrative State in Canada*. Toronto: University of Toronto Press.

Wilson, William J. (1987). *The Truly Disadvantaged: The Inner City, the Underclass, and Public Policy*. Chicago: University of Chicago Press.

Winham, Gilbert R. (1989). "The Prenegotiation Phase of the Uruguay Round." *International Journal* 44, no. 2 (Spring): 280–303.

Wolfe, A. (1989). *Whose Keeper? Social Science and Moral Obligation*. Berkeley: University of California Press.

Wolfe, D. (1984). "The Rise and Demise of the Keynesian Era in Canada: Economic Policy, 1930–82." In M. Cross and G. Kealey (eds.), *Readings in the Social History of Canada*. Toronto: McClelland and Stewart.

Wolfe, J. (1991). "State and Ideology in Britain: Mrs. Thatcher's Privatization Programme."
    Political Studies 39: 237–52.
Woodrow, R. Brian (ed.). (1990). *Uruguay Round Trade in Services Perspectives*. Proceed-
    ings from the First International Forum on Global Services Trade and Trade Liber-
    alization, Geneva, May 16–17. Geneva: Applied Services Economic Centre.
Woods, L.T. (1987). "Comparative National Approaches to Pacific Economic Cooperation:
    A Post-Fieldwork Report." Sydney: Research School of Pacific Studies, Australian
    National University, mimeo.
———. (1988). "Diplomacy and International Nongovernmental Organizations: A Study of
    the Pacific Economic Cooperation Movement." Doctoral dissertation, Australian
    National University.
World Commission on Environment and Development. (1987). *Our Common Future*.
    Oxford: Oxford University Press.
Yoffie, David B., and Joseph L. Badaracco, Jr. (1983). "Trade in Services and American
    Express." Cambridge, MA: Harvard Business School.
Yoffie, David B., and Sigrid Bergenstein. (1985). "Creating Political Advantage: The Rise
    of the Corporate Political Entrepreneur." *California Management Review* 28, no.1
    (Fall): 124–39.
Zysman, J. (1983). *Government, Markets and Growth*. Ithaca: Cornell University Press.

Index

About the Editors and Contributors

FREDRICK APPEL is a Ph.D. candidate in the Department of Political Science at McGill University. His research interests include political and moral philosophy, liberalism, nationalism, and intellectual history. He has published in the area of political culture and identity.

ERKKI BERNDTSON is Senior Lecturer of Political Science at the University of Helsinki. He has published several articles on the history of political science. His research interests include democratic theory and methodological foundations of political science.

NEIL BRADFORD has taught political science at the University of Western Ontario. He has published articles on Canadian political parties and the role of intellectuals in politics. He is currently working at the Ministry of Labour, Government of Ontario.

STEPHEN BROOKS is Associate Professor of Political Science at the University of Windsor. He is the author of several books, including *Public Policy in Canada* and *Canadian Democracy;* co-author of *Social Scientists and Politics in Canada* and *Business and Government in Canada;* and co-editor of *Social Scientists, Policy and the State.*

WILLIAM BUXTON works with the Department of Communication Studies at Concordia University. He is the author of *Talcott Parsons* and has published extensively in the area of communication policy.

ALAIN-G. GAGNON is Professor of Political Science and Director of the Quebec Studies program at McGill University. He is the editor of *Intellectuals in Liberal Democracies* and *Quebec: State and Society*. He is co-author of *Social Scientists and Politics in Canada; Quebec: Beyond the Quiet Revolution;* and *Allaire, Bélanger, Campeau et les autres*. He is co-editor of *Canadian Parties in Transition; Democracy with Justice;* and *Comparative Federalism and Federation*.

EVERT A. LINDQUIST is Assistant Professor of Political Science at the University of Toronto. He has contributed to *Globalization, Governance and the Role of Think Tanks* and *Social Scientists, Policy and the State*. Other articles and chapters have appeared in *Canadian Public Administration, Optimum, Knowledge in Society, Studies in Political Economy,* and *How Ottawa Spends*. He is currently the first Visiting Fellow to the Government of Canada's Treasury Board Secretariat.

STEPHEN D. MCDOWELL teaches at the School of Journalism and Communications at Carleton University. His research on international trade and investment issues has dealt with transborder data flow research programs in international organizations, trade in services, and India's policies for trade and investment in telecommunications and computer software services.

SUSAN D. PHILLIPS is Associate Professor in the School of Public Administration at Carleton University. Among her most recent publications is *How Ottawa Spends: A More Democratic Canada?* She has also published articles in the areas of the new social movements, democratic practices, and interest groups.

JOAN ROELOFS is Professor of Political Science at Keene State University. She is a Member of the International Political Science Association Research Committee on the Study of Political Science as a Discipline.

MARTIN J. SMITH is Professor of Political Science at the University of Sheffield. He is the author of *Pressure, Power and Policy: Policy Networks and State Autonomy in Britain and the United States*.